THE
RIVERS OF AMERICA

Edited by
HERVEY ALLEN

As Planned and Started by
CONSTANCE
LINDSAY
SKINNER

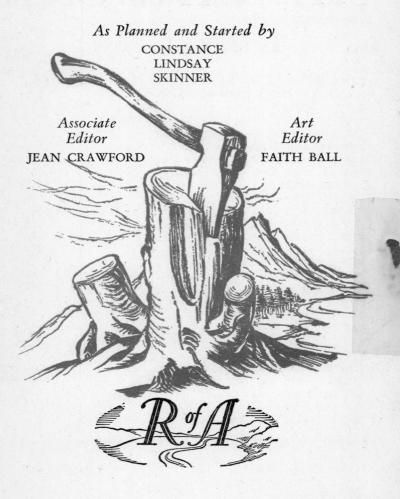

*Associate
Editor*
JEAN CRAWFORD

*Art
Editor*
FAITH BALL

The
SHENANDOAH

by JULIA DAVIS

Illustrated by Frederic Taubes

FARRAR & RINEHART, INCORPORATED

New York   *Toronto*

This book has been manufactured in accordance with the paper conservation orders of the War Production Board

To the memory of

STEPHEN VINCENT BENÉT

Who had the heart to understand
the voice to sing
America

Contents

PART I: PROMISE

1. SONG 3
2. THE UNRECORDED PAST 9
3. EXPLORATION 22
4. SETTLEMENT 31
5. PIONEERS 47
6. WASHINGTON 60
7. MASSACRES 70
8. FORT LOUDOUN 77
9. REVOLUTION 93
10. EXPANSION 110
11. INVENTIONS 121

PART II: HOLOCAUST

12. THE FATEFUL LIGHTNING 135
13. THE SWIFT SWORD 152
14. MARCHING ON 168

15. THE INVADED 182

16. VALLEY CAMPAIGN I 194

17. VALLEY CAMPAIGN II 205

18. VALLEY CAMPAIGN III 215

19. THE LONG YEAR 225

20. THE BURNING 242

21. THE STARVING CROWS 255

PART III: RECOVERY

22. THE HERO 271

23. THE FAITH 284

24. FOOL'S GOLD AND TRUE GOLD 295

25. PAST INTO PRESENT 306

26. VALLEY TOUR I 317

27. VALLEY TOUR II 327

28. VALLEY TOUR III 339

29. EPILOGUE 354

POSTSCRIPT 358

ACKNOWLEDGMENT 362

BIBLIOGRAPHY 363

INDEX 371

PART I

Promise

1. Song

Oh, Shen-an-doah, I hear you call me. A-way, you roll-ing riv-er! Oh, Shen-an-doah, I'm goin' to leave you. A-way, a-way, I'm bound to-go, A-cross the wide Mis-sou-ri:

I T IS A sailor's chantey, a lost and hungry chantey, a song of faraway men reminding themselves of things they have loved, a sea song to an inland river which never meets the sea. Its melody has the nostalgic music inherent in the name of Shenandoah—for the name and the song and the river have a talismanic quality.

The Shenandoah is a short river, a narrow river, a shallow river. No commerce rides the often muddy waters, no cities break the willow fringe along the banks. Yet to thousands who have never seen it the Shenandoah is music, the Shenandoah is romance.

The Shenandoah is a legend, and it deserves to be. There are names which ring like bells in history, and Shenandoah is one of them, for it is not only a river, but also a valley, a valley consecrated by the lifeblood of brave men.

During four autumns and five springs, Federal and Confederate, Blue and Gray, they died in the Valley for their country, for their homes, and the soil is sacred now to North

3

and South alike. Out of their courage and their pain on this symbolic battlefield, which changed hands more often than any other, rose a united nation welded by blood and fire. All this endured, we still remained one people. In the Valley of the Shenandoah we learned that we are indivisible.

The Shenandoah is a legend, and it is history. It is all the brave men who have loved and walked the Valley. The roster of great names is a long one: Spotswood and Fairfax, Washington, Jefferson, Madison, Andrew Jackson, Boone, the Lincolns, Houston, Sevier, Lee, Stonewall Jackson, Sheridan, Maury, Wilson, the Byrds. In all these lives the Valley has had a place. It has been a seedbed and a school for the expanding nation.

But the legend and the history do not account entirely for the nostalgia that haunts the name of Shenandoah. The Valley is the earth itself, fecund, rewarding, rolling in gentle checkered fields to the Blue Ridge which guards it like a wall. Blue is the color for the Valley, blue mountains in the summer haze, blue sky, and cornflowers catching the sky on their petals, blue-green orchards making a festival of spring.

The Valley is the old brick houses, with the tall trees around them, settled comfortably into the earth, each with a special flavor, an identity, an air of permanence and peace. The Valley is the pungency of box in half-neglected gardens, the cool springhouses, the watercress in little rushing streams, the old stone walls built by slave labor, the neat new fences of barbed wire. It is the climbing roses which crowd the honeysuckle, the honeysuckle loading the summer night with a delirium of fragrance, the hollyhocks clambering down the banks into the gray roads.

Through the long summer days when the heat shimmers impalpably over the rustling corn, and the buzzards hang high and still by magic in the empty air, the houses are dark and cool with their closed shutters and bare polished floors. At evening all the crows go home with a long level flight. Then the night air holds a balmy fragrance, and the canoes come out on the river like dark fish, guided into the willows, looking for the moon. The new sunlight of morning dapples the ground in oak groves which have never known an ax. There is no other sound at once so soft and so crisp as the rattle of the wind in the oak leaves, beneath the distant mournful clamor of the doves which haunt the groves.

In the Valley are old names, old places, an old and undemanding way of living. It is land which has been loved rather than exploited, and for that reason it has given to its owners the best that land can give: stability, and a treelike peace which has no cause to fear the slow swing of the seasons. Life moves at its own tempo in the Valley, not with the brief fevered grasping of an individual span. The Blue Ridge rocks are old, and the river has survived great changes. The earth is old to cultivation, but it is not exhausted, for it has been cherished.

More than history, the Valley is a way of life. It is the rich fields, and the mountains older than measured time. It is the stillness of a hot noon, or of moonlight, or of snow. It is the calm old houses, where the oak leaves and the doves have time to set up their music in the heart of a child.

The Valley is Home

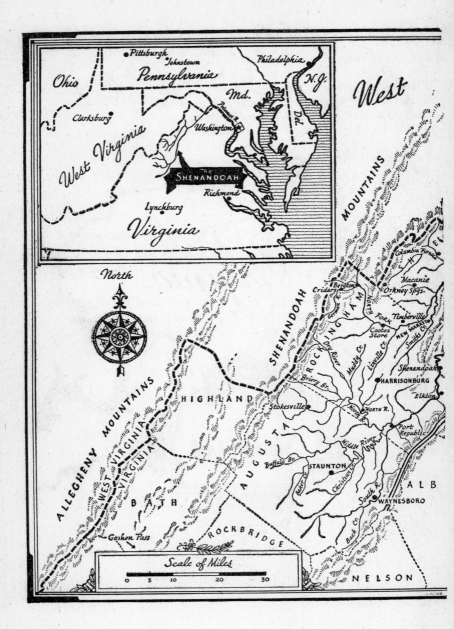

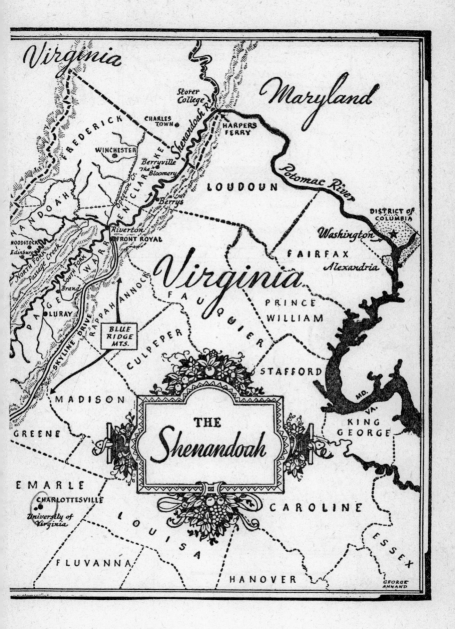

2. The Unrecorded Past

The hills are shadows and they flow
From form to form and nothing stands.
They melt like mists, the solid lands;
Like clouds they shape themselves and go.

THE Shenandoah River flows northward for one hundred and fifty miles through a valley in Virginia between the Blue Ridge and the Allegheny mountains, and meets the Potomac at Harpers Ferry, the convergence of Virginia, West Virginia, and Maryland, fifty miles from Washington. At Harpers Ferry it brawls noisily over a rocky bed, but higher up in places it is green and still, with splendid reaches where the willows and sycamores dabble in the silent water and the black bass leap abundantly. The Blue Ridge, covered with oak and hickory, hangs closely to the eastern bank, and the rich fields stretch westward. At Front Royal the river is split into two branches by Massanutten Mountain, a huge monadnock rising steeply from the Valley floor. Then the North Fork, narrow, sluggish, deep, drains the lush bottom land of the main Valley and loops itself into the spectacular Seven Bends near Woodstock. The South Fork, swifter and clearer, flows through the narrow Luray Valley on the eastern side of Massanutten, and its headwaters rise at last in the foothills only a mile or two from the headwaters of the James.

The Shenandoah is a short and friendly river to have so rich a history. It is narrow, it is often muddy, and even a canoe would have difficulty in riding the full length of its waters. It was no barrier to exploration and settlement, for it has always been easily crossed at many fords. The main road through the Valley rarely approaches it, and the towns follow the road, the Valley Pike. Commerce left the river fifty years ago when the last freight barge floated down. Nevertheless, the river has had a deep influence on the life around it.

It is the life stream of the Valley, hidden and beautiful, approached by side roads, encountered with surprise. The men rest and fish on it, the young people swim in it and camp along it, and the flow of its waters is mingled in their minds with the first stirrings of romance. They may stray far from the Valley, but not beyond the memory of glassy moonlit water broken at long intervals by a leaping fish, of swift green rapids, of dark mountains close at hand.

For two hundred years white men have loved the river, but through countless ages before they came the water carved the land and shaped it. The story of the Shenandoah is the story of the Valley which the river made.

Many of the scenic beauties on this continent are unappreciated because mankind has not praised them long enough—but the Shenandoah Valley does not suffer from this lack. From the earliest explorers on, visitors have launched into pages of description at the sight of it. Thomas Jefferson thought the view at Harpers Ferry "worth a trip across the Atlantic." Harriet Martineau, Count Castiglione, the Duc de la Rochefoucauld-Liancourt, all were loud in admiration. Washington Irving, who visited the Valley when he was preparing his biography of Washington, wrote in a kind of ecstasy that it was "equal to the promised land for fertility, far superior to it for beauty, and inhabited by an infinitely superior people,—choice though not chosen."

As for the native children of the Valley, born there, bred there, with the limestone in their bones and the river flowing through their hearts like their blood—when they contemplate their natal countryside, their pens take flight, and "garden of Paradise" is the most restrained term which to them seems adequate. Such descriptions leave a subsequent writer little to attempt. This much may be firmly said. The Shenandoah Valley is beautiful.

Seen from the new drive along the summit of the Blue

Ridge, the Valley is a long green trough between two mountain ranges, a checkerboard of green and brown and gold, on which the silver river writes in flowing curves. The small toy houses of the towns among the fields seem neat but unimportant, for this remains what it has always been—a countryside for farmers.

Along both sides of the gently rolling farm land, the wooded hills rise steeply like protecting walls. At no point in the Valley can one be unconscious of these guardians, yet they are not close enough to be oppressive. They are the ever-present backdrop of every scene. At the wide northern end the distance between the ramparts is so great that only one of them is visible at a time. At the southern end, from Staunton to Lexington, both ranges are close and lovely. The Shenandoah looks like a protected valley especially designed for security and peace. It is a valley with a long and bloody history.

The unexpected bulk of Massanutten, an isolated ridge forty miles long in the middle of the valley, increases the fortresslike aspect. Even today, Massanutten is so rugged that only two roads cross it, and its impassability has had a great influence on Valley history, for Stonewall Jackson made use of it, as will be shown. Inside the northern arms of Massanutten lies a dell ten miles square, completely hidden from the outside world, a little secret valley named Powell's Fort, which from the mountaintop seems as fair as Avalon. Legend says that George Washington dreamed of it as his ultimate retreat when the Revolution was going badly.

Valley people think in terms of counties rather than of towns. Strictly speaking, Lexington and Natural Bridge are on the waters of the James, yet their county of Rockbridge is so identified by tradition and feeling with the Valley that they must be included in the story. Rockbridge and Augusta, the next county down the river, were settled chiefly by Scotch-Irish, and are predominantly Presbyterian still. Then come the rich farm lands of Rockingham and Shenandoah, still predominantly German, then Frederick, Berkeley, Jefferson, and Clarke, where the English settlers of gentle blood built their fine houses and kept their slaves. On the other side of Massanutten, in the lovely Luray Valley watered by the South Fork of the Shenandoah, are Page and Warren counties, more mountainous and more remote. The Opequon River near Winchester is a tributary of the Potomac but, like Lexington, Winchester must be included in the history of the Valley—for the Valley, clearly defined by the mountains, is as unified a region as one can find in the United States.

Green, fair, and sweetly varied with field and meadow, mountain and living stream, the Shenandoah Valley has seemed a good land to all who have seen it—small enough between its mountains to be loved foot by foot with an intimacy denied to more sweeping landscapes, large enough to be welcoming. When Governor Spotswood of Virginia looked down from the Blue Ridge in 1716, he saw a promise in the grassy prairies edged with woodland. The early settlers found the promise true. "The gateway to the west [says James Truslow Adams] and a veritable land of Goshen, of all the frontier the Shenandoah Valley has given the developing America the grandest glimpse of what lay beyond." The Valley was indeed the West made visible.

Today the mountains are still so much a wilderness that they remain a botanists paradise, but in the Valley the buffalo grass has been crowded out by the bluegrass which the English settlers brought. Cornflowers and bouncing Bet along the roadside, blue thistle in the alfalfa, have replaced some native weeds in pleasing the eye and making the farmer curse. The heavy forests which once surrounded Winchester and covered much of the lower Valley, have been reduced to groves of noble oaks. The story of the Valley, from wilderness to frontier, to prosperity, to disaster, to prosperity again, has been a microcosm of American history. Most of our national problems have been reflected in the life there, and most of them have been survived.

And still the river flows on through the rich green fields, the guarding mountains change from green to blue as the air thins or thickens, and the smiling land extends its promise still.

It took a long time to make this simple smiling valley—
perhaps half a billion years of timeless processes.[1] Some of the
earliest shellfish have left their fossils in the Cambrian dolomite on the valley floor. Some of the first plants left the im-
prints of their fernlike leaves in the much later Carboniferous
shale. The Blue Ridge is made of primitive volcanic rock as
old as any in existence.

The encyclopedic mind of Thomas Jefferson studied the
gap at Harpers Ferry, and evolved this theory. "That the
mountains were formed first; that the rivers began to flow
afterward; that in this place they have been damned up by
the Blue Ridge of Mountains and have formed an ocean
which filled the whole valley; that continuing to rise they
have at length broken over at this spot, and have torn the
mountain from its summit to its base." The Indians, looking
at the long green trough between the ranges, said that it was
once a lake around which the stars sang every thousand years.
It is impossible at present to produce scientific confirmation
of the starry chorus, but the Indians were correct as to the
lake.

In the time which geologists call Archeozoic because it
antedates their first conclusions, a land mass stretched eastward over space now covered by the Atlantic Ocean. Beneath
it were the granite and the gneiss, once molten, which had
crystallized as the planet cooled. And there was no life anywhere.

For thousands of centuries the earth spun emptily.
Gradually a portion of this land sank below sea level, and the
waters from the southern Gulf and from the Atlantic seeped
into cover it from New York to Alabama with a huge land-
locked sea. When the Alleghenies of today were below the
ocean, the land to the east separated the Atlantic from this
Paleozoic sea. Then the rains fell, the winds blew, the lost
and traceless rivers ran, and the highlands slowly washed
away. Particle by particle, the mud, the sand, the gravel, sank

[1] Those who believe that the rocks of a region determine the character of
the inhabitants, may note that geologically the Shenandoah is slow-changing
and unhurried.

through the water until the sediment lay one mile deep, and the mountains had vanished. All this took time. Perhaps more than three hundred million years.

Conditions were not always what geologists call stable around the Paleozoic sea. For reasons indecipherable, the waters ebbed and flowed, and as they changed, the character of the sediment changed also. When the sea was muddy, it made shale; when it received the detritus from quartz mountains, sandstone was formed. When the clear and quiet waters filled with life, millions of tiny shells decomposed and hardened into limestone through the slow wheeling of the centuries. Silently and imperceptibly the strata formed, until six thousand feet had been laid down, and a new era dawned.

The area began to rise. Some incalculable force from the earth's heart pushed the rocks westward, folded them upon one another as if they had been dough. Earthquake succeeded earthquake, and the waters rolled away from the upheaving land. A new range of mountains lifted and began again to wash away under the sun. These were the "mother Appalachians," of which now only the roots remain. For rain and wind and the new rivers, ceaselessly eroding, leveled them again into a plain.

There is evidence that at least four times, during the Mezozoic and Cenozoic eras, the area was smoothed off, vertically uplifted, and worn down again. At a rate of perhaps one foot in every thousand years, all this took time. Perhaps one or two million centuries.

Since the granite Blue Ridge resisted all erosion, they are entitled to display what geologists call "the convex softened contours of mature mountains." On Stony Man, the highest Blue Ridge peak, now four thousand feet above sea level, are traces of the oldest plain created by erosion after the "Appalachian revolution," which first raised the land above the sea. The Alleghenies are made by a huge fold of sandstone harder than the surrounding shales and limestones, and the same hard sandstone forms Massanutten, which was part of the same range. Once it lay in a trough between two mountains, and

so it was protected from erosion while the peaks at either side quite literally washed away.

The streams of this region originally drained it to the east and south, but the Shenandoah, then a sporadic young torrent, began at Harpers Ferry with a gully which it made into a gulch, cut its channels up the Valley, and "pirated" the heads of the earlier rivers by undercutting and diverting their waters into its own. From this process came the numerous "wind gaps" in the Blue Ridge—which are now high and dry above the floor but were once the channels of vannished rivers. The Shenandoah has already beheaded in this way the Rappahannock, the Rapidan, and the Rivanna. The Seven Bends of the North Fork, where the river folds back on itself like a ribbon, show that it once meandered sluggishly through an almost level valley. When another uplift came, it cut its channel more deeply and entrenched itself along the established curves instead of changing course.

Water has ceaselessly sculptured more than the surface of the Valley. Under the ground uncounted rivers once ran through the limestone, dissolving the rock with the carbonic acid in their waters and hollowing out the caverns. Natural Bridge is thought to be a part of one such cave, with the roof fallen in. But water had not finished with the caverns when the rivers burst from them into the sunlight. Water continued to seep through them gradually, charged with lime from the stone through which it had passed, and each drop left a minute deposit on the underground floors and ceilings, building the stalagmites and stalactites of today.

Time measured by the rocks is endless time. There is no fever in it, nor does any mountain stand alone. Particle by particle, aeon after aeon, all has been built and shaped. Nothing by chance. All by immutable law. Thousands of small entities, ordered and placed, merge slowly into greater ones, and these in turn dissolve into their elements. The destruction of one is the beginning of another, for nothing ends. And at the last, the water, weak, fluid, nonresistant, is stronger than the stone.

The mountains stood still and the seas subsided, and the rivers cut their curving channels through the hills. Thousands of years passed like one night of impenetrable obscurity, and then there were men in the Valley.

No one knows how they came there, nor from what cradle of the human race they sprang, nor how the seas were parted by dry land to let them walk across. They had a more highly organized society than the tribes which followed them. They built cities which inclosed fifty acres behind earthen walls, they used copper and silver, pipes carved in shapes of tropical animals, ceremonial mounds symbolically shaped. Then they were gone, and the chance acorns fallen on their mounds had grown to trees that marked six centuries before the white man came. The Delawares and the Catawbas, the Algonquins and the Iroquois did not remember them.

It was not in the Shenandoah Valley that they built their pyramids, their ceremonial circles, their human figures seventy feet long, commemorating kings. But they lived in the Valley, and left burial mounds behind them. In the early eighteen hundreds a citizen of Winchester named William Pidgeon made himself into an amateur anthropologist. He opened a mound nine miles from his home and found a stone vault in the center, full of bones. The railroad destroyed it when they built their right of way, but after four hundred wagonloads of stones had been removed, it was still six feet high. Four miles west of Winchester, under another mound of stone, they found a limestone basin eight feet in diameter, deeply marked with fire. On the North Fork stood still another mound and on the South Fork a moat and a wall, the remnants of a ceremonial circle. The earliest historians of the Valley, writing more than a hundred years ago, mention these remains as having been "reduced by the plow." The seated skeletons, the earthen vessels, the pipes with twining serpents, were looked at curiously, and lost. A pioneer discoverer crushed one skull with an ax, declaring that he would give Indians no quarter, dead or alive. "They had murdered his mother, crippled his father, and shot at him. But he had bored nineteen holes in their hides and he would smash that skull and make it an even score."

When the white man came, he found the Valley almost empty, used as a hunting ground and a roadway between north and south. There was a well-marked trail along the top of the Blue Ridge, where the Skyline Drive now runs. There was another trail in the Valley, which is now the Valley Pike. The Shawnees maintained three villages near Winchester, three collections of bark huts near little clearings where the straggling corn and pumpkins grew rank in the summer and were abandoned in the snow. Another Shawnee village stood near Woodstock, and the Tuscaroras occupied the neighborhood of Martinsburg, where were found the giant skeletons, seven feet long, with three-foot thighs.

The first settlers heard legends of a tribe called the Senedos who had been exterminated by the Iroquois, and occasionally a trader found a tribal slave who claimed to have Senedo antecedents. The Cherokees had a tradition of having lived there until the northern Indians drove them farther south. There were also stories of a struggle between the Powhatans from the Eastern Shore and the Iroquois.

It was said that Opecancanough, son of Powhatan, made war in the Valley on the Iroquois chief Sherando, drove him out, and left his son Sheewanee in charge. But Sheewanee was not strong enough to face the counterattack, and soon fled back to the Tidewater. Opecancanough, informed by runners, swooped down on Sherando through a gap in the Blue Ridge, killed him, and re-established his son. The Valley Indians were known as Shawnees from then on.

The Monocans called Natural Bridge "the Bridge of God," for according to their tradition it had been thrown across the chasm for them when they were fleeing from the Powhatans. They had sent their women and children across it for safety, and then were able to hold it against the enemy.

All this the first settlers got only by hearsay. The Indians they knew in the Valley were the Delawares from the Susquehanna, the Catawbas from South Carolina, who passed to and fro hunting and fighting, and intermittently met and murdered one another according to their immemorial custom. The migrant Indians came and went, demanding bread and milk at the cabins where they stopped, regarded as nuisances, regarded as jokes, and boasting about their exploits.

They claimed to have fought a great battle at Painted Rock near Harpers Ferry, where their blood had reddened the stones forever. The Catawbas said they had buried a Delaware chief alive near Shepherdstown, and that Swearingen's spring flowed from the pulsing of his heart. At Parrill's farm near Winchester, thirty Delawares passed through with a Catawba prisoner, and soon the Catawbas were inquiring on their trail, followed them up the mountain, killed them, and stopped at Parrill's with their rescued comrade on the way south again. At another farm, the Delawares came through with a Catawba woman, tied with grapevines on the ends of which they slept at night to keep her from escaping. Near a settlement they sacrificed her and her child, and cut off the soles of her feet so that she could not follow them over the mountains.

Ignorant heathen, scarcely more human than the wolves, the white men thought them. Thomas Jefferson deduced that war must be the natural state of mankind, since these savages fought although they dwelt six hundred miles apart, with "no trade, commerce, or clashing of interests." The average pioneer kept out of their quarrels and gave them little attention, for he had much to do. To his eyes the Valley was empty. It must be made into a dwelling place for Man—and by Man he did not mean a handful of naked savages.

The Indians left little in the Valley—mounds to be plowed down, arrow heads, the dust of bones. They lived like shadows among the trees, like shadows they have passed, and even the terror they inspired is now forgotten. Only one imperishable trace of them remains, ringing down the centuries like distant music. They left the Valley its name, Shenandoah.

The name has evolved, like most American place names of Indian origin, coming down through old records in many phonetic spellings: Gerando, Gerundo, Shendo, Genantua, Sherando. Many meanings have been assigned to it. The most

CHIEF SHERANDO

romantic one, the one popularly accepted by the Valley people themselves, is "Daughter of the Stars." This meaning has been much beloved, and incorporated into the writing which every generation of inhabitants feels inspired to produce, but the basis for it has remained concealed from the present researcher. The name appears in books of Indian etymology as Schin-han-dowi, the River-Through-The-Spruces, (but spruces are rare in those mountains), or as On-an-da-goa, the River-of-High-Mountains, or as Silver-Water. The Museum of the American Indian in New York City believes that it is a word of Iroquois origin meaning Big Meadow. Or it might come from the fallen chief, Sherando, or from the earlier exterminated tribe, the Senedos. Most authorities agree that Massanutten means Potato-Ground.

But these discussions matter little. As Daughter of the Stars the river has been enshrined in the hearts of Valley dwellers, and Daughter of the Stars it will remain to them.

3. Exploration

From this discourse it is clear that the long looked for discovery of the Indian Sea doth nearly approach.
—JOHN LEDERER to WILLIAM TALBOT. 1670

Sic juvat transcendere montes.
—GOVERNOR SPOTSWOOD. 1716

THE white man had been fifty years established on the lowlands of the coast. The starving time had been forgotten, forgotten the "country sickness" which had decimated Jamestown. The foothold on the continent was secure.

In 1669 a German named John Lederer, born in Hamburg, "a modest ingenuous person and a pretty scholar," came to Sir William Berkeley, then governor of Virginia, and procured a license to trade furs across the blue mountain wall at the west of the colony. All reasonable people considered the mountains impassable. If this foreigner wished to throw his life away, no one would be the worse for it, and if by some chance he should succeed, the colony might benefit. When the March sun began to bring out a mist of young leaves over the forest, he left York River with three Indian guides and soon vanished in the tangled green thickets.

At that period everyone knew that North America was divided into three parts—"the flats, the highlands, and the mountains, called by the Spaniards Apalatean." The party made its way across the highlands, John Lederer on his horse, the three Indians on foot, swift and silent, nosing out a trail. They hacked their way through entwined creepers, they found a rattlesnake six feet long, they saw a deer killed by a wildcat, they picked up rocks containing isinglass and crystal. At night they lay on the ground and heard the wolves howling on the scent of the one horse, and the bears lumbering around them, "crushing mast like swine."

By March 14th they reached the mountain crest, and peered down out of the woods into a shining valley, green with young grass, and far across it in the hazy distance, climbing waves of purple mountain peaks. The three Indians prostrated themselves on the ground crying, "God is nigh!" John Lederer, from the advantage of his superior intelligence and education, sat his horse, contemplated the Valley, and congratulated himself on his first sight of the "Apalateans."

He took three days to reach them, and to climb a little way on foot, far enough to discover that they were apparently endless, range beyond range. Then he returned to tell the governor what he had seen.

On the twentieth of May he started out again, this time with a party: a Major Harris, "twenty Christian horse," five Indian guides. They came again over the mountains, and descended to a river which the astute major identified as "an arm of the lake of Canada." When he had seen this much he was ready to go back, for the biscuits had become moldy and they were living on parched corn; but that stubborn Lederer persisted in continuing, in following the river to the south. Major Harris stuck it out for two more days, then led his party homeward, and left his German friend to advance on foot with one Indian guide. He presented Lederer with a gun when they parted, and wrote him down as a lost man, a man about whom anything might safely be told, anything that reflected credit on Major Harris.

For two months Lederer made his way southward, living happily among the Indians, who received him everywhere with kindness. He discovered that they were not like the coastal Indians, but had been driven down from the northwest by their enemies or, as they liked to tell it, led to this green land by an oracle. They raised three crops of grain in a summer, lived in houses or arbors of watlings and plaster. Their kings wore strings of pearls, measured time with knotted cords, used hieroglyphics: a stag for swiftness, a serpent for wrath, a dog for fidelity, a swan for the English who had flown over the sea.

They were kind to Lederer, and he treated them with respect, never entering one of their houses unless he had been invited. When he saw strange things, he kept silent. He saw an ambassador and five other men of the Rickohockans arrive to treat with the Akenatzy. He saw the withy council lodge darkened by the smoke of a great feast, under cover of which the strangers all were murdered. Lederer saw this, and departed quietly with his guide that night, not troubling to say farewell.

The Tuscaroras, who were the haughtiest and the most serious, took his gun, but this did not alarm him, since he reasoned that one gun had no real value against so many savages. He journeyed on until he met a tribe where the women were the stronger sex while the men were lazy and effeminate, where peacocks were esteemed for making feather ornaments, and where he was told that the Spaniards lived to the southwest, only two days away. He was not afraid of the Indians, but he was afraid of the Spaniards, so he turned back, and came out in the end near Appomattox, "not a little overjoyed to see Christian faces again."

Even then, John Lederer had not had enough. He had found a pass through the southern Apalateans, and he thought that there must be one to the north. He reasoned that a branch of the long-sought Indian Ocean must surely lie beyond those endless ridges, for if there were anything there except salt water, the Canadian swans, ducks, and geese would not cross the mountains for their winter in the south. He suggested that a party of five or six bold men might safely try the crossing, notching the trees so that they could find their way back, and carrying hammocks in which they could sleep.

In August of 1670 he set out a third time, now with a Colonel Catlet, "nine Christian horse," five Indians. They rode straight westward from the Rappahannock, crossed the Blue Ridge easily at Manassas Gap, and descended into broad savannas, flowery meads, where herds of red deer were feed-

ALEXANDER
SPOTSWOOD

SIR WILLIAM
BERKELEY

ing. The grass which sprang from the limestone soil was so high that they could tie it across their saddles. Since the Indians burned this land over every autumn to make their game preserve, it was only lightly wooded with occasional groves of oak or maple. The prairies, where the red deer sprang away from the horses, were hot and fragrant, but the Apalateans proved still unyielding, still to be climbed only on foot. Before many days the explorers were weary of the laurel thickets, and again reduced to living on parched corn. Lederer was bitten by a spider, and although one of the Indians saved him by sucking the wound, after a slight illness he was persuaded to turn back.

This time he did not meet a pleasant welcome in Virginia. Major Harris had been explaining why he had given up when another man found it possible to continue alone, and Lederer was written down as a "presumptuous stranger." His persistence was held to be "the measure of his insolence," and from a storm of "affronts and reproaches" he fled to Maryland, where Lord Calvert received him more hospitably. Virginia and Maryland were then as ever in colonial days jealous of each other, and engaged in boundary disputes. Sir William Talbot, secretary of Maryland, wrote Lederer's story, and did not neglect the opportunity of putting the Virginians in an unfavorable light.

Finding him a modest ingenuous person, and a pretty scholar, I thought it common justice to give him an occasion of vindicating himself . . . for indeed it was their part, that foresook him in the expedition, to procure him discredit that was a witness to theirs.

*   *   *

Time passed into another century, and still the mountains remained a barrier to be crossed only by the occasional traders—quiet men who did not talk or write about their journeys.

In 1707, French Louis Michelle and a party from Annapolis came through the gap at Harpers Ferry, traveled south as far as Powell's Fort, that secret valley in the arms of Massanutten, and left a crude map of the region filed for posterity in the Public Records Office in London. They found a name, "Senantoa," applied to the mountains, they found evidence of silver mines, but they recorded nothing more. By 1716 they had been forgotten, if indeed the Virginians had ever heard of them, and time had ripened for another expedition.

This was to be discovery in a different style, in the grand manner, a definitive exploration with a dash and flourish rare in American annals, headed by His Honor the Governor of Virginia, in person.

Even the background of Governor Alexander Spotswood had a romantic richness. He was descended from a Scottish archbishop who had been deposed, but later compensated by burial in Westminster Abbey, and from a grandfather who had fought under Montrose. He himself was born in Tangier, wounded at Blenheim, fought at Malplaquet, rose to be quartermaster general for Marlborough at the age of twenty-eight. When he came to Virginia in 1710 he could and did "swear like our army in Flanders" at the obstinacy of his House of Burgesses, but he was ambitious for the improvement of the colony. He imported artisans, founded ironworks, and in 1716 boldly determined to attempt the passage of "the

Great Mountains," which were then Virginia's western wall, and in so doing to establish Virginia's western claims.

For an old campaigner like the governor, to determine was to act, but there was to be nothing inconspicuous, nothing unequipped about exploration as he saw it. Here was no solitary adventurer wandering into the woods so innocently as not even to provide himself with a gun. This would be official discovery, stamped with the royal seal.

Late in August, at Germanna on the Rapidan, His Honor assembled his party, fifty strong: gentlemen, servants, Indian guides, two companies of rangers, horses and pack horses with "abundant provisions." He wore a riding habit of green velvet, boots of Russian leather, a hat with a fine plume—not perhaps the most comfortable outfit for August in Virginia. The names of the gentlemen who rode with him read like a Virginia roster of today: Beverly, Robertson, Robinson, Taylor, Todd, Mason, Brooke, and young Ensign John Fontaine, who did posterity the kindness of keeping a diary.

First Fontaine listed the "abundant provisions": "several cases of Virginia wine, both white and red, Irish *usquebaugh*, brandy, stout, two kinds of rum, champagne, cherry punch, cider, etc." What "etc" could have been is not specified. Then he recounted how they had the foresight to shoe their horses with iron, for the mountain trails would be rougher than the sandy lowlands. This occupied the morning, but they set out at one, and by five the governor halted them to encamp beside a little stream. "We made great fires, supped, and drank good punch. By ten of the clock I had taken all my ounce of Jesuit bark, but my head was much out of order." (Reason not given.)

At seven on the morning of August 30th, the party sprang to life at the call of a trumpet, and "Austen Smith, one of the gentlemen with us, having a fever, returned home. We had lain on the ground under cover of our tents, and we found by the pains in our bones that we had not had good beds to lie on."

By nine, they sent the servants and the baggage forward, but the gentlemen remained behind to catch the governor's horses, which had strayed. By two-thirty they secured the horses, by three they mounted, by half after four they came up with the baggage at a small river, "which we call Mine River, because there was an appearance of silver in it." Somewhat exhausted by this arduous day of one and one-half hours travel, they found at the river "good pasturage for our horses, and venison in abundance for ourselves, which we roasted before the fire on wooden forks, and so went to bed in our tents," not without having "good liquor," and setting a sentry to guard the governor against the wilderness.

Next day, inured to woodland life, they covered fourteen miles, and so continued, until by September 2nd they found themselves actually toiling up the mountains. They passed over many small rivers, hornets stung their horses, they saw a small bear running down a tree, but forbore to shoot it on the Sabbath, although they had killed three the day before. Alas now for the riding habit of green velvet, the plumes, the boots of Russian leather—they tore their clothing, their saddles and holsters to rags in the thickets. "We had a rugged way."

They were not the men to turn back, however, and by September 5th they camped at the foot of the "Great Mountain" itself. Here some of the party had the humiliation of breaking out with measles, but the rest left their heavy luggage at "Rattlesnake Camp," flung themselves at the mountain, and by one o'clock looked out above the leaves at Swift Run Gap. Below them crouched the smaller hills like shaggy beasts, and beyond they saw a wide triangle of lush and fertile valley, against the blue background of another mountain (Massanutten). They were higher than a buzzard who floated past on silent outstretched wings. In the surrounding woods, the Virginia creeper, already touched by frosty nights, flung scarlet cascades down the trees, locust and shaking aspen, oak and white pine. The sumac had lit its crimson candles, and the goldenrod burst into ethereal fountains above the underbrush . . . but the smiling unknown valley lay in midsummer still.

His Honor observed the occasion properly. He called a halt, drank the health of the king, drank the health of the royal family, then led his party down the slopes between the crouching hills.

They found the descent harder than they had expected, for the little streams they followed led to precipices too steep for the horses; but at length they reached the Valley, pushed through the waving grass higher than the horses, and camped by a clear and beautiful river which they named "Euphrates." Fortunately Governor Spotswood was an explorer and not a settler, and this affected cognomen did not fasten forever on the Shenandoah.

The party crossed the river and buried on the other side a bottle which contained a paper claiming all this territory for His Majesty King George I. They feasted on wild deer and turkey which they killed themselves, and on the cucumbers, currants, and grapes which grew around them.

We had a good dinner, and after it we got the men together and loaded all the arms; and we drank the King's health in champagne, and fired a volley; and the Princess in Burgundy, and fired a volley; and all the rest of the Royal Family in claret, and fired a volley. We drank the Governor's health, and fired another volley.

After this glorious finale to a successful expedition, the young ensign had only one more entry. On the way back they stopped at a spring which they named after himself, and drank a bowl of punch.

In the pleasure of retrospect, Governor Spotswood wrote glowingly about his trip to what he called "World's End":

The chief aim of my expedition . . . was to satisfy myself whether it was practicable to come at the Lakes. Having on that occasion found an easy passage over that great Ridge of Mountains which were before judged impassable, I also discovered by the relations of Indians who frequent those parts . . . that from the western side of one of the small mountains which I saw that the Lake is very visible.

Encouraged by this outstanding bit of misinformation, His Honor hoped that they might soon establish an English trading post which would drive a wedge between the extremities of the French position. He ordered little golden horseshoes for the gentlemen who had gone with him, and inscribed them "Sic Juvat Transcendere Montes," in memory of their preparation for the "rugged way." And so with waving plumes and convivial volleys, the governor and his "Knights of the Golden Horseshoe" ride out of the story.

The Tidewater discovered, but the Tidewater did not settle the Valley. Spotswood rested content with laying formal claim to it, with proving that the mountains were accessible. The fair valley did not tempt his followers; on the contrary they were glad for the protection of the Blue Ridge.

Providence has secured us from the savages [wrote one Hugh Jonas, considering "the Present State of Virginia" in London eight years later] by a continued Ridge of vast high hills which through the care and conduct of the Hon Col Spotswood are secured for His Majesty, though not guarded as yet, which might easily be done . . . to the encouragement of Back Settlements.

Mr. Jonas added smooth words of comfort for the timid: "There can be no room for real apprehension of Danger of a Revolt of the Plantations in future Ages."

This was in 1724. Before ten years had passed, men would brave the danger of back settlements without waiting for suitable guards on the frontier; men who wore no plumes, no velvet habits, but who took what they wanted because they were sure that no one else would help them get it and were prepared to deal abruptly with whatever stood in their way.

4. Settlement

THERE were three great strains in the early settlement of the Shenandoah Valley: the Germans, and the Scotch-Irish, both Protestant, both with a long tradition of religious persecution, a hatred of European quarrels; and the English settlers of gentle blood. The Germans, among whom were some Swiss, came first.

In 1689 the Catholic soldiers of Louis XIV drove the Protestants from the Palatinate. Some fled to England, and then on to the New World. They sent back good reports and others followed.

These German Protestants were careful people, serious people, who intended to work hard and to establish their families on a solid basis. Their wives did not mind working in the fields, or pulling a plow when draft animals were lacking. They went into New Jersey, New York, and Pennsylvania, looking for good land which had not been taken up, and in Pennsylvania they heard fur traders extol the valley of the "Cenantua." Between 1726 and 1735, many of them gathered up their wives and families, children and grandchildren, to go there in small groups, independently, but all searching for the same thing: land. Land upon which they could settle. Land which could be improved.

They did not come into the Valley over the forbidding wall of mountains, but in a more natural way, down through the rolling fields of Pennsylvania and across the Potomac, near what is now Shepherdstown, which the Germans called Mechlenburg. An old tombstone indicates that there were settlers there as early as 1726, but their record has been lost. The pioneers found no town, of course, only a rich prairie with tall grass and flowering pea vine, good pasturage for cow or horse. They knew good land when they saw it, these Germans who had so little, who brought with them only their will to work, their strong wives, their healthy flock of children, a domestic animal or two, a few household utensils, and their massive German Bibles with the brass or iron clasps. They pushed southward up the Valley, and their children's children remain there to this day, holding still the two things left to them: the land and the heavy German Bibles.

Most of the settlers were obscure people, and their arrival is veiled in obscurity. It appears that the earliest, after those at Mechlenburg, was the Swiss Adam Miller, whose application for a naturalization certificate in 1731 stated that he had lived five years in the "fields of Massanutten" (the Luray valley). History records of him one other fact. The house he built for his family burnt down on the day he was ready to move into it, and he patiently began that night to build another.

John Van Meter, a fur trader, with his two sons Abraham and Isaac, saw the waving grasses five feet high, and obtained a grant in 1730 for 10,000 acres in the fork of the "Sherando." A year later, at about the same time that the Quakers began their settlement on the Opequon, Van Meter sold his grant to a German of some wealth and substance, Hans Jost Heydt.

Joist Hite, to Anglicize him as his neighbors promptly did, came from Alsace to Kingston, New York, in 1710. Family tradition says that he sailed in his own ships, the brigantine *Swift* and schooner *Friendship*, and that he carried his gold in sacks. Likewise it is told, on evidence which has not been produced, that he was a baron. With some frequency it appears that the early Americans escaped from the artificial distinctions of titles only to create them fairer still in the imagination. Baron or not, Hite moved southward little by little, crowded here, discouraged there by Indian raids, until in October of 1731, "cutting his road from York," he crossed the Potomac and settled near the Quakers, five miles southwest of the site of Winchester.

If the sacks of gold ever existed, there is no conclusive proof that he brought them to the Valley, but he did bring some evidence of wealth, and better still the native energy and sturdiness of his own character, and the strength of his blood. Of the sixteen families who came with him, three were families of his sons-in-law, George Bowman, Paul Froman, and Jacob Chrisman, and four were the families of his sons. In partnership with a Quaker, Robert McKay, and others he increased his holdings to 100,000 acres, and Governor Gooch confirmed the grant. This apparently regular proceeding gave rise to a classic lawsuit, which dragged on through the courts for fifty years.

In spite of legal troubles, Joist Hite behaved like a man who had come to stay. Each year he and his sons brought more land under the plow, enclosed new fields with saplings. At first he lived in a log cabin like the other settlers, but before long he began to quarry stones for the foundation of his barn, and then, after the stock had been taken care of, for his permanent stone house, the first built in the Valley. When his wife died, he soon married a widow, Maria Magdalena, and recorded a marriage contract in which he promised her "Christian love and faithfulness," while she promised him love, obedience, and all her worldly goods, the two mares, the colt, the pair of oxen, the household gear, valued at twenty-two pounds, seventeen shillings, and fourpence.

Joist Hite remained on his land. The courts could not unseat him, nor could Lord Fairfax. Later he gave more than a dozen grandsons to that Revolt of the Plantations which Hugh Jonas saw no room to apprehend. But that is getting ahead of the story.

The Germans in the middle of the Valley held stubbornly to their own ways. In some places they clung to their language for more than a hundred years, and newspapers were still being published in German during the early part of the nineteenth century. Some of the Dunkards in Rockingham County speak German still. For a long time they kept up their distinctive customs. They slept between feather beds, ate sauerkraut, wore short coats with long waistcoats above their breeches, trimmed their broad hats with heavy silver buckles.

Like all back-country people, their weddings were their great social occasions. When one of the Miller girls married near Woodstock, they danced for a week. Four maidens and four young men put on the white embroidered ceremonial aprons, and waited on the bride and groom. They had wine in stone bottles, beef, pork, fowl, cabbage and potatoes in wooden bowls and pewter dishes. The lads held the girls on their laps when they ran out of chairs. The groomsmen were supposed to keep the other fellows from stealing the bride's shoe, from snatching it off and dancing around with it. If one succeeded, he got a bottle of wine as a prize.

When the bridal couple went to bed, all the party poured into their room, and as they lay there, red-faced and giggling, rolled up the bride's stocking, and threw it at her over their shoulders. The one who hit her on the head would be the next one married. Then the guests whirled off to dance square sets all night, and in the morning to send up food and a bottle to the married pair. They ought to be hungry by then. They ought to be ready to hear the toast: "Here's health to the groom, not forgetting myself, and health to the bride, thumping luck, and big children."

The Germans loved their thumping big families, worked them hard, and built for their future. They might let their women work in the fields, but they housed their stock in the wintertime, and their fat cattle astonished their neighbors. Their "swisher" (Switzer) barns, with the overhanging second stories, were always larger than their square little houses. They paid for everything they got with their own produce, did their own work and rarely hired labor. Every two or three years they bought new land. They were the best of settlers, say the old records, because of their thrift and "their perfect submission to the civil authorities."

The Scotch-Irish, who for the most part settled in the upper Valley, may have admired this submissiveness, but they did not imitate it. It has been said that the Covenanters, whose descendants they were, had such a fear of God that it left no room in their hearts for any fear of man. Certainly man they did not fear, and persecution taught them only to adhere more firmly to their principles, their customs, and their faith.

From the persecutions of Dundee in Scotland they fled to Ulster. In this new refuge they soon quarreled with the Catholic Irish, but they survived the siege of Londonderry. Catholic monarchs tried to exterminate them. Anglican monarchs called them dissenters, held their marriages illegal, debarred them from office or military rank. Caught between Papist and the Established Church, they made no truce with either. If they could not live in Scotland, they would move to Ulster. If they could not live in Ireland, they would migrate to America. If they could not live in Pennsylvania, they would move to Virginia. More and more stringent religious tests were enacted to hold them under, and not only their religion but their livelihood was threatened. They made not the slightest modification of their beliefs, they bowed to no temporal authority. Still Presbyterians, they moved on to the south and west.

It could not be hoped that such a people, making no concessions to civil or religious authority, viewing all governments with a suspicious eye, and expecting only the worst from them, would become instantly popular in the communities where they wished to settle. When they began to arrive in Pennsylvania, attracted by its broad and tolerant policy, the secretary of that province wrote acidly: "It looks to me as if Ireland is to send all its inhabitants hither, for last week not less than six ships arrived . . . It is strange that they thus crowd where they are not wanted."

The Scotch-Irish were accustomed to not being wanted. They moved on again, this time to the almost empty Valley. By 1738, the year when the first Valley counties were established, they were there in such numbers that they sent the governor of Virginia a petition: "For those who are of the same persuasion as the Church of Scotland . . . to ask your favor in allowing them the liberty of their consciences, and of worshipping God in a way agreeable to the principles of their education."

The governor graciously replied that they would not be interfered with so long as they behaved peaceably, registered their meeting place, abjured the Stuart Pretender, the doctrine of transubstantiation, and the Pope at Rome. Nothing in this oath disturbed a Presbyterian conscience, and the Scotch-Irish in their turn agreed to pay their tithes to the Established Church so long as they did not have to go to it. His Majesty welcomed an increase in quitrents and the governor took pleasure in establishing a group of hardy people between the rich plantations and the frontier. It is possible that he also saw an advantage in removing to a remote area a number of rigidly devoted characters who did not fit in with the established order and might have caused some difficulty in more settled regions.

There was no one to object to the Scotch-Irish in the Valley, and this time they found rest; not only they, but numerous other small and unpopular sects, notably the Quakers, who started a colony on the Opequon, near Winchester. The Germans, called Dutch, and the Scotch, called Irish, were glad of neighbors. The Valley was long enough, and wide enough, and rich enough, for Lutheran, German Reformed, Quaker, Mennonite, Dunkard, and Presbyterian. Between the ramparts of the mountains, these descendants of persecution dwelt in peace with one another.

The Scotch-Irish looked backward with some homesick remembering, and named parts of their new country for the landmarks they had known. Near Staunton there are two hills called Betsey Bell and Mary Gray, named for two Irish mountains in County Tyrone. Betsey Bell and Mary Gray had crossed the water once before. In Perthshire, a hundred years earlier, the house of Lednock on the river Almond bore the name of Gray, the house of Kinvald the name of Bell, and Betsey and Mary were friends, and young, and one young man in love with both of them. During the pestilence of 1645 their fathers sent them for safety to a "bower" in the

mountains, but their suitor followed, bringing the plague
with him, and they died. The hills in Tyrone were named
for the hills in Perth, the hills in Virginia for the hills in
Tyrone.

First among the Scotch-Irish, like Joist Hite among the
Germans, was John Lewis, who founded the town of Staunton in 1732. Strictly speaking, he was not Scotch-Irish at
all, for he was of French descent, and his wife Margaret came
from Loch Lynn in Scotland; but he had lived in the north
of Ireland, and he had left in a hurry, for he had killed
his landlord, Lord Clonmithgairn. There had been an argument over rents, the courts upheld Lewis, the lord attacked
him in Clonmell Castle at night, and in the ensuing fight
Lewis lost his brother and Clonmithgairn his life. Lewis fled,
and found a refuge in Virginia. Many years later the king's
pardon reached him there, but by that time he was established,
and he never went back.

When he arrived in Virginia, he stayed in Williamsburg, with Governor Gooch, a friend of his wife's family,
and there he heard about the Shenandoah from John Peter
Salling, a Marco Polo of the wilderness. Salling has been captured in the Valley by some Iroquois who were passing
through, and carried out to the Mississippi over rather more
of the country than he had intended to explore. At the
Mississippi an itinerant Spaniard bought him from the Indians and took him as interpreter to the French in Canada.
The French sent him to the Dutch on the island of Man-
hattan, and thence he made his way back to Virginia—to
settle at last with Lewis in the lovely Valley, where his ad-
ventures had begun.

His story of the rich land induced John Lewis to obtain
a grant and to cross the mountains with about thirty of his
tenantry who had remained loyal to him. They set their cabins
in the flowering prairie, where it "unrolled like gaudy car-
peting around them," and where Snowdrop, the white cow,
came in at evening with her hoofs stained crimson by wild
strawberries. It was a fair land, fair, silent, empty, and far
from all that once had made life gracious for them. The

brave and gentle Margaret Lewis consoled her loneliness by keeping a diary, a "Book of Comforts," between the lines of an old ledger. A version of this diary has survived, probably not in its original form, and yet so packed with detail which other records corrobate that it cannot be dismissed as wholly spurious.

In it she tells how she set to work to make her home beautiful for her children, so that they might love to stay in it, "and learn beauty of soul by growing up with beautiful things." When she transplanted some of the wild roses to bloom around the door, Oroonah, the Indian chief who lived near by, told her that she should have let them alone, for the Great Spirit had put the flowers where he wanted them.

The Indians visited the settlers often, and Margaret thought they looked like painted mountebanks at an Irish county fair, but she never felt at home with them. Strange people, secret people, arriving unexpectedly, and vanishing among the trees again. The chief brought his son, Omayah, to play with the Lewis boys, and with little Alice, whom he called his "White Dove." Omayah made her crowns of flowers, and brought her a fawn which he had tamed. But John Lewis did not let this friendliness prevent his building a stockade ten feet high around his settlement, with a blockhouse at each corner. "It shall descend to his posterity," wrote Margaret proudly, "that John Lewis hath builded the first town in the Valley." They called the little cluster of log houses Staunton, after Lady Rebecca Staunton, wife of Governor Gooch.

On the day when Alice Lewis was fourteen, Oroonah, the outwardly accepted and secretly-laughed-at friend, arrived in a chieftain's dignity, to ask her hand in marriage for his son. John Lewis tried to make light of it, set her to play the spinet, said, "You don't want her. White woman good for nothing else." When the chief went away in silence, John laughed, but Margaret was full of fear. For some time Omayah came rarely, "sad, silent, and brooding." Still John Lewis would not see a danger, and took his young people to a picnic at Tower Rocks. Margaret stayed at home with her new baby, but Omayah went.

The Indian boy and the White Dove, still childhood playmates, wandered away from the others and crossed a little brook in search of "good luck plant." Then with a fierce suddenness the Indians swooped down, caught Alice up, vanished like ferrets into the underbrush. Alice screamed once. Then there was silence as the leafy curtain closed behind them. The white men pursued frantically, firing as they ran, but the forest still belonged to the Indians, and it sheltered them. That night John Lewis returned alone to comfort Margaret. Four days later his sons and the other men of the party, came back empty-handed.

I had never showed such grief before him until then, no, not when we made that little grave on the prairie and piled the white rocks upon it. I was striding the floor as he surprised me, wringing my hands, and, may heaven forgive me, almost reproaching the Most High that he had mocked me to hear my prayer and raise her up from that dreadful fever when she lay a little one tossing in my arms, getting ready for flight, I thought.

Twice while the men were searching vainly in the forest, the Indians attacked the fort, and were driven off. Their war cries did not frighten Margaret, for she was "already possessed with dread and anguish." After one attack, the defenders shot a stout Indian who was creeping toward the fort. The Indian fell and then they saw that it was no Indian at all, but mad Mary Greenlee, sister to one of them, a poor deranged creature whom some called a witch, who wandered the countryside at will, now with the heathen, now in solitude. While they dressed her wound, she gabbled out a strange tale of stealing the White Dove away from the tribe and hiding her in a palace underground, where the walls were silver and the floors were pearl. She said that if they would give her a horse, she would bring Alice home.

It was a story to be believed only by a mother who must catch at any hope, but Margaret gave her the horse, although others said that it had "gone for no profit." "Indeed she will be more angel in my sight than flesh and blood, if she talked not idly in the news she bears me."

Faith was rewarded, for the tale was true. Mary Greenlee brought Alice home, unharmed except for a fever into which the terror had thrown her. In her delirium she too talked of a marble palace with statues and fountains, interminable galleries, and stars and moon peering through the roof. The settlers set this down as fantastic nonsense, for it was to be another hundred years before the white men would blunder into a limestone cavern. Some insisted that Alice had been bewitched.

But Margaret would not have it so, and saw to it that Mary Greenlee came and went as it suited her. "Where her palace is it hath been her freak not to tell . . . but none of the Lewis name can forevermore carp at Mary Greenlee what she does. Blessed creature, I would walk on hands and knees to serve her to the latest day of my life." In her joy, Margaret even forgave Omayah, who came protesting innocence of the plot: "I am willing and glad to think the boy was not at fault. He hath been the playfellow of my sons so long . . . Tiger King professes great penitence, but in him I have less faith. In the old I look for more stability, in the young for more truth. This for red and white men."

Thanks to a spirit too sweet and strong to cherish bitterness, the incident was smoothed over, and the friendly relations between Indians and settlers were resumed. There was peace again in the flower-carpeted meadows between the mountain ranges—for a time.

The Scotch-Irish were religious and, some say, contentious, but they were not too grim to enjoy a wedding. Margaret Lewis went to the nuptials of John Peter Salling's nephew, where they had whisky in a barrel and a gourd for a ladle, where they danced reels and jigs and no one was allowed to sleep, and the fiddler played "Hang Out Until Morning." She saw the attendants ride up dressed in buckskin shirts and leggings, and the bride brought on horseback to the preacher's house, with grapevines tied across the trail to make it hard, and mock ambushes to see if the horses were frisky. On the way back to the bride's home, after the ceremony, the boys dumped the girls who were riding behind their saddles, and held a "race for the bottle," a mad dash over stumps, brooks, and stones, to the doorway where a friend stood holding the bottle tied in white ribbon. The winner carried it back to the party, for the bride must drink first, and then the others. There was not much left in the bottle by the time they reached the house.

Margaret gave the bride, Comfort, one of her gowns from former days, a yellow brocade (over which Mr. Parks from Williamsburg had upset the gravy boat on the day the surveyors laid out the town). She watched the rowdy festivities with some alarm, the wild dancing, the kidnaping and bedding of the married pair, the supper sent up to them consisting of Black Betty (another bottle), bacon, beef, and cabbage. "These New World manners are making queer innovations among our people," Margaret said.

Her baby, Charles, born in Virginia, she called her "New World child," but although she did not realize it, all her sons were New World children. This wilderness life, the harshness of which she attempted in her gentle way to modify, would claim them all. John Lewis lived long, builded more solidly than he knew, and when he died they carved on his headstone an epitaph like a trumpet call for days to come:

HERE LIES THE REMAINS OF JOHN LEWIS
WHO SLEW THE IRISH LORD
SETTLED IN AUGUSTA COUNTY
LOCATED THE TOWN OF STAUNTON
AND FURNISHED FIVE SONS TO FIGHT THE BATTLES OF
THE AMERICAN REVOLUTION

In 1736 Lewis was visited by one Benjamin Burden, an agent for Lord Fairfax, who was delighted with the Valley, and is said to have taken back a buffalo calf as a present for Governor Gooch. The governor rewarded him by a "minor grant" of 500,000 acres on the Shenandoah and the upper James, provided he could settle one hundred families on it

VIRGINIA AROUND 1730

within ten years—the standard procedure in those days of vagueness about the western lands. Each family would receive one hundred acres, with the privilege of taking up one hundred more as soon as five acres of the first had been planted in corn, and His Majesty got a quitrent of two shillings an acre. Since there were no surveyors to establish boundaries, successive governors granted land without regard to what had been done before, and thereby laid the foundation of many a bitter argument and of a conviction in American minds that royal government was something they could do without.

Benjamin Burden hurried to northern Ireland for his first shipload of settlers. Back with him came McDowell, McClure, Alexander, Wallace, Moore, Preston, Matthews, Campbell, Ramsay, Houston, Bell, Douglas—and the names are in the Valley still. Colonel James Patton, late of His Majesty's Navy, crossed and recrossed the Atlantic twenty-five times, carrying furs and tobacco, and bringing out healthy young people, many of whom were willing to work five years as indentured servants to pay for their passage, for their chance at a new life.

Like the Germans, the Scotch-Irish had come to stay.

Soon after John Lewis laid out Staunton, a group of Scotch, Welsh, and English settlers founded a town in the lower Valley. Their leader was a Colonel James Wood, who had been educated at Oxford, had served in the Royal Navy, and had come to the Valley in his late twenties as a surveyor for the state of Virginia. With some experience behind him, and the world to choose from, he chose the Valley, and in 1735 began to build his "seat," "Glen Burnie," beside a little brook. The stone walls around the garden, the springhouse, the cliff lilies, the cedar walk, were laid out in the English style. Inevitably, when he planned his town, he named it for his English home: Winchester.

"To Morgan Morgan, Thomas Chester, David Vance, Andrew Campbell, Marquis Calmes, Thomas Rutherford, Lewis Neill, William McMachen, Meridith Helm, George

Hoge, John White, and Thomas Little, *gentlemen,*" Wood
deeded twenty-two lots of half an acre each, crossed by two
streets thirty-two feet wide; on condition that they should
build on each one within two years a house not smaller than
twenty by sixteen feet, "of framed work or squared logs,
dovetailed." This title, said the deed with premonitory foreboding, was to be defended against all claimants except Lord
Fairfax (of whom more will be said presently).

Where were the Indians, while this was taking place,.
while their Valley of the Silver Water was given away and
granted, parceled out and settled? They were there. They
came and went in their shadowy way, disturbing the face of
nature as little as did the deer, making no greater change in
their environment than does a chipmunk when it builds a
nest. The Valley was their roadway and their hunting ground.
They did not have the drive which urged the white man to
remodel it.

Yet, though the wind sighed unchecked over empty
leagues of silent trees, there was no peace under the high green
forest roof. There can be no peace between a wildcat and a
rabbit, between a rabbit and a leaf, between a bluejay and
a butterfly. In nature's wilderness, life fed on life in nature's
way, beast against beast, man against beast, man against men.
Eternal vigilance was the price paid for survival, and the
forest kept its forces delicately balanced. Then came the
white man and overturned the scales.

At first the Indians respected the plowed fields, and no
longer burned the prairie every autumn to make good graz-
ing for the buffalo and deer. The game stayed away, and
between the cultivated strips the trees sent out the advance
cohorts of their seedlings and their saplings. The animals fled,
and the Indians grew restless. Still they were prepared to like
these settlers, who were not the dreaded Long Knives (the
Virginians, named for their swords), but who came from
Pennsylvania, where William Penn had established a good
reputation. The truce between red and white lasted for
twenty years.

Only one group thought the Indian should be considered, only the Quakers and Mennonites were so fantastic as to make serious efforts to purchase what they claimed. In 1738 Leader Thomas Chaulkley wrote an earnest letter to the colony on the Opequon, exhorting them firstly through eighthly to keep a friendly correspondence with the Indians:

> For as nature hath given them and their forefathers the possession of this continent . . . they had a natural right thereto in justice and equity.
> Therefore my Christian advice to you is, my dear friends, that the most reputable among you do with speed endeavour to . . . purchase your lands of the native Indians . . . Who would run the risk of the lives of their wives and children for the sparing of a little pains? . . . Consider that you are in the Province of Virginia, and the Virginians have made an agreement to go as far as the mountains and no farther, and you are over and beyond the mountains, and therefore out of the agreement. . . . Except you will go about to convince them with fire and sword, contrary to our principles.

Clearly this devout old man, with his talk about natural rights, agreement, purchase, lasting peace, was not in touch with reality, as his contemporaries saw it. Who could make binding agreements with savages? As for purchase, half the time there was no one about from whom a purchase could be made. Both of the two chief groups of Valley settlers had a comfortable conviction of God's guidance. Plainly the Lord God of Hosts (and of Battles) had led his children out of the hands of the Philistines to this Canaan which they would make to flow with milk and honey—or with blood if necessary. Lasting peace had no place in their creed.

5. Pioneers

As the years passed life took on a pattern in the Valley—a pattern of small log cabins in the clearings or the grasslands, of long laborious days, tuned to the slow change of the seasons, of lonely silent nights broken by wolves or whippoorwills. Try to imagine the silence of the Valley, where a man could work all day with his own hands for company, hearing the wind whisper, hearing the doves, hearing the corn stretch and crackle in the heat, hearing the singing silence of the earth itself. A man had his hands and arms for company, and his children helping in the fields; and for the evening, his children and his wife. His wife, and time to watch the blue deepen into purple, to see the darkness slowly cover the mountains and the trees.

Day ended with the darkness. There was no road to go on, and nowhere to go. There were no lights to read by, and no books to read. A man who had a Bible had a library. The more luxurious might add a copy of *Golden Apples in Silver Shells; Selected Passages from Holy Writ*. With darkness it was time to make the cabin fast against the night, to shutter out the wide black spaces where no lights glowed, the panthers, bears, wolves, wildcats, and the loneliness, the loneliness most of all. Man and his labors vanished in the darkness, and the wilderness flowed back, lapping the cabin threshold like persistent water, turning each home into an island in the night. During these hours men did not like to leave their families, but all slept close and warm together until day came through the chinks in the shutters, and called them to stir out again in the fresh morning.

In such a society everyone turned out to bid newcomers welcome. Weddings and buryings, harvesting, log rolling, house-raisings, these were the occasions for a gathering and a feast. A newly married couple could count on all the men and boys to help them build, to set the cornerstone and lay the sleepers, to raise the log walls, and lay the puncheon floor. A long porch across the front gave saddle storage room and shade in summer. When they had cut a loophole, hung an oaken door, built a stone chimney, and chinked the cracks, the work was done. A band of energetic men could finish a home in three days.

But after the wedding came the work. Then the countryside was lonely and quiet as before. From dawn to dark the husband dug and planted, hunted or harvested and the wife ground corn for journeycake and pone, cooked hog and hominy, milk and mush, spun and wove flax and wool for linsey-woolsey hunting shirts, and bore a long succession of children alone or with a helping neighbor woman.

Some children died in every family, but those who lived grew strong. The pioneers attributed the diseases of children to worms, and dosed them with the scrapings of a pewter spoon. For croup, the specific was onion or garlic juice; for fever, sweating with snakeroot or purging with walnut bark; for the itch, a salve of brimstone and hog lard; for burns, a poultice of Indian meal or slippery elm; for snakebite, anything and everything that an old wife or Indian could suggest. Erysipelas could be circumscribed by the blood of a black cat, and the Germans had incantations for hemorrhage, sprains, toothache, or bullets. The men developed rheumatism, for their moccasins, although warm enough when stuffed with leaves, became waterlogged on wet days. All backwoodsmen learned to sleep with their feet to the fire.

It was not a life for soft and easy people. There was the night loneliness and the wide dark, there was the endless laboriousness of the self-sustaining life, there was the dread of unattended illness, there was hunger.

When the Doddridges arrived they thought they had brought with them enough Indian meal to last until the first harvest, but when it gave out they had to depend on meat alone, for they did not know what roots and herbs were edible. They told the children that bear was meat, and the white breast of turkey was bread, but the children grew thin on the diet. Every day they went to watch the potatoes, corn, squash and pumpkins growing in the truck patch, but they grew so slowly! Some days it seemed as if they would not grow at all. What a jubilee when at last they could pull the young corn for roasting ears. And when it could be grated to make johnnycakes, "we became healthy, vigorous, and contented with our situation, poor as it was."

But the back inhabitants in the Valley had no intention of remaining in this primitive state for long. By 1734 so many of them had settled there that the Burgesses of Virginia established a county called Orange, and grandly declared that its borders should extend to the Mississippi. This did not serve, for the back inhabitants would not cross the mountains to attend court. In 1738 the Burgesses revised their gesture, set the boundaries of Orange east of the mountains, and divided the wild west, "unto the utmost limits of Virginia," into two new counties, named for the Prince and Princess of Wales, Frederick and Augusta. They appointed vestrymen of the Established Church, they exempted the people on the Mississippi from taxes for building courthouses in the Shenandoah, and they thriftily abolished the bounty on wolves' ears, which was proving too expensive for the government.

In 1743 courts were set up at Frederick Town (now Winchester), for Frederick County; in 1745 at Staunton, for Augusta. At Frederick Town, James Wood and his friends selected justices, elected a sheriff, and charged him to clear land and build a courthouse of forty-foot logs, a hut on Sheep Hill Common for the safekeeping of persons with the smallpox, and a jail, twelve by twelve, "he not to be answerable for escapes. To connect themselves with the world, they ordered a roadway cut "through the dense forest out to the grass land both to North and South."

Although the early courts sat at Glen Burnie until the courthouse could be built, they were no respecters of persons, for they soon presented and fined Colonel James Wood for getting drunk and swearing two oaths within six months.

Campbell presented Curtis for plowing on Sunday, and Curtis countered by presenting Campbell for drunkenness and oaths. Patrick Riley and Marquis Calmes obtained tavern licenses, allowing them to serve "hot diet and cold diet, Barbadoes rum, Rye brandy, and rum punch." A poll tax was collected in tobacco, and 1,283 souls were found in the county who could pay it. And for the spiritual welfare of the inhabitants, they indicted a Quaker for articles against the Established Church, and the Reverend William Williams for performing a marriage, "he being no orthodox minister."

The justices were not sparing in the lashes they ordered laid on at their whipping post outside the jail—twenty-five for a girl who had born an illegitimate child. They would have the court respected, and while it sat "no person should presume to strain either by pacing or racing through the streets." They built a ducking stool for scolds, a pit seven feet square, with a roof over it. Soon the lower Valley would have all the benefits of civilization.

Augusta did not lag far behind Frederick in these matters. In 1745, Sir William Beverly conveyed twenty-five acres of land for a courthouse in Staunton. The court passed a tax on tithables for the purpose of restoring that so necessary bounty on wolves' ears, for building roads and bridges, and for relieving the poor. They offered to pay one hundred pounds of tobacco for a wolf head, and in one month they had to pay on two hundred and twenty-five. Judging from the warrant books of the early sheriffs, law enforcement had its troublesome side.

> Elliott vs Johnson: Not executed by reason of the flux being
>   in the house
> Not executed by reason of an axe.
> Not executed by reason of a gun.
> Not executed by reason the defendant outrode me.
> Not executed by reason the fellow gave me heel-play.
> Not executed by reason the way was dangerous for Indians.
> Not executed by reason of the heathen Indians ranging so
>   that I can't get up there.
> Issue this against cousin again, and we may have better luck.

This is my friend's. Issue it again and I shall storm his castle
once more.
Issue this against the body once more, and I will lie at his
house all night but I will have him.

As might have been expected, the Presbyterian settlers
of Augusta had taken care of their spiritual welfare before
they organized their temporal affairs. As soon as they received
the governor's permission to worship freely, they began to
importune the Presbytery of Donegal in Pennsylvania to send
them a minister. In 1739 they were rewarded by being allowed to call the Reverend John Craig.

A young man more thoroughly fitted to bring a wilderness into order and its souls into the fear of God could not
have been discovered. In the story of his work, which he later
published, he said that he had been born in Ireland, educated
in Edinburgh, and "compelled at the age of five or six to
fly to God with tears and prayers in secret for pardon, peace,
guidance, and direction." He felt himself indeed directly
guided, for while still in Scotland he had seen his future
parish in a dream, and on the ship coming over, one monstrous
wave had swept him off the deck, so that he gave himself up
for lost, but the next one threw him back upon the vessel,
unharmed. He was convinced that he had been preserved for
some purpose, and he did not falter in pursuit of it.

When he dedicated himself "to be set apart for the work
of the Gospel ministry in the south part of Beverly's Manor,
the place was a new settlement, without a place of worship
. . . a wilderness in the proper sense, and a few Christian
settlers in it with numbers of the heathen travelling amongst
us, but generally civil, though some persons were murdered
by them about that time. . . . They march about in small
companies . . . and must be supplied at any house they call
at with victuals, or they become their own stewards and
cooks and spare nothing they choose to eat or drink." In this
wilderness, the Reverend John Craig rooted himself like a
tree, and "married a young gentlewoman of a good family
and character, by whom I had nine children."

By the time they built the Staunton courthouse, he had three congregations, and if he could walk five miles to preach, carrying his rifle, they could travel ten to hear him. When they arrived he gave them something worth coming for, preaching from ten in the morning until sunset, with an hour for lunch. One of his sermons had fifty-five heads. He began by preaching in the open air, but soon had his people building churches, and the Old Stone Church by the Valley Pike was the first of them, with walls thick enough for a fortress (a fact which proved useful later). All the men of the congregation worked on it, with their guns beside them, and the women brought the sand for the mortar on horseback from the river.

The reverend's life had some difficulties. Men qualified to be elders were scarce. "When I couldna get hewn stones," he said, "I tuk dornacs." His prosperous congregation at Tinkling Spring gave him more trouble than all the rest, for a spirit of true submission ever flourishes more in poverty than in riches. That session once dared to vote him down. He vowed "none of that water shall ever tinkle down my throat" and kept his word in spite of eight-hour sermons.

It must be confessed that the Scotch-Irish, who had disagreed with so many people, also disagreed among themselves. Before long a schism split the church, and the New Side referred to the pastor as a "poor blind carnal hypocritical damned wretch." Nevertheless, John Craig remained the shepherd and the leader of the upper Valley during four and thirty years.

It is plain from all this that the settlers in the Valley were a law-abiding people, determined to organize their new communities properly, and to do everything in an orderly manner. Nevertheless, in the matter of the grants, in the very fundamental titles to the land itself, there arose a confusion for which they could not be blamed, and against which they contended with all the strength of their characters.

The remote and uncertain control of the early days gave free rein to the quality which in successful ancestors is called mother wit. In the Burden Grant, a servant girl named Polly

Millholland dressed as a man, moved from cabin to cabin in the woods, claiming each in a different name until she acquired thirty holdings. Her industry was rewarded, although they found her out, for she held her land, married well, raised a fine crop of sons, and lived to be over eighty.

To the northeast, in the Luray valley, a Swiss named Jacob Stover took up five thousand acres in the names of his horses, cows, dogs, cats, as heads of families. Others bought from him, and in 1733 a moving petition reached Governor Gooch from the "fields of Massanutten," in the name of Abraham Strickler, and a small group of settlers.

That about four years past they purchased five thousand acres of land off one Jacob Stover, and paid him a great sum of money for same, amounting to upwards of four hundred pounds . . . They came and settled on the land . . . cleared several Plantations, and made great improvements thereon . . . Since when they have been informed that the said land is claimed by one William Beverly, gentleman, that should the said Beverly recover the said land he will turn your petitioners out of Doors by obliging them to give much more for the lands and Plantations than they are worth, which will entirely ruin your petitioners. And your Petitioners cannot recover anything of the said Stover, he being very poor and is daily expected to run away.

The governor upheld the petitioners, and both Stricklers and Stovers live today east of Massanutten on land which they named Egypt because of its fertility—prizing the land, and prizing their old Bible, printed at Zurich in 1536. Sir William Beverly, sitting comfortably at Williamsburg, did not prevail against them, although he was the great land-owner of the lower Valley as Fairfax was of the upper, and although he later aided the settlers at Staunton.

Thomas Lord Fairfax, gave the settlers more serious trouble. He was a grandson of that Lord Colepepper to whom Charles II had presented, with a more than usually inclusive sweep of the royal pen, a tract of land known as the Northern Neck. It began on the shore, between the mouths of the Potomac and the Rappahannock, and extended indeterminately westward over the better part of what are now twenty-two counties. Since no one knew what it contained, it was easy to give as to retain. Lord Colepepper willed it to his daughter, Lady Catherine, who married the fifth Baron Cameron, and in turn gave it to her son, Lord Fairfax.

It is probable that the early settlers never heard of him, and that it would have made no difference if they had. The noble lord lived in England, where he had land enough. Here lay rich meadows ready for the taking, uncalculated forest, living streams, a sweet and smiling virgin land. The settlers took it and possessed it with their labor and their love.

Tradition says that Lord Fairfax became interested in his Virginia lands by talking in London with a trader called John Howard, who had gone up the Valley, crossed the Alleghenies, descended the Ohio in a boat of buffalo hide, and taken ship at New Orleans. This is not too great an improbability in the story of a nation whose history is all improbable.

In 1736 Lord Fairfax came to visit his cousin William Fairfax at Belvoir on the James. He had not been long in Virginia before he realized that a great many people were living on his land without having taken the trouble to communicate with him. Many of the rather illiterate inhabitants had not even recorded their titles. He instructed his agents to get in touch with them and request them either to purchase the land or to pay him an annual quitrent of from two to twenty shillings for every hundred acres—moderate enough, in all conscience, but a pleasing income when multiplied by the hundreds of thousands. Those who would not agree to these reasonable terms would have to move.

To his astonishment, Lord Fairfax, upon asserting his legal rights, heard himself denominated a monster by those whose only claim to his property was their bringing it out of wilderness into production by their own enterprise, risk, labor, and sweat. They asserted that "he was exercising his insatiable disposition for the monopoly of wealth" and that his acts were "odious and oppressive." That stubborn old German, Joist Hite, not only refused to move upon his lordship's "caveat," but actually dared to bring suit against his would-be landlord.

The matter passed into the slow jaws of the courts. After a year or two, Lord Fairfax, in love with the scenery but disgusted with his lack of progress, returned to England to present his grievances at court. It was said then, and it has been said since, that America was no country for a gentleman.

In 1746, Lord Fairfax sent a party to survey his land and run the famous "Fairfax line" across the southern boundary. Thomas Lewis, son of John and Margaret, acted for him, and Peter Jefferson, father of the future president, for the crown. Most of the Valley north of Massanutten lay within this line, which also crossed the Alleghenies and took in the South Branch valley of the Potomac. The surveyors crawled through the countryside for a month, made a remarkable list of the trees to be found in the western mountains, and found the country exceedingly rugged. Thomas Lewis kept a diary which has recently been reprinted.

> Sat. 20th. the mountains made
> Such a dismal appearance that John
> Thomas one of our men took Sick on
> the Same and So Returned home.

In 1747, Joist Hite finished his permanent stone house upon the disputed land, and his sons also began to build in stone.

By this time the settlers of Frederick and Augusta could take pride in the progress of their Valley. They had a ferry across the Shenandoah at its confluence with the Potomac, and an iron furnace at Old Bloomery. They exported hemp, furs, and whisky, floated on barges down the river or carried on creaking oxcarts over the mountains. Increased communications brought a different class of settler, and the wills of important people began to list such luxuries as china cups and saucers, looking glasses, three silver spoons. In 1747, Lawrence Washington, who had a young half brother named George, bought 700 acres in the Valley, and 1,300 the year after.

In 1748, Lord Fairfax arrived to assume personal supervision of his property, and of those whom he was pleased to

LORD FAIRFAX'S OFFICE AT GREENWAY COURT

call his "retainers." In that year the Virginia Assembly confirmed his claim, and he refused to grant to that annoying
German, Hite. Hite did not move; on the contrary, he instituted a new suit, praying that his lordship might be decreed
to make him deeds.

This was a different and an embittered Fairfax. Tradition says that he had been jilted by an English lady, and
blamed his mother and grandmother for her loss. Disappointment made him a misogynist. Within a year of his arrival he
established himself on his "Manor of Leeds" (between Winchester and Berryville), at his hunting lodge "Greenway
Court," a one-story log house with a long veranda. He put
a White Post at the crossroads to guide his visitors, but he
never allowed a woman on the premises. There he lived for
the remaining years of his long life, wearing elaborate coats of
green and scarlet silk, laced with damask, waistcoats of scarlet plush or gold tissue, black velvet breeches. But he ate with
his cats and dogs, and slept in a log hut twelve by twelve,
apart from the larger cabin which was his home. His portrait
has survived, a young, pouting, corpulent face, wearing an
expression of petulant astonishment.

From Greenway Court he issued statements to the "retainers" on his Manor of Leeds, and he was shocked at the spirit in which they were received. Even the educated men in Frederick Town, which Colonel Wood had not as yet named Winchester, replied with a subversive document.

. . . having been truly informed of Thomas Lord Fairfax's intention of making us pay a yearly rent of five shillings each for our lots, and we not being willing to come under that yoke, have taken this method to make known the same by subscribing our hands hereunto.

What a country! Where people talked about coming under a yoke when asked to pay a moderate and perfectly legal rent! They negotiated all summer, but in September the politic Colonel Wood effected a somewhat stiff-necked compromise.

9/14/1749. Colonel James Wood offered my Lord Fairfax to comply with the rules of his office, though he did not think himself bound by the decrees of King and Council, and that he would pay him the composition of . . . quit-rents from 1745, provided he would let him have all within his old lines, including the town.

Not bound by the decrees of king and council! What impertinence! However, it was better to agree than again to try the laborious processes of the courts. Evidently Joist Hite thought so too, for he and one of his sons signed the compromise for the town, although not for his own land.

Colonel Wood's working agreement did not mean that he was subservient, nor did it guarantee the lord proprietor (self styled) any peace of mind. Lord Fairfax wanted the hamlet of Stephensburg, more properly near to Greenway Court, for the county seat. Along came Colonel Wood, got hold of one of the justices, brought him around over a bowl of toddy, and fixed the seat at Winchester. Lord Fairfax never spoke to the justice again.

Lord Fairfax wished to be fair, and even generous. He granted the town additional acreage, and the Assembly decided that he might lay off the lots, but they confirmed Colonel Wood's choice of a name. He gave to the churches;

THOMAS LORD FAIRFAX

he was active in promoting the defense of the frontier. He charged the orphans of Martin Coffman a quitrent of only one peppercorn a year, to be delivered on the day of their patron saint, St. Michael.

By his own standards he was a very public-spirited man, but in the wilderness he was an anachronism. The back inhabitants were not his "retainers" and had no intention of becoming so. They were men who had preferred independence to servility, who had taken risks rather than accept limitations, and he embodied for them the Old World from which they had fled. They wished neither for his bounty nor for his assistance. They intended, and they made their purpose clear, to maintain their right of *doing for themselves*. "Lord Fairfax never *gave* the Valley anything," they said. "The court records show him a litigant unceasing in his efforts to disturb and destroy the first settlers by his exactions in collecting his rents."

Surrounded by such people, it is no wonder that Lord Fairfax looked surprised and petulant. Nevertheless, in spite of loneliness, of an uneven climate, there was a sweetness in the air, a breadth in the vista rolling to the mountains from Greenway Court. The nights were fragrant, and the days were bright. His lordship fumed and fretted, argued and sued, but he did not depart. Without his own volition, like many an emigrant before and since, he had been captured by Virginia.

6. Washington

IN 1748, Lord Fairfax, pursuing the regulation of his affairs, sent two young men to survey the northern end of his Valley property. One was a cousin, George William Fairfax, the other a youth of sixteen, who in the light of subsequent events seems an odd choice for the champion of inherited privilege to have made.

The youth was tall, strong, serious-minded, and as the eldest son of a widow had a lively sense of the necessity of making his own way. He came of what Virginians call "nice people." His older half brothers, one of whom had married a Fairfax, could make good connections for him, but he intended to improve his opportunities by his own application to work. His name was George Washington.

Like many an earnest young man, he was acutely interested in a world where every experience seemed a novelty, and he kept a diary of his trip, of his "Journey over the Mountains."

On the eleventh of March they mounted at Alexandria and rode forty miles to Bull Run. Next day they crossed the Blue Ridge, swam their horses over the Shenandoah, and spent the night with a Colonel Ashby. From there an easy day's ride took them across the Valley, "through most beautiful groves of sugar maples," to Greenway Court.

"We spent the best part of the day in admiring the trees, and the richness of the land." To planter Washington, good land would always be the most charming thing in the world. The fertility of the limestone soil enchanted him, after the sandy lowlands, and he marveled at the abundant crops of grain, hemp, and tobacco. Beyond White Post, however, the country grew wilder, the inhabitants fewer, the Alleghenies nearer, and his first night in the field taught him some of the difficulties of wilderness life. With a cheerful disregard of grammar, syntax, and spelling, he recorded his introduction into the backwoods of which he was to learn so much before he had done with them.

Tuesday, March 15. We set out early with the intent to run around the said Land, but being taken in a Rain and it Increasing very fast obliged us to return it clearing about one o'Clock and our time being too Precious to Loose we a second time ventur'd out and Worked hard till Night and then retired to Pennington's. We got our Suppers and was lighted into a Room, and I not being so good a Woodsman as the rest of my Company striped myself very orderly and went into the Bed as they called it when to my Surprise I found it to be nothing but a Little Straw Matted together without Sheets or anything else but only one thread Bear blanket with double its Weight of Vermin such as Lice Fleas, etc. I was glad to get up, (as soon as the light was carried from us) I put on my Cloths and Lay as my Companions. Had we not been very tired I am sure we should not have slep'd much that night. I made a Promise not to Sleep so from that time forward chusing rather to sleep in the open Air before a fire as will appear hereafter.

With unabated industry, the party finished their work in that region next day, and "Travelled up to Frederick Town where our Baggage came to us we cleaned ourselves (to get Rid of the Game we had catched the Night Before) and took a Review of the Town and thence returned to our Lodgings where we had a good Dinner prepared for us Wine and Rum Punch in plenty and a good Feather Bed with clean Sheets, which was a very agreeable regale."

They continued on, day after day, with nothing of note except the occasional advantage of a good bed to lie on. They swam their horses over the Potomac, they traveled "the worst Road that ever was trod by Man or Beast," and in the raw woods they met the savages.

Rained till about 2 o'Clock and cleared when we was agreeably surprised at the sight of 30 odd Indians coming from War with only one Scalp. We had some Liquor with us of which we gave them Part it elevating there Spirits put them in the humour of Dauncing of whom we had a war Daunce.

Round and round the fire sprang the Indians, against a background of black dripping twigs, shaking the scalp that was their only trophy, and their feet pounded on the soggy earth like the sullen pulsing of a savage heart. It vastly amused young Mr. Washington. He had of course seen an occasional Indian, but never a whole group of them in woods wild enough to be their natural habitat. Too well brought up to laugh openly at anyone, he concealed his mirth by staring into the wet trees or the fire.

There music is a pot half full of water with a deerskin tied over it, and a gourd with some shot in it to rattle and a piece of a Horse's tail tied to it to make it look fine . . . They hopped and carried on in a most comical manner.

Not only the Indians diverted Mr. Washington. Ten days later the party passed one of the German settlements, and the inhabitants turned out for them, and accompanied them through the woods, "showing there Antick tricks." "I really think they seemed to be as Ignorant a Set of People as the Indians. They would never speak English, but when spoken to they all speak Dutch."

With such encounters to break the monotony, the surveying party spent a month in the woods, saw the forest change from bleak March to tender April; ate wild deer and twenty-pound turkeys which they had shot. "Our Fork a split Stick, our plate a wooden chip, our Bed the ground . . . with neither a cloth upon the Table nor a Knife to eat with, but as Luck would have it we had knives of our own."

At last it was over, and on April 13th, "Mr. Fairfax got safe home and I . . . to my Brother's which concludes my Journal." It had been hard work and it had been interesting, but Mr. Washington's diary does not indicate that he enjoyed it. Nevertheless, he soon returned to the same work, this time without Mr. Fairfax, and this time to remain for several months. The backwoods might not be very agreeable—a favorite word of his—but he was a widow's son, and there were several other children younger than he. During this period of exile, his letters to his friends, to his brother Jack, to Mistress Sally Fairfax, wife of George Williams, are poignant.

As its the greatest mark of Friendship and Esteem you can show to an absent Friend by often Writing to him, so hope you'l not deny me that Favour as its so ardently wished and Desired by me . . .

Since you received my Letter in October Last I have not slept above 3 Nights or 4 in a Bed but after walking a good deal all the Day lay down before the fire upon a Little Hay Straw Fodder or bairskin whichever's to be had with Man Wife and Children like a Parcel of Dogs or Catts and Happy's he that gets the Birth nearest the fire . . .

Theres nothing would make it pass off tolerably but a good Reward a Dubbleloon is my constant gain every Day that the Weather will permit my going out, and sometimes Six Pistoles . . .

I have never had my Cloths of but lay and sleep in them like a Negro except the few Nights I have layn in Frederick Town.

In fact young Mr. Washington was profoundly homesick for quiet houses, polished floors and white-clothed tables, for good food and pleasant voices, for dancing, laughter, and light witty talk. And when in one household he met "an agreeable young lady" . . .

It was only added Fuel to the fire it makes me the more uneasy for by often and unavoidably being in Company with her revives my former Passion for your Low Land Beauty whereas was I to live more retired from Young Women I might in some measure alieviate my sorrows by burying that chaste and troublesome passion in the grave of Oblivion.

To Mrs. Sally Fairfax, who was always to be for him the symbol and epitome of gracious living, he wrote: "I could wish to be with you down there with all my heart." But it is notable that he did not go, this homesick youth in a job he did not like. The work must be finished, and there was that important matter of a doubloon ($3.72) a day. He completed his surveys, and the names in his notebooks are in the Valley still: Arnold, Baker, Calmes, Campbell, Carter, Hite, Hoge, and many others. Although surrounded by comical Indians, and barbarians who could not even speak English (against whom he seemed to have the typical Anglo-Saxon prejudice), he performed his task in such a way that he gained the friendship of Lord Fairfax, and retained it all his life, despite their differing political beliefs.

When he went home at last, with accomplishment behind him, he thought he had forever finished with the backwoods life. He would go to sea, as he had always wished to do. As a start he would go to Barbadoes with his ailing brother, Lawrence. Adieu then, and cheerfully, to the tall silent trees, the barbarous mountains, the grassy prairies; adieu to the nights full of the cries of wild animals, the days of all too silent sunshine. Adieu, and may it be forever, to the savage and half-savage people.

But destiny, which is rarely obvious, had other arrangements. The forest, the Indians, and the frontier inhabitants, had not finished with young Mr. Washington.

It was in 1754 that the Indians left the Valley—without a word and without an explanation. For more than twenty years they had come and gone peacefully among the settlers. Then suddenly they were no longer there. No one could put a finger on the date of their leaving, but for a long time no settlers saw them. It was as if the woods had suddenly become empty of deer.

The Valley people, who had had no trouble with the Indians, felt in this something strange and ominous, and wondered among themselves what it could mean. They soon found out. By blood, by fire, by terror, they went on finding out for twelve long years.

At bottom, this trouble was an echo of a European war. The French instigated the attacks in their efforts to hold the Ohio against English claims, bringing their rivalry rather than their settlers to this wild green land. It must be admitted that they found no great difficulty in stirring up the Indians against the English, who had been bad neighbors, never keeping a bargain, but continually thrusting forward where they had promised not to go. "The French came and kissed us," said an Indian chief, speaking out of the bewildered heart of his people, "they called us children and we found them fathers; we lived like children in the same lodge."

The French and Indian wars were not continuous. There were in the Valley no pitched battles, no lines of men opposing one another. The victims of the conflict were not soldiers, but old men, farmers, pregnant women, babies. The Indians appeared out of the silence, in daylight, struck, and disappeared, struck again, and vanished. Not twice in the same place, sometimes not twice in the same year, but often enough to keep the terror living, to keep the people "forted up," to give a lasting name to a beautiful and treacherous season—Indian summer.

Through the cold months the Indians lay around their fires in smoky lodges, stirring only to procure essential food. When the cold came, the settlers ventured out of the forts, carried their families back to neglected homes, back to a life which at least had privacy, if not comfort. Then would follow the warm and dreaming days of late October or November, an unexpected and unwanted summer. The Indians would sweep down through the blue haze in the open woods, kill, and be gone before an alarm was sounded.

If the red man had been left to himself perhaps it would not have been so hideous, but he was ever goaded from the west into new outbreaks. There was a Frenchman killed with a war party on the Opequon, and the French order for blowing up Fort Loudoun found in his pocket. There was a bounty of three pounds on the fair English scalps.

Major George Washington, who had accepted a commission in the provincial army instead of going to sea, knew something about the machinations of the French. In 1753 he passed through Winchester again on his first military mission. The English intended to build forts for the protection of their traders on the Ohio, and they were notifying the

French to withdraw. Major Washington dined with the French officers at Venango. "The Wine, as they dosed themselves pretty plentifully with it, soon banished the restraint which at first appeared in their Conversation . . . They told me that it was their absolute Design to take possession of the Ohio, and by God they would do it."

When Major Washington carried this message back to Governor Dinwiddie, the governor raised an expedition and put him in charge of it, with the rank of lieutenant colonel. On this trip he fought his first battle, and although later defeated, retired with honor. The Virginia Assembly voted him thanks, and at twenty-three he found himself something of a hero in the small circle at Williamsburg. "I heard the bullets whistle," he wrote his brother Jack, "and believe me, there is something charming in the sound."

All this, however, had in no way relieved the frontier, and something must be done. Behold then, in the May of 1755, Lieutenant Colonel Washington waiting at Winchester for a general named Braddock. Now the English were sending a general of His Majesty's Army against the French, with a force of regulars, supported of course by a provincial regiment or two. Virginia asked Washington to recruit for her share of the expedition but, true to the habits of governments as he came to know them, did not send him a sixpence to pay the men. At the end of a month he wrote from "this vile post": "You may with almost equal success attempt to raise the Dead to life again as the force of this County."

But the young lieutenant-colonel, instinctively and unconsciously brave, sincerely patriotic, and not without ambition, felt optimistic about his prospects. He was treated with respect and freedom by the general and his family, and he intended "to improve an acquaintance which might be serviceable if I can find it worth-while pushing my Fortune in the Military way."

Alas for his hopes, the expedition was ill-starred from the beginning. General Braddock tarried in Winchester until July, in spite of all that could be said about giving the French time to reinforce their garrisons; he had trouble with contractors and supplies, and damned the whole colony for it with an inclusiveness which Colonel Washington deplored. When at least he started, the mountains did not suit him, and his heavy supply train did not suit the Virginians. "There has been vile Management in regard to Horses," Washington wrote. "They were halting to level every Mold Hill and to erect Bridges over every Brook, by which means we were 4 days in getting 12 miles."

No less a sage than Benjamin Franklin had suggested to the general that a long supply train made a choice target for lurking savages, and Braddock had replied with a smile—endearing himself to the colonists as many an Englishman has done before and since: "These savages may indeed be a formidable enemy to raw American militia, but against the King's regular and disciplined troops it is impossible that they should make an impression."

As luck would have it, Colonel Washington fell ill of a fever, an ague, and the bloody flux, had to be carried along in a wagon, and the general was thus deprived of advice which he indubitably would not have taken. Washington returned to duty just before the advance on Fort Duquesne, in time to have two horses killed under him during the battle and four bullets sent through his coat.

The well-known story of Braddock's defeat has no place in this narrative. The general died, murmuring, "Who would have thought it possible," and his body was buried in the roadway so that the feet of the retreating troops should obliterate the grave and conceal it from the Indians. The general died, leaving behind the bloodstained sash in which he was carried from the field—to be a relic borne by schoolgirls in the Winchester appleblossom festival; leaving his sash, and his name on half a dozen country lanes in the Valley, all claiming to be "Braddock's road."

It was very disillusioning to a young man thinking of "Pushing his Fortune in the Military way" and looking to the English army as a model. Colonel Washington did not mince words when he wrote to his mother and brothers concerning this occasion.

Honored Madam,
  As I doubt not you have heard of our defeat, and perhaps have it represented in a worse light, (if possible) than it deserves; I have taken this earliest opportunity to give you an account of the engagement. . . .
  Dear Jack,
  We have been most scandalously beaten by a trifling body of men . . . The Virginia Companies behaved like Men and died like Soldiers . . . The dastardly behaviour of the English Soldiers exposed all those who were inclined to do their duty to almost certain Death . . . They broke and ran as Sheep before the Hounds.

Now indeed something must be done. The Virginia government saw that it could not depend on either the English or the Pennsylvanians for support. Governor Dinwiddie determined to send Colonel Washington to Winchester, the principal frontier post, in command of some troops for the defense of the back inhabitants. Although the young man was only twenty-three, he had shown mature judgment, his courage was unquestioned, and he had had some experience of the country and the people.

Washington hesitated before accepting the governor's offer. He wrote a feeling history of his brief and painful military experience to his brother Augustine: "I have been upon the losing order ever since I entered the Service which is now two years; so that I think I can't be blam'd should I, if I leave my Family again, end'vr to do it upon such terms as to prevent my suffering. (To gain by it is the least of my expectations.)"

He then laid down some stiff conditions to Governor Dinwiddie. He must be able to appoint his own officers, he must have funds to defray his expenses, he must be able to make objections "as my Reason and my small experience have pointed out." The governor agreed to it all with a facility that should have alarmed him. He decided to accept, and wrote a brief note to allay his mother's fears, explaining to "honored Madam" that, if his country (Virginia) called him, his duty was to go.

In charge of all frontier defenses for Virginia, he arrived in Winchester in the September of 1755, now a full colonel, and no longer amused by the war dances of the Indians. There he embarked upon three years of as grueling instruction in the school of experience as ever fell to the lot of a young and enthusiastic officer. It was there that he learned to make bricks without straw, to deal with an indifferent civil government, to hold an army together without pay and without equipment, to act on his own responsibility when orders were not forthcoming. And all America one day had cause to be thankful for his training.

7. Massacres

After Braddock's defeat, many of the back inhabitants gave themselves up for lost. In Pennsylvania and Maryland the frontiers were almost deserted, but the settlers along the Shenandoah were made of sterner stuff. It is true that some did leave, and many considered it, but when in Augusta County the timorous congregations asked for the advice of the Reverend John Craig, he spoke out strongly:

Some of the richer sort that could take some money with them to live upon were for flying to a safer part of the country. My advice was then asked for, which I gave, opposing the scheme as a scandal to our nation, a falling below our brave ancestors, a making ourselves a reproach among Vandals, a dishonor to our brave friends at home, an evidence of cowardice, want of faith, and of a noble Christian dependence on God as able to save and deliver us from the heathen. It would be a lasting blot to our posterity.

Having thus gently admonished, the Reverend Mr. Craig set his people to fortifying their stone churches.

It was not of shadows or of rumors that the settlers were afraid. They had seen things happen. They knew the stark facts which cannot be embroidered, the truth so dreadful that the statement of it stops the mind.

The Indians came to Frederick in the spring, when the oak leaves were a little bigger than a mouse's ear and the ground dried out enough for planting. Eighteen or twenty of them crossed the North Mountain at Mills Gap, found Patrick Kelly plowing, and killed him; found his wife milking, and killed her also. One of the children got away to give the alarm, crouching and running through the underbrush like a little animal.

Each family that heard the news rode or ran for John Evans's fort near Martinsburg. The more improvident had laughed at him when he laboriously cut saplings for a stockade, but they were glad enough to use it now. His own brother did not start in time, for there was enough thin green in the woods around his house to make a little cover, and as the Indians burst out of it Tom had barely time to run in and slam the door. He fought them off, and when they went for reinforcements, he took the desperate chance of trying to reach the fort before they got back. His wife ran, carrying the two least children. The man ran, carrying his gun. The other children stumbled after them.

The Evanses arrived safely, but Polly Martin was not so lucky. On her way to Strodes she met little Joe Hackney, who told her that everybody had already gone to the fort, but she would not pay attention to him. Beyond the grove she could see a thin column of smoke curling into the blue spring air, and she wanted to reach friends quickly rather than run the uncertain miles alone. She was over the rise when she saw that the smoke came from a burning house instead of from a hearth. And then the Indians were around her, their black masks grinning, and she too frozen with fear to speak or run. She was a likely looking girl, and they took her along.

The people crowded into the fort, and nothing happened. A day passed, and a night, and nothing happened. The children grew restless, rolling on the ground like puppies, driving their mothers wild. After a while the men said it was a shame to leave Patrick Kelly lay like a hog, and him a Christian, and they made up a party to go and bury him. Several hours after they left, a lookout saw the black head of an Indian creeping through the tall dried weeds left from the summer. Then the Indians yelled.

Inside the fort everyone was quiet. Even the children did not scream. They just stared, big-eyed, at their mothers, and their mothers looked back with nothing to say to them. It was Mrs. John Evans who saved them. She grabbed up a gun and gave a gun to every woman who could fire one. Those who were skeered o' shootin' she set to rammin' bullets.

"You, little Joe Hackney, get that drum, and beat 'to arms' on it. Beat as loud as ever you can. Then everybody fire. Make it sound like a lot of men."

They kept on shooting as fast as they could load, and in the end the Indians ran away.

At Nealy's on the Opequon, the people did not fare so well. The Indians burned that fort, and left most of them dead and bleeding in the ashes. They took both of the Cohoons away with them, and their surviving children. They took little George and Isabella Stockton. Mrs. Cohoon tired easily because she was pregnant, and when she stumbled going up North Mountain, the Indians looked at her sharply. They made Mr. Cohoon go on ahead, a long way ahead, but still he was not out of earshot of her screaming. He escaped that night, crept back and found her, but she was cold and stiff, with her brains on the trail beside her. He sat by her for a while, then went alone back to the settlements.

George Stockton had just turned eleven, and Isabella was nine, with pretty curls which had been her mother's pride. George hoped the Indians would not hurt her. When she cried, he shook his head at her. Mustn't make them mad. He tried to leave a trail by breaking the bushes as they passed, but Black Wolf, who was in charge of him, tapped him on the shoulder. He tried digging in his toes to make tracks, but Black Wolf tapped him again. At night he and Isabella had grapevine halters put around their necks, with the ends tied to Black Wolf's wrist. For three days they had no water except what they could suck out of poplar bark. On the other side of the mountains the Indians killed a buffalo, and made it last a week. After traveling for twenty days, still bound with grapevines, they crossed the Ohio on a raft, and reached a Shawnee town.

These details are not fiction. George spent three years with the Shawnees before he could escape and tell his story of the trip. Polly Martin also returned after several years of captivity. The Shawnees sold pretty Isabella to a French trader who treated her cruelly. When she was about thirteen, he took her to Canada, and there another Frenchman, who according to the story bore the Spanish name of Plata, fell in love with her and asked her to marry him. Isabella, with a propriety which seems incredible under the circumstances, replied that she could not marry without her father's consent; and Plata, more incredibly still, took her home over hundreds of wilderness miles in order to get it. But the elder Mr. Stockton, an intractable man and evidently not a romantic, asserted that he would as soon see her married to the devil as to a Frenchman and obstinately maintained his position against every argument. Plata then suggested an elopement, and Isabella, now not so dutiful, agreed. They fled on two of her father's horses, but made the error of allowing themselves to be overtaken by her brothers. Some say that Plata was killed, and others that he was driven off by threats, but it is incontrovertible that Isabella was brought home alone by her brothers. For a time she tried to pine, but the back-country atmosphere was not conducive to languishing. Later she married a man named McClary, "removed and settled in the neighborhood of Morgantown, and grew wealthy."

Every year lengthened the tragic roll. Colonel James Patton, he of the twenty-five Atlantic crossings, was surprised by six or seven Indians as he sat at a writing table, with his sword lying on it in front of him. Although he fought like a demon and accounted for four of them, they killed him.

There was Mrs. Brewbacker, who insisted, on looking out the door one evening, that she saw Indians cooking their supper on Massanutten, two miles off. No one else could see them, and when she begged her husband to take her away, he dismissed her story as "mere superstition." Fortunately she remained on the watch, and when the Indians did indeed come the next day, she saved her children by hiding them.

There was Mr. Wolfe, whose faithful dog kept him from walking into an ambush by repeatedly standing up and putting its paws against his chest. There were Mrs. Sheets and Mrs. Taylor, who were attacked on their way to the fort with their husbands and children, at the Narrow Passage, where the Indian Road ran on a thin ridge between the North Fork and Passage Creek. Sheets and Taylor were both killed at the first volley, but when the Indians grabbed the wagon, Mrs. Sheets laid about her to such purpose with an ax and Mrs. Taylor whipped up the horses so zealously that they brought the children safely through to Woodstock.

The list grows too long for the telling of individual stories.

"Mrs. Horner was the mother of eight children. She never got back to her family."

"Mr. Williams, after killing five Indians, was quartered and hung on the four corners of his building, and his head on a stake in the fence."

"Mrs. Smith, after an absence of three years, returned home and presented her husband with an Indian son. Mr. Smith received his wife, and never maltreated her on this account, but he had a most bitter aversion to the young chief."

"It was often remarked by Mrs. Thomas's acquaintances, that after her return from captivity she would minutely relate the circumstances attending the murder of her husband and children without shedding a tear."

They came to George Miller's house in Shenandoah County while all the family were spreading flax except for one little girl, sick at home. She slipped out the back and ran to a neighbor's, but the rescue party found the others "weltering in their blood and still bleeding." The Indians had gone, but they had tried to set fire to the cabin by sticking a live coal in the family Bible. Then they had killed the cat and thrown her on top of it, and her weight had put out the fire. The Miller family preserve the charred Bible to this day.

George Painter built a stone cellar under his house near Woodstock, and all the neighborhood took shelter in it, but it did not save them. When Painter lost his nerve and tried to run, the Indians shot him, dragged his body back, threw it in the door, and set the house on fire. The others came out then, and surrendered. Four of the women had babies in their arms. The savages seized the babies, hanged them in trees, shot at them in sport, and left the bodies dangling. For no reason save a joy in cruelty, they fired a stable full of sheep and calves, and the bellowing and bleating of the roasting animals mingled with the human screams. When they left this scene from hell, they drove forty-eight prisoners with them. Two of the Painter boys escaped, but they could not persuade anyone to follow the trail, for the Indians were too numerous.

After six days the Indians and the living prisoners reached the villages beyond the Alleghenies, and there the captors held a council and a drunken feast. They ordered little Jacob Fisher to collect a pile of dry wood.

"Oh, my God, father, they are going to burn me!"

"I hope not, son. Do what they tell you. Don't make them mad."

The Indians piled the wood in a wide circle around a sapling, and tied him to the tree with one hand. He was a roly-poly child of twelve, always joking, and it made them laugh to look at him. They set fire to the wood, and poked him with sharp sticks until he ran into the flames, then back, and wound up to the tree, then out again. They sang and danced around him, and when the braves fell down drunk, the squaws kept the fire ablaze. It took him a long time to die. All this his father and his brothers had to watch.

Mrs. Painter and one daughter came back alive to tell the story. Back too came Mrs. Smith, she who had the Indian son. But the three youngest Painter girls forgot their English, fell in love with savage life, and never returned to civilization.

Not until 1766 did the terror stop. The last raid struck a Mennonite preacher, John Rodes (Hans Roth). He was standing in the doorway of his house on the South Fork of the Shenandoah when they shot him, and he fell forward, his white hair like a flag of truce across the threshold. His wife and son were shot as they tried to lift him, and another son when he climbed a tree to see what was happening at home. The eldest daughter caught up the baby, and escaped through the barn into a field of hemp which concealed her until she could get across the river.

After ten years and more of this, an Indian in the woods could expect no more quarter than a panther or a wolf, and John Walker fed his dog on Indian flesh. Even after the peace, when a settler was jailed for killing an Indian, the neighbors rose in a body and set him free.

The Indians had a music, a deep and breathing harmony with nature and their forest, but the white man could not hear it. His poetry was different, an epic of striving, of heroic determination. The Indian could not hear that either. Lost in their mutual deafness, they found no alternative to a struggle for survival which lunged on across the continent through new scenes, new tribes, new battles, until the white prevailed, and the Indian vanished as a potent entity.

8. Fort Loudoun

WHEN Colonel Washington took charge at Winchester in the September of 1755 he found the countryside in confusion, and he reported on it to Governor Dinwiddie in his own vigorous style (with spelling which by now approximated the conventional):

> The Blue Ridge is now our Frontier, no man being left in the county except a few who keep close with a number of women and children in the Forts. The supplicating tears of the women, and moving petitions of the men, melt me with such deadly sorrow that . . . I could offer myself a willing sacrifice to the butchering enemy, provided that would contribute to the people's ease.

Since such a measure would obviously be useless, the practical colonel set out to make soldiers of his new and undisciplined men, teaching them to drill and to shoot, forbidding drinking, swearing, and the use of an obscene language. He sent officers to find recruits between sixteen and fifty, who could meet physical requirements which were not excessive. They must not be under five feet four inches (unless well made), they must not have old sores upon their legs, nor be subject to fits.

So far so good, but within the first two weeks the colonel wrote the governor a rather anxious and certainly prophetic letter. He was having trouble with Mr. Dick, the commissary, who did not want to provide more food and clothing until he had been paid. "The soldiers will soon be barefooted, which always pleads exemption from Duty." Recruiting went slowly, and to draft them would answer no end, unless they were brought under better regulations. The colonel took the

77

liberty of suggesting that His Honor should instruct Mr. Dick not to detain the king's stores. Or let him resign and another be appointed.

When he had placed these matters squarely before the governor, the colonel had the optimism to order privately his own new uniforms: "Regimentals of good blue cloth, faced and cuffed with Scarlet and trimmed in Silver, a Scarlet waistcoat with Silver lace, blue Breeches, and a Silver laced hat, if to be had, for camp or Garrison Duty, Also a common Soldiers Dress for Duty in the Woods."

Colonel Washington's suggestions did not cause supplies to be rushed across the Blue Ridge. The vagueness of his instructions, the vagueness of the Tidewater about the frontier, now began to make itself felt. The situation was desperate, and the measures taken to meet it were inadequate. Colonel Washington had little more than one hundred men in his command, and was expected to bring it up to regimental strength by recruiting. In addition, his forces were to be augmented by militia companies, voluntary organizations from the lowland counties, entirely independent, and not answerable to anyone save thir own officers. It had not been decided whether he was to lead an expedition against the Indians or whether he should build a fort, and if the latter, whether it should be one strong fort or a chain of smaller ones. He knew nothing definite as to the moneys or supplies he might expect. The amateurish attitude of both his officers and his men was distressing to a professional soldier; the apathy and timidity of the inhabitants whom he defended was disheartening to a man of courage. The full extent of his difficulties dawned slowly upon the optimistic colonel. As month succeeded month and realization came, he felt himself entitled to express opinions based upon knowledge which did not endear him to his superiors. But let Washington himself tell his story through his letters.

On October 8th he repeated his complaints about the commissary. As preliminary measures of defense he explained that he was trying to arrange for some friendly Indian scouts (so far without success), and he had ordered his ranger captains, on outposts in the forest, to fall *no* farther *back.* He asked that the militia might be placed under a military law. When this produced no answer, he wrote the governor again:

I would again hint the Necessity of putting the Militia under a better Regulation; had I not mentioned it twice before, and a third time may seem Impertinent. No orders are obeyed but what a Party of Soldiers or my own drawn Sword enforced. I can plainly see that under the present Establishment we shall become a Nuisance, an insupportable charge to our country, and never answer any one expectation of the Assembly.

Having relieved his feelings by this mild hint, the colonel called his junior officers sharply to order for delays and disobedience ("Your crime is sufficient to break the best Officer that ever bore a Commission"). He reproved Ensign Dennis McCarthy, who had been recruiting by confining and torturing those who would not voluntarily enlist, "a method very unacceptable and of infinite prejudice to the Service." Worse still were the other recruiting officers who had been out for two months without getting a man, "spending all their Time in the gayety of pleasureable Mirth, with their relations and Friends." The colonel was "surprized" to see that some of his officers had not provided themselves with uniforms. He was also surprised by the arrival of a Captain Dagworthy from Maryland, who held a king's commission and consequently thought himself above taking orders from provincial officer Washington.

As for the soldiers, they were to cease pillaging and plundering or receive five hundred lashes. Each company would be allowed three women and *no more,* and the women were to wash for the soldiers and behave themselves orderly. If the town council of Winchester would not house their defenders (when drunk) in the jail, Colonel Washington would build his own.

In the midst of this refreshing attention to discipline, the colonel found himself once more forced to remark that he lacked everything from tents to ammunition, and that his beeves were dying of "absolute poverty," because the commissary was slow in bringing up supplies.

By November the Assembly took some notice of his hints and put the troops under martial law. Colonel Washington, a young man capable of considerable firmness, lost no time in tightening his regulations. He put the soldiers on bounds and ordered five hundred lashes for quarreling or fighting, two hundred for drunkenness. He sent Captain Ashby's wife home, suspended Captain —— who had cheated at cards. He instructed the officers to return a daily list of their recruits or be arrested, and to appoint some new sergeants instead of "the old dirty ones." Officers were reminded to spend their spare time studying the art of war, for something more was expected of them than the use of their titles. He sharply threatened the commissary, and he announced that deserters would be hanged. (But for this he soon found he did not have the authority.)

As the winter wore on, Colonel Washington learned more about the difference between what should be done and what could be done. If he could not hang his deserters, he would have to go on in the old way of *whipping* them stoutly. If he had not enough money to pay all his men, he would dole it out to the neediest. If he had no artillery, he could not take the field, no matter what the governor expected. If Captain Dagworthy would not take Virginia orders, he would not be issued Virginia provisions. *And* "I cannot help observing that Your Honor, if you have not seen the clothing lately sent up, has been imposed on by the contractors."

Above all, he kept urging the governor to tell him whether he was to prepare for offensive or defensive war, "because the steps for the two are very different." On this point the governor did not care to commit himself. Dinwiddie began to find Washington importunate, and refused him leave to come to Williamsburg and talk things over.

By March, after a long dull winter, Captain Dagworthy's pretensions had become so insupportable that Colonel Washington arranged a hurried trip to Boston, to see the new commander in chief for the colonies, Lord Loudoun, and settle the question once and for all. He kept a careful account of his month's journey, in currency of Pennsylvania, New York, Rhode Island, and Massachusetts, computing the value of it all in Virginia pounds. He bought a new uniform with the silver lace he had been wanting, took some ladies to the Microcosm, lost moderately at cards. Lord Loudoun completely confirmed him in command, and he returned in good spirits, only to find that the Indians had broken out again.

Now it was essential for him to know whether to take the field or to build a fort, "though I have often troubled Your Honor on this head."

Being in a state of uncertainty . . . reduces me to great straits and leaves me to *guess* at everything. Orders that are absolutely necessary on one day, appear the next as necessary to be contradicted . . . So much am I kept in the dark, that I do not know whether to prepare for the offensive or the defensive; and what might be absolutely necessary in the one would be quite useless in the other.

He thought first of marching against the Indians. For an expedition, he would need two thousand good marksmen, so he appointed a time for a rendezvous, and got fifteen volunteers. Fifteen volunteers, and the *militia*. "Whooping, hallooing *gentleman* soldiers," he called them in a climax of disgust.

He was obliged to point out that the commissary was deplorably slow in bringing up supplies. He had only two barrels of powder at Winchester. He could not get new wagons until he had paid for the old ones, and he had no funds. He could not even pay his junior officers. He wrote Governor Dinwiddie that he would be inclined "at any other time than this of imminent danger, to resign without one hesitating moment my command."

Since he could not resign and could not be equipped for an offensive, he strongly urged the wisdom of building a stout fort at Winchester. Fort Cumberland, the outpost in the Alleghenies, should be abandoned, as it was too remote. A fort at Winchester would guard the main road of communications with the west. If the settlers had a safe place to leave their families, they would be more ready to take the field against the enemy. He *must* have a fort at Winchester.

It was April and then it was May. Murders continuing, and nothing done. Colonel Washington despaired of the governor, and began to address himself to John Robinson, speaker of the Assembly, who since he was a colonist might be more sympathetic. To Mr. Robinson he reported that the commissary was all too slow in bringing up supplies; and that the clothing for the soldiers was so poor that they quite properly resented having tuppence a day deducted from their pay for it. Again he must remark on the *superlative insolence* of the militia, who thought that "they had performed a sufficient Tower of duty by Marching to Winchester." If they grew tired, they went home. When he put one of them in the guardhouse, the others got together and tore it down. When there were Indians about on May 17th, the militia of Louisa and Stafford counties deserted in a body. It was time to follow the example of the mother country, and enforce discipline in the army.

Mr. Robinson took an interest, and some useful measures were put through the Assembly. The colonel received permission to build his fort at Winchester. He might also draft men for his army instead of depending on recruiting, although they were only to serve until December—not long enough to make soldiers out of them.

Washington set to work at once. He selected the highest hill, the most commanding position in the vicinity for his fort, and began to blast a well in the limestone. He issued new regulations against drinking, gaming, and swearing, and had a sergeant shot for running away with his party in the face of the enemy. He forbade giving liquor to visiting Indians, "for the ill consequences of that are well known to all who have ever heard of an Indian."

In the midst of this heartening activity, Colonel Washington was delayed by a custom which has since become firmly rooted in the mores of his country, and which, since it antedated the Republic, may well survive it. The Assembly decided to send an investigating committee to the frontier. These "gentlemen Associators," most of whom had never crossed the Blue Ridge, were to inspect the front and select the sites for forts. If Colonel Washington thought the money for their tour might be better spent in paying his soldiers, it was not his place to say so. He bestirred himself to get ready for them, and some weeks later wrote with a slight acerbity to inquire why they took so long to arrive. When they did come they were a cross to him, for he desired two strong forts, one at Winchester and one at Staunton, and they recommended a chain of what he called "little Paultry forts very expensive to Maintain."

In spite of interruptions, he was very busy. The first draftees came in on the twenty-fifth of June—not two thousand good marksmen, but two hundred and forty-six, of whom several deserted at once, more had to be discharged as unfit, and seven were Quakers, who blandly and impassively and without raising their voices, refused to co-operate. Washington, who had no sympathy for the idea of nonresistance to Indians, asked Dinwiddie what he should do with them, and was told to make them work on the fort or confine them on bread and water. But the Quakers would not work on the fort. They elected to sit in the guardhouse through a broiling July, meekly and stubbornly eating their bread and water.

The long slow summer rolled hotly over the fields. The fort rose, foot by foot. The colonel would order his officers *once* more to make returns for their men. Twenty-five with the cat for swearing, and fifty for shamming sick, but in spite of everything desertions continued. The Quakers could not by any means be brought to terms. They chose "rather to be whipped to death than to lend assistance on anything of self-defense." Tired of seeing their meek hot faces in the guardhouse, he discharged them to the custody of friends. When he again asked the governor for permission to abandon Fort Cumberland, he received a politician's answer which could mean either yes or no. In the midst of enforcing discipline, he really could not blame either officers or men for losing heart when they were asked to serve without supplies or pay.

"I am wandering in a wilderness of difficulties," he wrote John Robinson.

The end of September found him laying in twelve months' provisions for a thousand men, without knowing whether he would have them through the winter or not. The militia were worse than ever. "Of no service to the people and burthensome to the country, who would *sooner* starve than carry a few days provisions on their backs, and when their month was out, go they must and did." He wrote a scathing note to the major of the Albemarle contingent: "I presume, Sir, it will be needless to acquaint you that the intent of sending men hither was to protect the frontier inhabitants . . . which cannot be accomplished while you remain in a body forted in as if to defend yourselves were the sole end of your coming."

A less stouthearted man would have been totally discouraged. Washington poured out invective, sarcasm, and importunity, but he kept his rangers active and he built his fort. It gave him some satisfaction to hear that Virginia was holding her frontier better than Maryland or Pennsylvania.

Then came the warm and dreaming days of October, and the Indians reappeared. The commander of exposed Fort Cumberland wished to withdraw, and Washington thought that he should, but Dinwiddie and Lord Loudoun refused to allow it for the clinching reason that it would not look well at Home. Worse still, His Honor decided now to discipline a young provincial officer, who had been most annoying with his refusal to remain quietly in the woods and look busy without bothering anyone. He ordered Washington to take one hundred men, go himself to Fort Cumberland, and stay there.

The colonel protested. He apologized stiffly for "anything which might have had an *air* of pertness or freedom," and proceeded with all rapidity to repeat the offense of thinking for himself. He would obey orders quite literally, he said, and would leave Winchester destitute of protection. All the

public stores would of course be stolen. He would comply
with his orders.

But by December 2nd he had not complied. He wrote
the governor that since the drafts had gone he had only
eighty-five men. What should he do with the stores? He himself would like to go, "for I am sick of this place, the inhabitants and the life I lead here," but he thought it his
duty to point out the consequences. By December 10th he
was still delayed, this time for want of tools.

On receipt of this letter, Dinwiddie lost his patience entirely. He ordered the smaller forts abandoned, the men with-
drawn to Winchester, and he informed the inhabitants of this
before he informed Washington. Lord Loudoun concurred.
Washington had to go to Fort Cumberland then, but he did
not go in silence.

If the stockade forts are all abandoned there will be more
men than required . . . for Fort Cumberland and Fort Loudoun
and the communications between, eighty miles unguarded and without a settler. But I mean nothing more by asking this question than
to know Your Honor's intention, which I would willingly pay
strict attention to.

He wrote also to Lord Loudoun, recapitulated his complaints, and offered to resign. His men were naked and suffering in the cold, he had no cash to pay them, and they
thought themselves "bubbled." He was not allowed to enforce discipline, no provision was made for his wounded. He
felt obliged to mention that he had had some trouble with the
militia. BUT, if he could get three thousand regular soldiers
he would be overjoyed to take the field in an offensive action,
for March was approaching, when the Indians would move
again.

March passed, and nothing happened. In April, Colonel
Washington wrote his story to the Assembly, which responded
by voting him less salary, ordered him to stay in Winchester,
and relieved him of the conduct of Indian affairs.

By June the county reaped the harvest of this neglect,
for the Indians were seen moving openly through the woods.

The inhabitants hurried to the forts, and, from Cumberland, Captain Dagworthy began to call for aid.

Washington acted in a prompt and soldierly manner. He sent a courier to Colonel Stanwix, of the Royal American Regiment, asking for support, and he called out the militia ("without much hope"). His spirits rose at the prospect of action, and he wrote that the alarm had so stimulated the building of the fort that he thought three hundred men would be able to finish it by October.

The alarm proved false. Captain Dagworthy had got the wind up for nothing, "a surprising mistake for an officer to make." Colonel Stanwix ignored the request for support. The militia arrived without arms or ammunition and refused to work on the fort. As routine, Colonel Washington wrote to Governor Dinwiddie and asked him for more arms, more men, more money.

By now His Honor was so tired of these importunities that he was ready for an open breach. When Washington inherited Mount Vernon about this time, he was refused leave to come down and settle his affairs. He turned again with his requests to John Robinson. "I have mentioned this to the Governor, but on this head as on most others he is silent."

July dragged on amid alarms from Captain Dagworthy. In spite of threats and whippings, the men were not satisfied in their service without clothing and without pay. Out of four hundred drafted, one hundred and fourteen deserted. Washington decided to hang two or three as an example, "if I can be justified in the proceeding." He built a gallows forty feet high, and hanged two men, but this severity did not check the "infamous practice." On August 27th he wrote that sixteen new drafts did not replace the number who had deserted since his last letter. He sickened of severity and let the earlier culprits out on promise of good behavior. One of them rewarded him by deserting again that night. "In short, they tire my patience and almost weary me to death."

As he entered the third year of this exasperating duty, he faced a new irritation—a malicious rumor that he was fabricating the alarms in order to obtain more money from the Assembly. He protested passionately. In a letter to Dinwiddie, which still heats the pages, he deplored his loss of the governor's friendship, defended himself against the imputation of insubordination, or ingratitude, "a crime I detest." "No one has ever had the Interest of the country more at heart."

By now Dinwiddie was preparing to return to England, and wished to leave only good feeling behind, so he replied soothingly that Washington should "try to forget it." Washington caught at the perfunctory olive branch, and answered with a list of matters he would like to have the governor settle before his departure. Dinwiddie bluntly refused to permit him to come to Williamsburg and talk things over. Washington wrote him again, and to John Robinson, and to Colonel Stanwix.

It was not to enjoy a party of pleasure I wanted leave of absence. I do not know on whom this miserable and undone people are to rely for redress. . . .

In my estimation, the *only* defense for the frontier would be an expedition to the Ohio.

It was at about this time that a citizen of Augusta County was brought into court because he had "damned Robert Dinwiddie for a Scotch peddling son of a bitch." The court found him guilty, but indicated their opinion by allowing him to apologize and go free. Dinwiddie sailed without replying to Washington's last letter.

Soon after, Washington fell ill with dysentery, and went down at last to Mount Vernon where he spent a lonely winter of profound discouragement in trying to get well. In his depression, he thought of resigning his commission to someone else, who might "have his endeavors crowned with better success." "Because of the obstinacy of my disorder, I have now too much reason to apprehend an approaching decay."

That was in March, but April found him back on the frontier, full of renewed hope and energy. The Assembly had worked this miracle by augmenting the frontier troops to two thousand, and placing Washington in command of them with the rank of brigadier general. The long wished-for offensive expedition was to be undertaken at last, headed by General Forbes and Colonel Stanwix with His Majesty's regulars, assisted by provincial regiments from Virginia and Pennsylvania.

Once again General Washington was optimistic. He wrote to the English officers with whom he had been associated under Braddock and asked them to mention him to Forbes, "not as one who has a favor to ask, but merely to be distinguished from the motley herd of provincial officers, since he had been in the service longer than any of them." He outlined the measures which he thought would be necessary to ensure success, and the officers appeared to agree with him. For the moment he seemed to be getting along well with everyone. He rose above the discouraging fact that he must again start recruiting without funds. But, tutored by experience, he absolutely refused to take the responsibility of ordering out the militia.

A month passed. Almost two months passed, and the young general encountered fresh postponements of his hopes. May found him still at Winchester, still recruiting without funds, still uncertain as to whether or not he should finish his fort. At the end of June, by which time the friendly Indians were tired of waiting, he was at last ordered to proceed as far as Fort Cumberland, eighty miles away. His spirits rose, and he wrote a hasty note on the eve of departure, to the widow Martha Custis (for all the winter in the lowlands had not been wasted in spite of illness).

We have begun our march for the Ohio. A courier is starting for Williamsburg, and I embrace the opportunity to send a few words to one whose life is now inseparable from mine. Since the happy hour when we made our pledges to each other, my thoughts have been continually going to you as to another self. That an all powerful Providence may keep us both in safety, is the prayer of your ever faithful and affectionate friend.

With high hopes the Virginia troops arrived at Fort Cumberland on July 2nd, and remained there doing nothing until September 15th. The English officers decided that instead of using Braddock's Road to the Ohio they would take time to build a new one from Bedford (then Raystown) in Pennsylvania. General Washington differed with them sharply, and as usual did not conceal his opinion. They now had the men and the equipment, already lurking Indians were killing off their stragglers, he knew from experience that winter campaigns were all but impossible in the mountains. Surely, he thought, it was shorter to go one hundred and forty miles on the old road than to cut one hundred miles of the new through mountains and forests.

And now we begin to observe the making of a good revolutionary in General Washington, a second time disappointed in the efficiency of the king's troops, and for nearly three years driven to an extremity of impatience by royal governors. He had seen the fatal results of delay before, and thought himself condemned to watch it again. He pushed his protests to the point of insubordination, and General Forbes found his conduct "very little soldierly." Work on the new road began. "It might be the better plan, but I shall believe it when I am an eye-witness to it," said the unconvinced George Washington, and he continued writing to everyone who had any influence.

All is lost! All is lost by heavens! Our enterprise ruined, and we stop'd at the Laurel Hill this Winter; not to gather Laurels, by the by.

Everyone knows what could have been done on the old road, few can guess what will be done on the new. . . . That appearance of Glory once in view, that laudable Ambition of serving our Country and meriting its applause, is now no more. Every f--l will have his Notions, prattle and talk away, and pray why may not I? . . .

The conduct of our Leaders is tempered with something I don't care to give a name to, indeed I will go further and say they are d--ps or something worse to P-s-v-n Artifice . . . for nothing now but a Miracle can bring this Campaign to a happy Issue. It has long been the luckless fate of poor Virginia to fall a Victim to the views of her Crafty Neighbors.

While he thus fumed to no avail, in Winchester his private affairs took an interesting turn. He had in his absence been put up for election as a member of the Assembly, although he had informed his friends that he ˌwould have no time to campaign for himself because he could not leave his troops. He had in fact run once before and had been defeated, but this time the adroit Colonel Wood handled the matter for him, and with success. Washington wrote to thank his friend, and to reimburse him for thirty-nine pounds spent on liquor and on dinners. He was determined, he said, once this ill-starred campaign had ended, to take up politics and renounce forever the military life, where all was vexation and disappointment, and "backwardness appears in all things except in the approach of winter: that jogs on apace."

By September 1st, forty-five miles of the new road had been cut. Word came that Fort Duquesne was garrisoned by only eight hundred men. The Assembly began to lose interest in an expedition which accomplished nothing. A new governor, Fauquier, arrived in Virginia, and promptly received a letter from a young provincial officer:

Honored Sir: If you are surprised to find us still Incamped at this place, I shall only remark that your surprise cannot well exceed my own. The General, I daresay; for his good character; can account fully for these Delays . . . but I really cannot.

This also had no effect, for it may be presumed that Governor Fauquier knew what General Washington did not: that there were negotiations going forward with the Indians and the French which made delays advisable, and might save many lives.

On September 15th, orders to advance at last were issued, but joy was tempered by the news of a disaster. Major Grant of the Highland Battalion had attacked Fort Duquesne with eight hundred men ("what to do there unless to meet the fate he did I cannot certainly tell you") and had been defeated and captured. Andrew Lewis, son of John and Margaret, also was captured, to the dismay of Augusta County. He had gone cheerfully to the fight, said the reports, although he had constantly reminded everyone, in that irritating provincial fashion, that he did not approve of the maneuver.

Washington proceeded to the advance post, Loyal Hanna, finding the new road incredibly bad, and sure that "after a month's further Tryal, and loss of many more Men by the Sword, Cold, and perhaps Famine, we shall return to the Inhabitants condemned by the world and derided by our Friends." At Loyal Hanna he learned that he and his men had been selected to open the new road through the winter woods as far as Fort Duquesne. He went to work, not neglecting to inform his superior officers that he did not think it a good idea.

November 18th found him thirty miles from his objective, with his men cold, hungry, naked, and fatigued, cutting the road as rapidly as the snows permitted, and much annoyed at having to build a stone chimney at each camp so that General Forbes might be comfortable when he got there. And then occurred the miracle, "which alone could have saved us . . . a fortunate, and indeed unexpected success of our arms." When he was within one day's march of Fort Duquesne, the enemy set it on fire, and "ran away by the light of it down the Ohio."

By December 9th, Washington had his troops back in Winchester, having successfully protested that they were in no condition to remain in the west on garrison duty. He then resigned, not without a last plea for them, and his officers gave him a banquet and a farewell speech.

How sensibly we must be afflicted with the loss of such a commander, such a sincere friend, and so affable a companion! . . . Adieu to that superiority which the enemy have granted us . . . and which even the Regulars acknowledge! Our unhappy country will receive a loss no less irreparable than ours. Where will it meet a man so excellent in military affairs? Who so much respected by the Soldiers?

Although touched, General Washington did not alter his fixed determination. For a second time he said farewell to the backwoods. Again he had finished, and now more firmly than ever, with the military life: with the hard bed on the cold ground, rough food or none, delayed campaigns, uncertainty, discouraged men, lax subordinates, blundering civilian governments. He would take his seat in the Assembly, marry the widow Custis, and above all, plant his fields.

He married in January of 1759, and soon after arrived in Williamsburg. When he rose in the Assembly to make his maiden speech, the courage which had stood by him in the forest suddenly deserted him and he turned crimson, unable to utter a sound. His old friend John Robinson leaned forward in the speaker's chair and addressed him kindly:

"Sit down, Mr. Washington. Your modesty equals your valor, and that surpasses the power of any language I possess."

9. Revolution

FORT LOUDOUN stood on its hill, completed at last in spite of governors and commissaries. Its eighteen cannons made it so formidable that it was never attacked. In 1763 the treaty of Aix-la-Chapelle brought peace between the French and English in the New World as well as in the Old. In 1764, Colonel Bouquet negotiated with the Shawnees for the return of ninety Virginia prisoners, many of them taken in the raids which have been described. Quiet brooded over the Shenandoah for a decade, and a new type of settler began to come over the Blue Ridge.

These were gentlemen, intending to seat themselves properly on the sort of estate no longer available in the settled lowlands. Carter, Burwell, Nelson, Meade, Randolph, Page, Yates—the English names arrived and have remained. They did not start from scratch as the earlier inhabitants had done. They brought wainscoting from England, they had taste, they built sound comfortable houses of brick or stone, with lovely doors and mantels. The northern end of the Valley attracted them, where the good land spread for thirty miles between the mountain ranges.

Some of the amenities of life began to appear. Visiting friends and relatives braved the bad roads in their carriages, and drove across the Blue Ridge. They drank tea, they quoted the Greek and Latin classics. On the shelves of Mr. William Riddle's store appeared a cosmopolitan mixture of "Irish linen, Russia sheeting, German rolls, India nankeens, Bohea tea, French brandy, Spanish indigo." The "nice people" brought their good horses and their English silver. They also brought a small unnoticed portent of disaster. They brought the slaves.

Slavery was never widespread along the Shenandoah. The thrifty Germans found it wasteful; the Scotch-Irish used but few. Here were no great manor houses resting on the labor of a thousand blacks. Here no one had ambitions beyond a few house servants or field hands, and scarcely ten per cent of the population went so far. No one saw in the Negroes anything ominous. They were the friends and children of the family—well housed, well clothed, in the main well treated, joked with, after a fashion loved. No one saw in their black smiling cordial faces a portent of doom. No one heard the cannon thunder in their singing, or saw the flames behind their heads.

George Washington had a great faith in the Shenandoah, and represented Frederick County for two terms in the Assembly, where he put through measures for the public good such as forbidding hogs to run at large in Winchester. On his advice, two of his younger brothers came to settle: Samuel, who had five wives, left a numerous progeny, and built Harewood, where James and Dolly Madison were married; and Charles, who laid out Charles Town, and named it for himself.

One evening in a Williamsburg tavern, a gentleman "who had been sporting" paid his debts by auctioning off a grant of thirteen thousand acres in what is now Jefferson County. On the advice of George Washington, a Mr. Ralph Wormley, after "regaling himself with a social glass," bought it in for five hundred guineas. With the morning came sobriety and repentance, but when Mr. Washington heard of his regrets, "he waited upon him at once, and offered to take it off his hands for what he had paid, but at the same time urged him to hold it, as it would be the foundation of an independent fortune for his children." Mr. Wormley heeded the advice, and a fortune it was, but his heirs dissipated it as heirs sometimes will.

Along the lower reaches of the Shenandoah a marked civility of living now made its appearance, but all was not graciousness and ease. Not then, not ever. Battletown (now Berryville), originally the home of a retired Major Charles Smith, a veteran of Braddock's expedition, became notorious for its brawls on Saturday night. Front Royal was called Hell Town. The South Irish and the Germans rioted in Winchester, parading each other's patron saints: St. Michael with a necklace of sauerkraut, St. Patrick and "his wife Sheely" (St. Sheila), with an apronful of potatoes. In 1771 smallpox broke out again, and the justices of Winchester forbade Mynn Thurston, Samuel Washington, and others, to have their families inoculated; and revoked the licenses of Drs. John McDonald and Humphrey Wells for attempting the hazardous practice.

In 1774 there was more Indian trouble on the Ohio, and the Shenandoah was still too close to the frontier not to be involved. Colonel Angus McDonald, an intractable Scot, whose home was "Glengarry," near Winchester, took a party west to survey the bounty lands granted to veterans of the French and Indian War, and was molested all the way by savages. He had fought in those wars, he had left Scotland abruptly after fighting at Culloden, he had re-established himself in Frederick as a vestryman of the Established Church and sheriff of the county. He was not a man whom Indians could annoy with impunity.

When he reported his difficulties to Lord Dunmore, he was allowed to head a punitive expedition which accomplished little beyond burning some empty villages of mud and bark; but knives were out again, and the brief episode known as Dunmore's War began. The governor raised troops, most of them Valley men, commanded one detachment himself and placed the other under Colonel Andrew Lewis, who had been exchanged after his capture at Fort Duquesne and had returned to Augusta County. Lewis fought a hard battle against Chief Cornstalk at Point Pleasant on the Ohio, and lost many men, among them his young brother Charles, Margaret's "New World child." After this costly victory, it enraged the soldiers from the Shenandoah to find that Governor Dunmore, instead of coming to their support, had made a treaty with the Indians without consulting them.

When Andrew Lewis was ordered to march home without further fighting, he refused to move until Dunmore rode to his camp and told him in person that the war had ended. The frontiersmen had no faith in treaties. Only if the Indians were driven out, dead, *gone,* could a man be sure of safety for his family. The land lay waiting and they meant to have it. Lord Dunmore considered that he had avoided bloodshed by his negotiations, but the Valley saw in them another deep-laid machination to confound and weaken the colonies.

All through the New World, men were beginning to feel that the mother country did not have their welfare at heart. A Valley boy, Jacob Bumgardner, happened to be in Boston with his father's team when some tea was dumped in Boston harbor, and brought back an eyewitness account. When the port of Boston was closed, the missionary impulse, later to flow so disastrously southward, for once flowed north. The people of Augusta sent one hundred and thirty-seven barrels of flour by wagon to the hungry New Englanders.

As early as June, 1774, a committee at Winchester solemnly protested against the closing of the port of Boston: "that such acts would have a necessary tendency to raise a civil war, thereby dissolving that union which has so long happily subsisted between the Mother country and her colonies." Isaac Zane, Angus McDonald, Mynn Thruston, Samuel Beall, Alexander White, and George Rootes, signed it with a flourish. A visiting tutor, Philip Vickers Fithian, described the rising tide of war, the Valley men gathering in hunting shirts, cockades, and "Bucks Tales," "hardy and invincible Natives of the Woods of America": "Mars the great God of Battle is honored in every Part of this spacious Colony, but here every Presence is warlike, every sound is Martial! Drums beating, fifes and Bagpipes playing, and only sonorous and heroic Tunes."

Then as now, however, the heroic note was difficult to sustain and a closer acquaintance with the heroes forced Fithian to qualify his approval: "Instead of military Exercises,

Drinking and Horse-racing—Hollowing, Carousing,—but most thirsty for News . . . Talk of supporting Freedom by meeting and practising Bacchanalian Revels,—preposterous and vain are all such pretensions."

When the news of revolution at last reached the people of the Shenandoah, they knew what to do about it. Although disillusioned and unruly, they fought gallantly on every front and produced six generals for the cause. Less than a month after the battle of Bunker Hill, the first troops raised in Virginia left the Valley to join Washington at Boston. Captain Daniel Morgan organized one hundred sharpshooters, led them out, and by a remarkable series of forced marches arrived there on August 7, 1775.

Washington's first weeks in Boston must have been lonely. No one knew better than he how great the odds the colonies had to face. With his first shot he had broken his life in two, broken with the military tradition in which he had been reared and with the country he had been taught to call home, although he had never seen it. No one had grown up with more respect than he for the regular British Army and no one knew better than he how disunited the colonies were among themselves, how raw the volunteers whom he would have to mold into an army. The Virginia Riflemen arrived and he came out to review them. Many of them he knew. From Daniel Morgan down, the majority had served with him in other campaigns, under Braddock, under Forbes. They were a long way from the Shenandoah now but they were still fighting together. Tradition says that he shook hands with each of them in silence and that when he tried to speak to them the tears ran down his cheeks.

The story of Daniel Morgan is in the best American poor-boy-makes-good tradition. His parents were Welsh iron-mongers who emigrated first to New Jersey and then to the Shenandoah, and remained always a dim background for their famous son. The legend is that he began to emerge from obscurity while a teamster for Braddock, when the captain of his company had trouble with a bully in the ranks and Morgan thrashed the bully. Certainly he had good practice in the

rough-and-tumble. After the Braddock campaign Major
Charles Smith gave him room for a house on the estate of
Battletown. Danny Morgan used to lay down a pile of stones
by the roadside on his way to the tavern of a Saturday night
for ammunition to cover his retreat. The court records at
Winchester note numerous fines for misbehavior. In his last
illness his doctor noticed a badly twisted toe, and asked with
the respect due an aged hero if it was a relic of his Revolutionary service.

"I broke it kicking Bill Davis at Battletown," said the
general.

As the years went on he built a small house called "Soldier's Rest," married, begot two daughters, and began to
achieve respectability. The year 1766 saw him overseer of
roads for Frederick County, and by 1773 he owned both land
and slaves. Prosperity did not make him afraid of risk, as
his prompt arrival in Boston demonstrated.

Morgan's Riflemen were to have a glorious history. They
went through the snow with Arnold to Quebec, where Morgan and many others were captured. In time he was exchanged, and, when he disembarked at New York, tradition
says that he knelt to kiss the soil of his own country. Promoted to colonel, he led his reorganized and reinforced command to Saratoga under General Gates (a neighbor in the
Valley), and there his sharpshooters earned a large share of
the credit for the victory. Morgan's men began to have a
reputation. They were the boys who never missed with their
long muzzle-loading rifles. They were the boys who shot their
squirrels only in the right eye. When Washington wanted
them with him against Howe, General Gates protested,
"Would you ask me to give up the corps which the army of
Burgoyne most fears?"

As soon as Burgoyne surrendered, the Riflemen started
a forced march down the Hudson to join Washington, but
arrived too late for Germantown. When fighting suspended
for the winter, Morgan, who had served three years without
a furlough, went home in charge of several hundred Hessian
prisoners quartered at Winchester.

Without English to make themselves understood, fighting a war they had entered without conviction, the Hessians were acutely homesick. Morgan had them build him a stone house which he named "Saratoga." If they protested against labor, he had a simple rule—no work, no food. Most of them were glad to be occupied, and many stone walls and buildings which they constructed still stand in the Valley of the Shenandoah. They also left the Hessian fly to eat the wheat.

When Morgan, now a brigadier general, returned to active duty, he transferred his Hessians to James Wood, son of the first James, who was delighted to stay at home with his young wife. "My dear, my lovely Jenny, I did not know how dear you were to me until this separation. Indeed I cannot live without you. Do write and send me a plat of your hair." James Wood had been homesick too at Germantown.

By 1780 the Revolution had dragged on for five years with no sign of ever ending. Some said the commander in chief had not sense enough to give in. General Morgan took his Riflemen to fight with Gates in South Carolina. After Gates had been defeated at Camden, Morgan fought Tarleton at Cowpens, in January, 1781. "Morgan has never been licked," he told his men.

His command consisted of the Riflemen, some cavalry, and some militia. General Washington had not revised his opinion of the militia, although now he expressed it in more dignified terms. "No militia will ever acquire the habits necessary to resist a regular force. Regular troops alone are equal to the exigencies of modern war, and when a substitute is attempted, it must prove illusory." Dan Morgan knew what they were like, and made allowance for it. They had run on Gates at Camden and ruined him, but they were not going to run on Danny Morgan.

He retreated until a river behind him cut off retreat. Then he stationed the militia three hundred yards ahead of his picked troops, ordered them to fire twice and then run like the devil. Tarleton's dragoons came charging down as usual. The militia fired twice, did their running with real enthusiasm, and the dragoons spread out and overextended themselves in pursuit just as Morgan had expected. When they were well scattered, his Riflemen and his cavalry charged and soon had the British regulars begging for mercy. Morgan lost only twelve men.

Soon after Cowpens, the Virginian term of service expired, as terms then had a way of doing in the midst of a campaign. The men insisted on going home, for they had not been paid in a year, and the climate of South Carolina was doing them more harm than the British. "Go they must and did," and with them General Morgan, now a rheumatic cripple, but they took along enough prisoners to raise the total in the Valley to sixteen hundred. The British prisoners complained that the Hessians were given more privileges and freedom than they. The Hessians had learned to make themselves useful.

Morgan did no more active service, except to lead a brief expedition that summer against the Tories on the South Branch of the Potomac across the Alleghenies. The summer of 1781 was a dark one, for Cornwallis had landed in the Tidewater, and Tarleton swept up from the south as far as Charlottesville, looting, burning, and carrying off thirty thousand slaves, of whom two-thirds died of smallpox. The Virginia Assembly sat at Staunton in old Trinity Church that summer, having fled there in such haste that Patrick Henry left one of his boots behind. The Tories in the South Branch (Potomac) valley came out of hiding, refused to pay taxes, and organized a company to join Cornwallis.

Morgan and others from the Shenandoah crossed the mountains and spent ten days chasing them, killed one, shot another in the leg, branded a third on the posterior with a red-hot spade, and gathered up many pigs and calves. "They had feasted the Tories, now they could feast the Whigs," said Morgan.

Down in Augusta County the citizens made ready to defend themselves if Tarleton should cross the Blue Ridge. The old men and boys took up arms and went to the mountains. The sons of John and Margaret Lewis were already fighting, and now the grandsons went, down to the ten-year-old. But the tide turned back, for Tarleton did not invade Augusta, and the Assembly found a refuge in the old church.

Augusta's most distinguished contribution to the Revolution had been made in the first year of the war, when Brigadier General Andrew Lewis and Lord Dunmore met again. This time it was not the colonial who had to retreat before he was ready.

Lord Dunmore, after his unpopular "war," had given the Virginians new offense in the April of 1775 by seizing all the gunpowder in Williamsburg on the pretext of preventing a slave uprising. The slaves were quiet, and the Virginians knew it. Patrick Henry led their protests, and in the end the governor paid for the powder but kept it in his own hands, and they had no way to replace it. Then Lord Dunmore, "in order to have the privilege of wearing his head," took refuge on his ship and went down the coast rousing the slaves himself. More than a thousand joined him (and were later rewarded by being sold again in the West Indies). He burned Norfolk, and with a fleet of fifty small boats took his stand on Gwynns Island, at the mouth of the Rappahannock. General Andrew Lewis, who had never forgiven him for his failure to pursue the Indians after the battle of Point Pleasant, had the congenial duty of driving him out of this position in the summer of 1776.

Dunmore fled with those of the blacks who had not died of fever, and never showed his face in Virginia again. Even the Virginians who had condoned his negotiations with the Indians could not pardon him for rousing the slaves. In the Shenandoah Valley a new county had recently been taken from Frederick and called Dunmore. The name was quickly changed to Shenandoah, so that even his memory might be obliterated.

The new Shenandoah County also produced its Revolutionary hero. In the village of Woodstock, in the middle Valley, lived the Reverend Peter Muhlenberg, Pennsylvania born and German educated, ordained in the Established Church and pastor of the Lutheran flock. He interested himself in the Revolutionary movement and took part in the Virginia Conventions of 1775. On the Sunday after his return to the Valley, he mounted the pulpit dressed in his usual somber black gown and preached a stirring sermon on the text: "For everything there is a season, and a time for every purpose under heaven . . . a time to keep silence, and a time to speak . . . a time for peace, and a time for war." At the most dramatic moment, he threw off his gown, revealed himself in the uniform of a Virginia colonel, and proceeded to recruit the nucleus of a regiment from his congregation. Known as the German Regiment, it did excellent service, notably in South Carolina, and the good pastor, after many a fight, ended the Revolution as a brigadier general.

The shrewd and salty Morgan, the frontiersman Lewis, the fighting parson Muhlenberg, were types of the New World, committed to the theory that a man may make of himself whatever he wishes to be provided he has the innate capacity. Children of the Western Star, they prospered, and their later lives were full of honor. At the northern end of the Valley, however, lived three men whose prospects at the beginning seemed far brighter but who failed in the new because they could not altogether relinquish the old. Horatio Gates, at "Traveller's Rest," Charles Lee at "Prato Rio," Adam Stephen who laid out Martinsburg, all had homes within a few miles of each other, were far above the usual rank of frontier settler, rose to be major generals, and all three were disgraced and retired before the end.

It must be admitted that they began the Revolution in a blaze of patriotism: "I am ready to risque my life to preserve the liberty of the Western World," wrote Gates while the trouble was brewing. Charles Lee talked of declaring independence long before most colonists had accepted the idea. Adam Stephen wrote to his neighbor Angus McDonald, and urged him to take up arms:

Your Highland pride may stare you in the face and bellow out "Shall I serve under ——? It is incompatible with my mistaken honour, merits, etc". I beg you will remember that in 1776 I was nothing in the military way,—in less than a year I was a colonel, brigadier, and major general. Had not my attachment to the interest of America been superior to all scrupulosity, I would now have been poking at home about the mill.

Gates had come to the Shenandoah as a major in the regulars under Braddock, and had liked the country well enough to settle there after the campaign and to persuade his colleague Charles Lee to follow him into the neighborhood. Although his parents had been only servants in the household of the Duke of Leeds, Gates had one foot in the great world, for Horace Walpole was his godfather and some said his father. He began the war as Washington's adjutant general and displayed a real talent for organization; but both he and Charles Lee suffered from feeling themselves superior to their commander in chief and in the end their careers foundered on that rock. They could not forget that they had been regulars when he was only a provincial officer.

As early as 1776, General Gates found time to inform Congress of Washington's strategical mistakes. His defeat of Burgoyne at Saratoga confirmed his good opinion of himself and, while Washington held on through the winter at Valley Forge, Gates headed a faction which complained that the country was being ruined "by a weak general and bad Counsellors." Washington, who had set his course with the tenacity he had shown at Fort Loudoun, took no notice of this disloyalty beyond letting it be known that he had heard of it and later put Gates in charge of driving the British from the Carolinas. There Gates got himself soundly beaten by Cornwallis, abandoned Charlotte, and fell back to Hillsboro. Congress relieved him of command. Gates retired in dignified silence to his Valley plantation where the Virginia Assembly sent him a consoling resolution and his caustic neighbor Charles Lee, who was there before him in disgrace, commented on his exchange of "northern laurels for southern weeping willows."

The rise of tall, gaunt, sardonic General Lee had been even swifter and his fall more steep. The son of a general in the British Army, brilliant, well educated, and acutely conscious of it, he was too bright to consider himself bound by the ordinary laws of politeness, too bright not to see the mistakes of his superiors, and much too bright to conceal his observations. His military experience covered many fields. After Braddock's defeat he had served in the Mohawk Valley, "married" an Indian girl, and earned the all too appropriate tribal name of "Boiling Water." After fighting under Burgoyne in Portugal, he expressed his criticism and was dismissed for writing against the ministry. He went to Russia and became a general. He then tried to rejoin the British Army; when they refused to have him, he returned to America and espoused the Revolutionary cause. At the onset of war he was second in command to Washington himself.

His successful defense of Charleston made him a hero to the public although his ingrained belief in British superiority had almost induced him to order his soldiers to spike their guns and retire after the first volley. When on the night before the battle he had visited his raw troops for the purpose of improving their morale, he was audibly astonished to find that it needed no improvement. He reported officially that the regiments raised in the Shenandoah Valley were "disorderly, mutinous, and dangerous in disposition."

During 1776, when defeat followed defeat, when the patriot army seemed to be melting away, when Washington himself is reported to have said, "My neck does not feel made for a halter. In the last resource we must retire to the mountains of Augusta and try a predatory war," many citizens demanded a "more firm and decided" general. Charles Lee modestly intimated that he would serve if called. Retreating too slowly across New Jersey, he let himself be captured by the very company of dragoons he had commanded in Spain fifteen years before. While a prisoner in New York he was well treated and the ever-forgiving Washington procured his exchange in the spring of 1778.

During his imprisonment he had urged Congress to send him a committee "to confer on a subject of importance to the country." He told British General Howe that he hoped to work out a compromise; he told the Americans that he meant to disclose to them the British plan of campaign; and he drew

a map for the British showing them how to take Alexandria
and the Chesapeake Bay. What he meant by all this, only
Charles Lee knew. In his heart he could not believe that the
Americans could win. Perhaps he had never believed it. By
the time he rejoined Washington at Valley Forge he was talking openly in favor of compromise.

When Washington fell back to Princeton, he ordered
Lee to delay the enemy, but at Monmouth Court House Lee
was so impressed by reports of British strength that he retreated instead. He was falling back in some disorder when
he encountered Washington and the main body of the army.
That was the day when Washington swore. "Yes, sir," said
one of his generals afterward, "he swore once. At Monmouth
Court House on a day that would have made any man swear.
He swore on that day until the leaves shook on the trees,
charming, delightfully. Never have I enjoyed such swearing
before or since. Sir, on that memorable day he swore like an
angel from heaven."

On the wings of his wrath, Washington rode up and
down the lines, re-formed his men for battle, and at this
show of opposition the supposedly irresistible enemy withdrew. The day was saved, but Lee had had a public dressing
down and he could not let it rest. He kept writing for "a
justification" and even suggested that his censure was caused
by "dirty earwigs" in the neighborhood of the general. He
demanded a court-martial so loudly that Washington at last
let him have it, with the result that he was suspended for a
year "for disobedience of orders, misbehaviour before the
enemy, and disrespect to the commander-in-chief." The find-
ings were sent to Congress for confirmation and Lee again
cut his own throat by hastening to Philadelphia and talking
so much that they retired him to the life of gentleman farmer,
for which he was singularly unfitted.

Adam Stephen, who had been "nothing in the Military
way," did not rise so far as his two neighbors, and consequently his descent was more cushioned. He had a degree in
medicine from Edinburgh, he had lived twenty years in the
country, had served at Great Meadows and under Braddock,

had run unsuccessfully for the Assembly against Washington. He was astonished to find himself a major general, and not too astonished when in a fog near Germantown his troops collided with those of Mad Anthony Wayne and he was dismissed for the error, which some were ungenerous enough to attribute to John Barleycorn. With the air of a cheerful philosopher he retired to his estate and laid out the town of Martinsburg, apparently not at all in disfavor with the community. Later he was a delegate to the Virginia Convention which ratified the Federal Constitution.

Charles Lee proposed a toast to the three of them: "To the one who was drunk when he should have been sober, to the one who advanced when he should have retreated, to the one who retreated when he should have advanced." It is to be hoped that the others appreciated his wit. It is to be hoped that Mrs. Gates, who was something of a scold, did not feel too much resentment when he told her at her own dinner table, "Madam, you want my opinion and you shall have it. My candid opinion is that you are a tragedy in private life and a farce to all the world." General Lee did not make a comfortable neighbor.

General Gates bore his downfall in silence and was rewarded by reinstatement in 1782, in time to be at Newburgh. He lived on quietly in the Shenandoah for ten more years, then moved to New York. But Charles Lee never forgave and never accepted his fate. When Washington once tried to call on him after the Revolution, he closed his shutters, locked his door, and put up a sign: "No Bread or Bacon baked here today." He so despised his surroundings that he never bothered to build partitions in his house, but divided it into four compartments by chalk lines on the floor—living room, bedroom, kitchen, harness room. "The most convenient arrangement possible, for I can without a moment's effort supervise it all."

Disappointed, bitter, never considering himself appreciated, always turning ugly when unrecognized, the son of a general, the husband of a squaw, Charles Lee went to Philadelphia for the purpose of selling his Valley property and died there. In his last delirium his mind reverted to happier days when ambitions seemed more attainable, and he kept calling: "After me, my brave dragoons!" He left Prato Rio to his two Italian servants, and even in his will he could not forego one last bitter fling:

I desire most earnestly that I may not be Burried in any Church or Churchyard or within a mile of any Presbyterian or AnaBaptist Meeting House; for since I have resided in this country I have Kept so much bad Company when living that I do not chuse to continue it when dead. I recommend my soul to the creator of all Worlds and all Creatures, who must from his visible attributes, be indifferent to their Modes of Worship or creeds, as a weak mortal can no more be answerable for his Persuasions Notions or even Scepticism in religion than for the color of his Skin.

With three successful generals and three failures, the record does no more than balance, but the glory of the Shenandoah during the Revolution was not in its general officers, but in its men. The long green trough between the mountains did not in this war become a battleground, but it sent soldiers to every front. There was a remarkable unanimity among the Valley people as to the advisability of the fight for independence.

Tories were rare among them. The few who existed were haled into court, tried, released under bond, and mildly treated. In Rockbridge, Mary Walker paid fifteen pounds and spent four days in jail and Moses Whitley's three slaves were seized. Felix Gilbert in Rockingham had to give bond. In Augusta, the Reverend Alexander Miller must have been more intractable, for he was fined one hundred pounds and spent two years in jail. The most prominent Tory of them all, Thomas Lord Fairfax, withdrew from the county court in Frederick but lived on unmolested at Greenway Court.

The Quakers, Mennonites, and Dunkards opposed violence as usual, and made their customary struggle against bearing arms. Some Valley Quakers, and others sent down from Philadelphia, stubbornly sat in custody at Winchester as their fathers had done on a previous occasion. The county lieutenant did not know what to do with them. He tried to release them under bond but they refused to swear an oath. He confiscated their property and that did not shake them. At last Alexander White was paid one hundred pounds in Virginia gold to go to Philadelphia and negotiate their freedom, which he succeeded in doing to the relief of all.

Not even all the Quakers could hold out so stubbornly against the concerted patriotism and warlike temper of their Valley neighbors. Like wealthy Isaac Zane of Frederick, many a one declared himself "a Quaker for the times." Zane served as an officer of militia and in his iron furnace and foundry at Marlboro turned out both cannon and cannon balls.

There were of course some slackers, as there are in every war and every era, but the Shenandoah had in the main been settled by men fully prepared to fight for their independence. No men were drafted in the Valley under the law of 1778, for the quota had been filled by volunteers. They joined Washington in Boston, they met Cornwallis in the Tidewater, they went south and west against the Cherokees and the Shawnees. They fought from Quebec to Georgia, from King's Mountain to Yorktown.

They were valiant but not amenable, wonderful shots but not in love with discipline. General Washington had to remind General Morgan that the Riflemen must be subject to regulations like the rest of the army. They were heroes at Cowpens and Saratoga, villains when they murdered Chief Cornstalk, who had come to their western fort under a treaty of peace. They fought on without shoes and without pay, but they reserved to themselves the right to go home for a visit when they felt like it and punishment did not deter them. Beyond all rights they cherished the right to complain, and complain they did. They might be "disorderly, mutinous, and dangerous in disposition," but they were still fighting after the critical General Lee was forced to quit.

In the overdramatization of our national legend, it should not be forgotten that eight years elapsed between the first shots at Lexington and the final treaty of peace; and that at no time during that period, in spite of individual successes, did the general situation look bright for the colonists. This does not minimize the American achievement, but enhances it. By the time a soldier has endured eight years of hardship, he is not fighting for excitement, for glory or for any other illusory reward. Fair-weather patriotism will have long gone by. It must be a strong faith that sustains him.

Every effort was made to divide the colonies by offers of peace, to separate diplomatically the Americans and the French; and all were failures. In the end it was the British who fell apart by interior pressure, by differences among themselves. It was the British who decided that the struggle was not worth continuing, and who turned their hopes of empire to India and the East rather than to the unruly West, where men had forgotten how to give in.

The Americans looked weak and they were; looked disorderly, uncouth, untutored, and were all of these things; but they were sustained by the most potent dream for which man has yet to die. They had imagined a strong and indivisible country where every man could walk in freedom, with justice and opportunity for all according to their merits. Even the most ignorant felt this dream stirring within them although they could not articulate it—and the land lay waiting.

The surrender of Cornwallis was not by two years the end of the struggle, but it was the omen of success. General Washington permitted himself a brief gleam of optimism while he pointed out the difficulties still ahead. In the Shenandoah Valley a leading exponent of the old order heard the news from Yorktown, and knew what it might mean.

"Help me to bed," said the octogenarian Lord Fairfax to his servant, "it is time for me to die."

10. Expansion

A FINISHED WAR is just a story for old men. When the Revolution ended and the soldiers of the Shenandoah Valley came home to see what had happened to the country they were fighting for, they found it in terrible shape. An era had ended, an era began, and new times brought new troubles. Inflation mushroomed until seventy-four continental dollars equaled only one dollar in silver, and the phrase "not worth a continental" passed permanently into the national argot. The ex-soldiers discovered that such meager pay as they finally received bought nothing, and they migrated in droves to their bounty lands to the west. Then came the depression. Wheat sank to three shillings a bushel, and merchants refused credit, "even to the Best Men."

The Valley people, no more unworldly than anyone else, had wished "to reap all the advantages and enjoy all the sweets of the desirable and glorious change." They found taxes higher, markets reduced, Maryland astride the Potomac, and interstate duties making trade impossible. When the newspapers came out for free trade between the states, the conservatives condemned such hopes as chimerical. Scarce coin was replaced by barter, and even taxes, twenty-five shillings for a slave, ten for a horse, had to be paid in tobacco, deerskins, or hemp instead of specie.

Everyone was in debt: Isaac Zane, Adam Stephen, Thomas Lewis, Alexander White, Archibald Stuart. General Gates said that he could not pay his creditors until he could collect from his debtors, and if he were to sue, the courts would take seven years to reach a decision. Judgments were enforced by "firearms, clubs, axes, drawn swords, and fixed

bayonets." Joseph Moore was sworn in as sheriff of Rockbridge County while in jail for a debt of fifty pounds.

Plainly, the Valley was ruined. Everything would be
swept away in this economic confusion, nothing would be
left. But the Valley was not ruined. The crops continued to
push up imperturbably through the generous soil, the doves
sang in the oaks, the fructifying sun evoked abundance. The
Valley began to come back.

No one expected that recovery would take place all at
once, but trade expanded gradually. Cattle, flour, whisky,
ginseng, beeswax went over the gaps, and clothing, hardware,
salt, and spirits traveled back. President Washington interested himself in opening the Potomac, the James, and the
Shenandoah to navigation, and Thomas Lewis told him that
the Shenandoah might be made usable for one hundred and
fifty miles. Although this was optimistic, they did open the
James River canal, and the legislature voted Washington one
hundred shares in it. In accord with his policy, "to shut my
hand against every pecuniary recompense," he promptly gave
the shares to the Rockbridge academy, Liberty Hall, and the
school changed its name to Washington College.

The hard sense of the Valley people rejected two measures of superficial relief: paper money, and a repudiation of
debts to British creditors. They held payment essential to
"national honour and justice," and won their point in the
Virginia legislature. They petitioned also for a better representation in their state government, and might have gained it
if they had not been opposed by that champion of liberty,
Patrick Henry. They did, however, secure some improvements in which they were peculiarly interested. The Presbyterians and other dissenters obtained a guarantee of their religious liberty, and tithes went out with the Revolution and
were never revived. In 1786 the Court of Appeals handed
down a final decision in the fifty-year-old case of Hite versus
Fairfax. Fairfax was dead, Hite was dead, but the land was
secured to the descendants of the plaintiff.

When in 1788 the Virginia Convention voted on the
Federal Constitution, the Shenandoah Valley cast its fourteen

votes solidly for ratification; for the Constitution embodied just such a compromise between progress and conservatism as suited the realistic Valley temperament.

At Winchester they held a celebration in honor of the event. "A select number of *pure* Federals" gave a banquet, followed by fireworks and toasts. They drank the first to George Washington, and put their hearts into it. The second was to His Most Christian Majesty, The King (of France). The third was to Lafayette, the fourth to Benjamin Franklin, the fifth to the memory of the American worthies who fell in the Revolution (and hardly an eye was dry), the sixth was to the United States, and called for a cheer to follow, the seventh was to the Fourth of July, and called for two or three cheers; someone suggested Patrons of Freedom for the eighth, and that put them in mind of Friends of the Federal Constitution for the ninth, and for the tenth they were on their feet and waving their glasses, "May the manufacturing spirit increase as the Federal Union becomes permanent and respectable" (who in the devil thought of that one, eh?), and they drank an eleventh to the majority of the Virginia Convention, and a twelfth to the Federal Pillars, with a red, white and blue display at the end of the garden, and the thirteenth to Peace, with gestures, "May the sword never be drawn again"—and so, rejoicing, home to bed.

Yes, there was gaiety as well as patriotism and progress in the Valley. Winchester streets might still be mudholes in the winter, the water supply might still be flowing from the spring through a log pipe, but they had two newspapers, three schools, and five taverns. The merchants advertised "duffel and rose blankets, negroes, cottons, bath coatings, callimanicoes, wildbores, ladies fashionable hats, ribbons of newest taste"; and in addition that most stylish novelty, "a consignment of India rubber shoes." "Females are becoming to exhibit a little more prudence in the winter apparel, and it is likely that the bill of mortality would be most happily less were this gum elastic shoe substituted for the fashionable sandals which are now in use." Mr. J. Moriarity begged leave to inform the ladies and gentlemen of the community that

he would teach dancing in the modern method of Europe—
while his rival, Mr. McMahon, would instruct (to the strains
of the best white music) in minuets, Allemands, cotillions,
and country dances, "The Innocent Maid" and "True Fe-
licity." The taverns—the Black Horse, the Golden Buck, the
Red Lion, the Golden Sheaf, the Indian Queen—did a rushing
business.

At the Black Horse one evening some young men were
debating the merits of the Christian religion when an old
man drove up in a shabby gig. He came to the fire, and they
ignored him. After they had argued from six in the evening
until eleven, one of them laughingly asked him for his opinion. At that the silent old gentleman sat up in his chair and
spoke for an hour. He took up each suggested point in turn,
summed up, gave a considered judgment. When the young
men had recovered from their stunned and total silence,
they ventured to ask his name, and found that he was Chief
Justice John Marshall, whose father had once been county
clerk at Woodstock.

Distinguished visitors also came to the Golden Buck,
kept by Philip Bush, an old German of violently republican
tendencies. Two gentlemen arrived in a fine carriage, and
after looking around with a highly unsatisfied expression,
ordered their suppers served in their rooms. Mr. Bush said
that he did not serve meals upstairs.

"My good fellow, you do not realize to whom you are
speaking. This is His Majesty Louis Philippe of France, and
I am the Duc de Chartres."

But Mr. Bush did not fall back in the expected delight.
On the contrary, he was now convinced that he would not
serve meals upstairs.

The Duc de Chartres, growing more and more coldly
aristocratic, but keeping his voice down and his vocabulary
simple, pointed to the sign outside the inn.

"Your sign declares that you are a place of public entertainment, and so you are obliged to take such orders as
the public wish to give."

Philip Bush was red in the neck by this time; but if

that was it, he knew what to do. He went out and grabbed an ax. When he returned he did not pause to look at his pride, his joy, his pretty little gilded deer.

"Come down, buck," said Philip Bush, and chopped it down.

The distinguished travelers had to go elsewhere, but other visitors met with better reception, now that Jefferson was the richest county west of the Blue Ridge, and the springs at Bath (now Berkeley Springs) had been improved with a hotel. Dr. Johann David Schoepf, surgeon to the Hessians, observed two things in particular: that the people in this new country were all bent on providing for their children something better than they had themselves and that the Virginians read but did not study. The Count Castiglioni had an eventful trip when he went by Staunton to visit Monticello, for the Shenandoah was in flood and he had to take refuge in a near-by house and wait for the waters to subside. When the "good man of the house" advised him that he might try, his servant stripped himself and ventured in (on horseback) with the carriage, but the river turned it over and swept him down, so that all were saved with the greatest difficulty. "I resolved never again to trust to the advice of these wild pioneers." Next day they crossed, and then went over the North River in a flat canoe, the horses swimming beside them. But as the unfortunate wayfarer journeyed on down the Valley of the "Shenandore," the bad road between Staunton and Winchester jolted his calèche so to pieces that he had to abandon it, and the "country of many delightful prospects" hardly recompensed him for the trip.

Captain Ferdinand Marie Bayard of Paris spent the summer of 1791 at Bath with his wife and child, escaping the heat of Baltimore. He found Bath gay with a troupe of Irish comedians, a dance every week, billiards, and so much play at the taverns that a planter might arrive with a carriage and attendants and go home with only a horse. This was the first of the Virginia Springs, the world of fashion flocked to it, and its gay reputation gave an impetus to all the others.

At Bath it is the custom to drink tea at five o'clock. Everything is very ceremonious. At the right of the lady dispensing tea are ranged in a half circle all the other ladies. A profound silence follows the entrance of each invited guest; all the ladies as grave as judges on the bench. A small acajou table is placed before the dispenser of tea. Silver pots contain the coffee and the hot water, which serves to weaken the tea or to receive the cups. A domestic brings on a silver waiter the cup, the sugar dish, the cream pot, the butter balls, the thin slices of ham. A Frenchman is embarrassed at the necessity of watching his cup and saucer in one hand, and with the other receiving a tart or a slice of very thin ham.

In sending back the cup the spoon must be placed in a manner to indicate whether you will begin again, or have finished drinking. A Frenchman on one occasion, unfamiliar with English and ignorant of this polite sign language, was overcome at seeing the sixteenth cup arrive, which having emptied, he hit upon the device of stowing it in his pocket, dreading a seventeenth.

Captain Bayard wished to see more of "this region where, beneath skies almost always serene, the inhabitants cultivate a generous soil," so he tore himself away from Bath and rode off to visit a planter near Winchester. "As you draw near the town, many well stocked farms appear. On the slopes range long wooled sheep, not afraid of wolves during the summer. Such war is made upon the wolves that even in this heavily timbered country there is little danger from them, except when the snow lies deep upon the ground. It is a magnificent country about Winchester. The men are tall, well made, of strong constitutions and ruddy. The horses and cattle have the eye and gait of health."

He was delighted with the planter, his manners, his conversation, the whisky distilled on the place, and the plans for the mansion, which like so many things in America lay in the future. He liked the moonlight, the flowers, the music of the whippoorwill, and "the blacks coming in from the fields singing behind the slow horses, fatigued with the day's work." At church on Sunday he saw the blacks again, sitting in the gallery, and he noted with dismay the American custom of reading the Bible all through Sunday afternoon, behind closed doors. By the time he set out for gay Bath in the early morning, he was deeply impressed with the peace and poetry of the New World life. "A light fog covered the valley, resembling transparent gauze, through which appeared the tops of trees, houses, and cabins, the cabin chimneys already smoking. The squirrels were early awake."

If one believes the local legends, not all the visitors to the Valley during this period were earthly, for supernatural visitants appeared as well. One night a stranger came to the house of Adam Livingston, near Middleway, and asked for shelter. Since he was evidently ill, they took him in and nursed him but when it became apparent that he was dying, he confessed that he was a Catholic and asked them to call a priest. Good Adam Livingston demurred. Catholics were still under a profound suspicion. Only a few years before it had been impossible for one of them even to give testimony in court without an oath denying transubstantiation and renouncing the pope. Livingston would have no truck with popery, and he told his visitor so.

The stranger died unshriven, and then strange things began to happen on Adam Livingston's farm. His candles would not burn, he heard horses galloping in the night but when he went to his barn he found them all in their stalls. His cattle sickened and died of mysterious ailments, his barn burned down, and when he and his wife went to put on their best black Sunday clothes, holes in the shape of crescents had been cut in both. Then in a dream he saw his visitor again.

By now he had learned a more tolerant attitude. He sent for the priest whom he had refused to call, and made him a present of a field which the Church holds to this day and on which a service is still held once every year. A mass was said for the dead man and the disturbances ceased, but Middleway had earned the name of Wizard's Clip, and as such was long known.

The visitors to the Shenandoah in the early nineteenth century found life there settled and agreeable. It had fulfilled the promise which had called the pioneers into its sheltered prairies and its forests, and the frontier had moved on westward. Within the memory of some still alive it had been wild, unknown, apparently untamable; now it was quiet, gracious, full of beauty and a serene charm. The sons and grandsons of the pioneers, moved by the classic American restlessness, began to seek *their* promise farther to the west, and many who left the Valley were such men as make history.

A Valley boy, John Sevier, founded Tennessee. A Valley boy, Sam Houston founded Texas. Such familiar names as Bryan, Boone, Lincoln, and Bowman were carried to Kentucky by the sons of Valley families.

Daniel Boone married Rebecca Bryan from the upper Shenandoah. At Strodes, also in Rockingham County, a couple of Irish indentured servants worked for a year and bore a son named Andrew Jackson before they moved west. John Lincoln took up six hundred acres on Linville Creek, in Rockingham, and his son Jacob built a good brick house where his children and grandchildren lived and were buried with their slaves beside them. Jacob's brother, Abraham, moved to Kentucky when his son Tom was four, an unsatisfied man who signed early petitions for better conditions: "We have stated the poor man's case." In Kentucky the unprosperous Tom allowed a second Abraham to be born in a log cabin, but it was not the comfortable Virginia Lincolns who made the glory of the name.

John Sevier was born in 1745, son of an innkeeper on a frontier farm near New Market. At twenty-five he moved to Woodstock, but that was not wild enough for a man of boiling energies, and he soon took his family on into the Great Smokies. There he and the men who followed him drew up in 1772 a form of territorial government as rough-and-ready and practical as themselves. At the outbreak of the Revolution they joined North Carolina in attacking the British at King's Mountain, only to find themselves ceded back to the Federal government when North Carolina decided to economize. Then the angry frontiersmen formed the state of Franklin, elected John Sevier governor and took care of themselves for four years. When at last in 1796 Franklin became the state of Tennessee, Sevier served as governor for three more terms, and later went to Congress. Time and two wives and eighteen children sobered him and watered down his roaring fighting qualities. Old age found him a respectable churchgoer in a blue broadcloth swallowtail coat, trustee of Washington College at Lexington, and of a college in Tennessee.

Samuel Houston's grandfather John was one of the first elders of the Reverend John Craig's Old Stone Church, his father was one of Morgan's Riflemen. Samuel was born in 1793 in a log house near Timber Ridge, and went to Tennessee at twelve, when his mother married again after the death of his father. His early life was chaotic. For a time he lived with the Cherokees, then studied law, went to Congress, and was elected governor of the state in 1827. He might have lived in Tennessee all his life and never have been famous, but for an unfortunate marriage which lasted only a week and caused him to resign and return to the Indians. During four years he disappeared into the twilight of their tribal life, then emerged in Texas, where his story is too well known to need repeating. After securing the independence of Texas he became its president in 1836, and later its senator. At the outbreak of the Civil War he was its governor, but was removed from office because of his opposition to secession.

Not far from the Houstons, in Rockbridge County, lived the McDowells on the land which Ephraim McDowell took up when he came from Londonderry in 1737. His son John was killed fighting the Indians, his grandson Samuel moved to Kentucky with his family in 1783. Another Ephraim, ninth of eleven children, was twelve at the time of the "removal." He took a degree in medicine at Edinburgh, returned to practice in Kentucky, and there in 1809 performed what is considered the first successful abdominal operation, although the honor is contested by another Valley doctor, Joseph Bennett. A woman had a tumor and McDowell undertook to remove it while the townspeople waited outside to lynch him if the patient died. "The intestines as soon as an opening was made, ran out upon the table, remained out about thirty minutes, and being upon Christmas day, they became so cold that I thought proper to bathe them in tepid water previous to my replacing them." Amazingly enough, the woman recovered and Dr. McDowell continued the practice of abdominal surgery, preferring always to operate on a Sunday so that he might have the prayers of the congregation during his work.

The two great strains in American life, the pioneer and the homebuilder, were nowhere more mingled than in the Shenandoah Valley during the half century when the great roads to the southwest ran through it, and in the upper Valley bisected the road from north to south. If much spirit and enterprise went from the Valley westward, so also did a ruthless and unruly element, and as they moved away the temper of the people gradually approximated the serenity of the landscape. In the first fifty years of the nineteenth century the region of the Shenandoah lost forever all resemblance to its pioneering days.

The people were still ready enough to fight, but fighting no longer seemed so pressing a duty. When General Morgan led a small force to the Whisky Rebellion in Pennsylvania and came back without firing a shot, President Washington twitted him gently: "It must have been an arduous campaign to walk up hill and down again." That was not war as teamster Dan and a young provincial colonel had learned it in '54, but those days were long ago, long even in an old man's memory.

When they fought the British again in 1812 the war was far from the Valley, although they raised their regiments and sent them into battle, and Angus McDonald, son of Angus, died as the result of a forced march near Buffalo. The Federalists opposed the war. A depression preceded it, an inflation followed it. Still the Valley continued to grow, not suddenly, not due to booms or mineral wealth, but slowly, steadily, and continually as a tree grows in rich soil.

When Washington Irving visited the Kennedys at Cassilis and wrote his name on Nellie Custis's door at Audley, he called the Shenandoah a glorious valley, "equal to the promised land for fertility, far superior to it for beauty, and inhabited by an infinitely superior people—choice though not chosen."

No one believed that the tranquil fields might ever again be the scene of organized murder, danger of battle seemed impossible. The Indians were remote, the British back on the other side of the Atlantic, the French transformed by the mysterious alchemy of time into friends and allies. The region had inherited its patrimony, and must consolidate it. For the inhabitants of the Valley, expansion had ended, development should begin.

11. Inventions

Some had industrial ambitions for the Valley, hopes of improving the navigation of the river, where barges regularly floated down but could not be poled back up; hopes of large-scale smelting of the iron ore found in the mountains. Fernando Fairfax, great-nephew of the baron, published "for the attention of monied men of discernment," a neat prospectus of the 20,000-acre iron estate which he wished to incorporate. He told how flour barges were already on the river, a furnace had been installed, the mountain trees would furnish tanbark, and the ore was to be mined not more than twelve miles above Harpers Ferry, where the United States armory turned out a thousand rifles a month.

It sounded like a glowing prospect, and in the main a prospect it remained. The Valley ore was indeed mined and smelted for a hundred years but, although moderately profitable, it made no millionaires, created no industrial overdevelopment. The first furnace was near Harpers Ferry; then came the Bloomery, near Berryville. At the time of the Revolution, the Zanes were molding cannon balls and salt pans. Near Luray, in Powell's Fort, near Browns Gap, over on the Allegheny side, the furnaces and the forges started up, but none of them fulfilled the expectations of the overambitious.

The ore was not rich enough, the river was not deep enough, the gifts of the Valley were not to be seized by such methods. Its way was to give slowly, growing as trees grow—never great wealth, but competence, peace of heart, and time: time for a man to develop what lay within him. If a man had long dreams, he could dream them there, where nothing moved much faster than the thin spears of the grass thrusting through the limestone outcrops. It was through the dreamers that the Valley made its contribution to the century of industrialization.

To Shepherdstown, shortly after the Revolution, came a man possessed by a dream of a boat which should move against the current without oars or sail. The neighbors called him "Crazy Rumsey." James Rumsey persisted. He did not do well at anything else. Son of a Maryland farmer, ex-soldier of the Revolution, he first tried milling as a partner of George Bedinger, a year later he set himself up as a merchant at Bath, another year and he was running a boardinghouse. But whatever he did to earn his bread, the experiments on the boat went on. In 1784 he showed a model to George Washington, and obtained a certificate.

I have seen the model of Mr. Rumsey's Boats, constructed to work against stream; have examined the power upon which it acts; —have been an eye witness to an actual experiment in running water of some rapidity; & do give it as my opinion (altho I had little faith before) that he has discovered the Art of propelling Boats by mechanism & small manual assistance against rapid currents;—that the discovery is of vast importance—may be of the greatest usefulness in our inland navigation—& if it succeeds, of which I have no doubt, that the value of it is greatly enhanced by the simplicity of the works, which when seen and explained to, might be executed by the most common mechanics.

Given under my hand at the town of Bath, County of Berkeley in the state of Virginia, this 7th day of September, 1784.

Armed with such a testimonial, Rumsey obtained from the Virginia legislature an exclusive right to construct and navigate boats on Virginia waters for the next ten years; and with the help of General Washington and General Gates he became superintendant of the Potomac Company, an organization to improve the upper Potomac. This post gave him a great deal of trouble and two hundred pounds a year, but after fourteen months he left it. He must have all his time for his boat, in which he now planned to use steam. He began the actual work on it in the summer of 1785, but ice in the river stopped his trials. He went on again the following spring, and it moved. It moved, but the boiler burst. He tried again with a new boiler, but the steam melted the solder on the machinery. He tried again with hard solder, but by now it was December and drifting ice carried the boat away and damaged it severely.

Not until 1787 was he ready, ready and this time so confident that he invited the public to witness the demonstration. A large crowd gathered one raw December day on the bluffs above the Potomac near Shepherdstown—General Gates, Major Bedinger, Colonel Darke, Captain Shepherd, and many more. Ladies were invited aboard, and several had the hardihood to accept the invitation. Mrs. Bedinger sat on the afterdeck, intrepidly knitting. A friend took the helm, another assisted with the engine, the fire burned brightly under the boiler, and James Rumsey set the machinery into noisy motion. After a breathless moment the boat began to chug upstream. General Gates tore off his hat and shouted, "My God! She moves!"

Move she did, upstream and down, for two hours at an average rate of three miles an hour. They called it the "flying boat." A week later, although in the meantime the pipes had frozen, burst, and been stuffed with rags, Rumsey got her up to four miles an hour. Then he set off in triumph for Philadelphia to seek fame and fortune.

No less a personage than Benjamin Franklin, a tinkerer himself, consented to become the president of the "Rumseian society" of backers. In the spring of 1788, with letters to Dr. Benjamin Rush, James Watts, and others, Rumsey went on to London. In England, however, the delays and disappointments began all over again. James Watt declined to help unless Rumsey would sever connections with all former backers, which he was too loyal to do. The patron he found went bankrupt while the boat was being built, and Rumsey borrowed to pay for it and borrowed again to pay his creditors. When the first trial of the *Columbian Maid* was a failure, Rumsey spent some time in hiding to avoid the debtors' prison. Soon he found work superintending the construction of a canal in Ireland, and returned to London in December of 1792 convinced that his great moment had arrived, only to have the *Columbian Maid* attached by creditors just before the public trial on the Thames. A week later he was lecturing to the Society of Mechanic Arts in London, in the hope of raising funds, when he murmured something about a violent pain and fell unconscious from a cerebral hemorrhage of which he died the following morning. The House of Commons ordered him buried in St. Margaret's, Westminster.

A few weeks later the *Columbian Maid* moved successfully up the Thames without her inventor, but there the matter ended except for a gold medal awarded to Rumsey's son and namesake in 1839 and a monument which now stands near Shepherdstown. Rumsey is credited with the discovery of jet propulsion, now applied to airplanes, but his name is little remembered outside his own locality. It is a curious circumstance that he wrote from London of meeting a young New Yorker, Robert Fulton, who had come over to sell a torpedo boat to the British government, and who until that time had not been interested in steam.

Thirty years later, at the other end of the Shenandoah Valley, another and luckier inventor lived. It was still possible in the Rockbridge County of that day for children to be chased by wolves on their way to the one-room school—but the fleet of six-horse wagons which plied the Valley Pike, and the pony riders who would carry a letter for as little as twenty-five cents, maintained a steady contact with the outside world. The upper Valley was a country of small farmers and of rocky farms, beautifully framed by close and lovely mountains full of bears, full of trout streams where boys could fish with loops of white horsehair. A few of the farmers owned slaves, but the sons of the family worked with them in the fields as soon as they grew strong enough. From such stock, active, shrewd, independent, Cyrus McCormick came. He was nineteen when he began tinkering with a mechanical reaper which his father had unsuccessfully tried to make. There were many things to distract him, the farm, the mountains, the presidential campaign of 1832 when Andrew Jackson's supporters carted around a hickory tree mounted on a wagon and decorated with silver dollars which jingled in the wind. It was three years before young McCormick had a crude contraption on which he could take out a patent.

No one except Cyrus took it seriously. Life flowed on at Walnut Hill, and the family worked the land which their ancestor had bought when he arrived from Londonderry. Cyrus kept on tinkering, assisted by a Negro slave, Joe Anderson, in the log and stone workshop near the brook. Five more years passed before he felt ready to make a public demonstration in a neighbor's oatfield. "The subscriber," said the printed handbill with which he advertised the event, "in consequence of other engagements, and the failure of the crop of grain, has done nothing with the machine for several years, until recently, since when he has made some improvements on it."

Young McCormick had the luck to arrive at exactly the right historical moment. The great West, the lush bottoms of the Ohio, the Missouri, and the Mississippi were opened at last. The nation was growing apace, and it was hungry. Already there had been bread riots in New York for lack of flour. Now only the lack of labor prevented the satisfaction of that need. The sky was the limit, the vast pale dome-

CYRUS MC CORMICK, HIS REAPER AND HIS WORKSHOP

like prairie sky, above the flat horizon of the grasslands, end-less as the sea.

The reaper took hold at once. For several years Cyrus McCormick made the machines at home, and sold as many as he could turn out. Then he realized that most of the de-mands came from the West, and that since transportation was difficult he should establish himself more centrally. In 1848 he moved to Chicago, and there built up one of the historic American fortunes. A native of a slave state, as-sisted by a slave, he had liberated the coming generations of farm labor by his invention.

The history of the Shenandoah Valley's contribution to the industrial revolution would not be complete without a

mention of James Gibbs, a Connecticut Yankee living in
Rockbridge County, who with his partner Wilcox became
famous for his improved sewing machine, and named his
house Raphine Hall, and the near-by village Raphine, after
his needles. He was in business in the North when the War
Between the States broke out, and he came back to throw
in his lot with his adopted people of Virginia. After the war
he would have shared their ruin had not his sewing machines
gone on earning money for him so that he found $10,000 to
his account in Philadelphia when it ended.

But it would still be early to speak of ruin in the Valley,
in the comfortable 1850's, when the sound small houses had
just settled maturely into their groves. The frontier was a
hundred years behind them, and no one remembered it. The
houses all had names—Belle Grove, Rion Hall, Carter Hall,
Claymont, Media, Saratoga, Graystone, Flowing Spring—
and in most instances the names were more pretentious than
the houses. They had no window screens or bathrooms, but
each had a distinct identity, and since roads were bad and
public amusements scanty, house parties and visiting made
the people happy in their homes. The big bedrooms seemed
to have unlimited capacity, and it was not uncommon for
families of five and six to visit other families, not for a day
or a week, but for a month or a summer. This was not an
unmixed blessing.

Ned brought Adeline up here in a carriage the day after you
left [wrote one wife to an absent husband] and she has been here
ever since. I did not know she was coming until she was on her
way, and I am very much afraid she will not get away until after
her confinement. I feel so rebellious at the thought of having to
nurse her through the experience, that I am afraid I commit a sin
about it. John and Phoebe also arrived this morning, you may be
surprised to hear. I do not know how long they intend to stay.

There would be a crowd every night for music and
singing, or for dancing on the polished floors. In the summer
the moonlight poured through the wide windows and in the
winter wood fires burned brightly on the hearth. Young

ladies learned to ride in spite of corsets. They did not learn to walk, and those who had Negroes did not learn to cook. If they could play "The Maiden's Prayer" on the piano, do needlework or paint china, they were accomplished. In the less prosperous families, which were the majority, they still needed the old-fashioned arts of spinning and weaving, and rich and poor alike must learn to sew. The young gentlemen rode hard and well, shot straight, were touchy on points of honor. They went to study at "the University" (of Virginia), at Washington College, V.M.I., Princeton, or West Point, and came home to run their places, or to read law in the offices of their father's friends, and gallantly to court the girls. "Aren't boys fun?" wrote one young lady, "and don't they like to flirt?"

The romances of Walter Scott found their perfect audience in the Valley, and chivalry became not only a fashion but a way of life. Some communities held yearly tournaments on horseback, where the mounted knights jousted for rings which they caught on their lances and presented to the Queen of Love and Beauty with her court of Maids in Waiting. Turner Ashby of Loudoun County often came to compete in these contests and was the paladin above all others, so successful that at last they made him ride without his saddle and still he won.

In 1834 a Baltimore and Ohio Railroad train steamed into Harpers Ferry with a hundred passengers. It had left Baltimore at eight o'clock that morning and spent six hours in covering eighty-two miles. A year later a branch line was opened between Harpers Ferry and Winchester, thirty-two miles of track. They celebrated the opening with a band, salvos of artillery, speeches, and a banquet. When the engineers surveying for the main line of the B. & O. got as far as Martinsburg, the Lafayette Guards gave a ball for them, and when the first engine came through some of the local boys were so exhilarated that they took a wagon which was standing behind a patient jackass in the courthouse square, dismounted it and mounted it again in the church steeple with the jackass braying in the belfry.

In 1854 the Virginia Central Railroad, now the Chesapeake and Ohio, came across the Blue Ridge as far as Staunton. While it was building there occurred an episode which Augusta County referred to as the "Irish Rebellion." The laborers on the railroad were all "Corkonians" when there arrived a party of North of Ireland people whom the others called "Fardowners," and who occupied a big frame house while they built the section near Fishersville. The boys from Cork warned them off; when they did not go, they attacked them. Loud and fierce was the struggle, the peaceful citizens of Augusta heard that many had been killed and that human heads were rolling like pumpkins. The local militia was called upon for assistance, the drum was beaten, and most of the young men fell into line. When they arrived about dark at the scene of the disturbance, they found the frame house burned and the enemy vanished. Later that night they caught and arrested some of them at Waynesboro. No one had been killed, and the Irish took such pleasure in the subsequent trials, and proved so witty while they were going on, that the whole episode ended in laughter.

Indeed, all classes had a good life in the Valley, plenty of hard work but well salted with amusement. No one starved and no one lived in idleness. It was gay and gracious, and the culture if not profound was charming—yet there was a shadow on the land. No one would recognize its presence, still less admit it as a threat. Nevertheless, a reckoning would be required, and not yet has the bill been paid in full. Not yet.

There were comparatively few slaves along the Shenandoah. Only twenty-four per cent even in wealthy Jefferson owned slaves, and ten to a family was considered a large number. In the upper Valley the proportion of black to white was not more than one in five and the Germans had never considered it economical to own Negroes. As early as 1832 Augusta County elected a pro-emancipation member to the legislature. Many slaves were allowed to buy their freedom, many were freed in wills. In 1860 a freed slave, Mary Phelps, filed a petition at Winchester to have herself and her two children reduced to slavery in the household of a Mrs. Avis, so that she would not have to move away, for free Negroes were not allowed to remain in Virginia more than a year.

"Nice people" shrank from the realities of the system and, rather than use the harsh words "slave" and "nigger," commuted them politely to "servant" and "colored man." The servants did not live in the "big house," but had their own cabins at a safe and sanitary distance. The flies went freely back and forth, but typhoid, dysentery, and even Asiatic cholera were scourges of God, meekly to be endured. The servants carried wood and water, made beds and cleaned, served abundant meals of excellent but limited menus from the food raised on the places. They were supposed to enjoy the fuss and stir of company, and they did. They wore black suits and boiled shirts for Sunday, and sat in the galleries of the churches where their masters went. They harvested to the rhythm of their singing, and the master presided at the harvest feast. The children of the family loved them, and were loved, and from their gentle teaching came that emphasis on "pretty manners" which Northerners held suspect then and after. They never knew want, never knew hunger, were taught in childhood, nursed in illness, and retired in old age.

All this is true, but it is only half the story. They were well treated, yet they ran away. They were secure, yet in their anguished and aspiring songs the longing for freedom took the fear away from death. "I'll go up to my Lord, and be *free!*" That is the shout which follows the harmonic moaning.

Gentlemen did not whip their servants, but they expected the overseers to maintain discipline and preferred not to know too much about it. An owner known to be harsh to his "people" was ostracized by his own class, but the early historians give some ghastly pictures of "tickling up old scabs," by successive beatings on successive days, or beatings by two on three men in turn, with a jug of whisky among them to keep it going.

The courts dealt with offenders whose crimes were worse

than laziness. A Negro belonging to General Gates was hanged for stealing some clothing from his cellar; the Negress Nell received thirty lashes for petty larceny, and was branded on the hand. At Belle Grove, where James and Dolly Madison spent their honeymoon, a Negress fell upon her mistress in the cellar and beat her to death with a shovel. Negro John killed a man, and was condemned after due trial. He went to the gallows singing "When I can read my title clear to mansions in the skies" and was buried under the scaffold, but disinterred and dissected by the doctors. The master of another slave, hanged for murder, was reimbursed by the state to the amount of $333.33.

Most notorious was the murder of a Dr. Berkeley, husband of one of the Carters, on his estate near Winchester, in 1818. Three of his slaves, Landon, Randle, and Sarah, were brought to trial, and they told the manner of it. Randle had run off, but came back again to Sarah's cabin, and the two of them sent Landon up to tell the master he was there. Dr. Berkeley came down at dusk with a pistol on him, but Randle was a powerful man, armed with a club. The doctor fell and they thought him dead. When they heard him groaning, Randle beat him again until the groaning ceased. It was night, and the other slaves came and went in the darkness, Ralph and Barnaba, Fanny, Tom, Robbin, whispering, staring. What should they do? Should they take the body out on a horse and drop it by the roadside? Should they sink it in the pond?

"The devil is dead," said Sarah. "We will burn him up."

They cooked him all that night on the wide open hearth, taking turns bringing in wood. At daylight they buried the bones behind the cabin. Sarah made Fanny bring from the sideboard the black bag in which the doctor kept his money. Then they all went about their work, cooking for the family, plowing, washing—and no one told. No one said a word.

But the white folks had ways of finding out, of knowing without a need for telling. The bones in the ground and the blood on the floor bore witness. They tied Landon up alone, and he lost his nerve and confessed.

The court appointed one of the best attorneys in the community to defend the Negroes, and he saved all from hanging except Sarah, Randle, and Landon, who had made the plot. Ralph and Barnaba were transported to the Dry Tortugas. The others were sold south. It was testified at the trial that Dr. Berkeley had been an indulgent master, but it was not the slaves who said so.

The story is dark, but it is orderly. No insensate mob tried to revenge itself upon the Negroes. There was never a lynching in the Shenandoah until after the Civil War. The Negro got justice in the ante bellum courts. In 1860 a free Negress killed a white woman in Winchester, was defended by no less a person than Colonel Richard Byrd, and was condemned, but secured a stay of execution on the ground that she was pregnant. An effort was made to have a committee of eight women determine her condition, but none would serve, and she remained in the Winchester jail until the Federal soldiers came through and released her.

All this means little. The injustice of the system lay deeper than the courts could reach, deeper than pride, too deep to be watered by the dews of mercy. Occasionally in the old records appears an item that seems a distillation of the bitterness, as in this advertisement for a runaway slave from a Winchester paper of 1858. It was not written to be poignant, and in that lies its tragedy. It was evidently written by a kindly man, somewhat confused in his thinking, and wholly positive in his conclusions, as confused people often are.

He had red hair and blue eyes, and he might come in of himself, for he wanted to be sold to me. He had three shirts, two working shirts and one for Sunday. He shall have a reward if he comes of himself.

He is as white as any man on earth, but a slave for life.

There they stand before us—the master, humane, well meaning, but himself imprisoned in an institution he did not inaugurate and dared not analyze; the slave, encased in utter hopelessness which only violence could shatter. And the gulf between them is full of blood and fire.

PART II

Holocaust

12. The Fateful Lightning

I N THE SUMMER of 1860, a professor from the Virginia Military Institute in Lexington, a Major Thomas Jonathan Jackson, went north to take his usual cure for the "nervousness and cold feet" which afflicted him; and came home full of foreboding. He wrote his sister Laura:

> It is painful to discover with what unconcern they talk of war and threaten it. I have seen enough of it to make me look upon it as the sum of all evils. . . . I think we have great reason for alarm, but my trust is in God, and I cannot think that He will permit the madness of men to interfere so materially with the Christian labors of the country.

Already the major, a veteran of Mexico, had played a small part in the prologue to the tragedy, when with Colonel Preston he had brought the corps of V.M.I. cadets to guard the execution of John Brown at Charles Town on December 2, 1859.

In June of 1858 a young man from Connecticut came to the town of Harpers Ferry, boarded with a widow, and married his landlady's daughter. He was, he said, a book agent, and his name was John Edwin Cook.

Harpers Ferry began then, as it does now, near the top of a Blue Ridge mountain and tumbled down steep streets to the roaring junction of the Shenandoah and the Potomac. The riven hills are shaggy still with trees and broken by jutting cliffs, upon which in that unenlightened day no enterprising hand had as yet painted the merits of Mennen's Baby Powder. In spite of such modern improvements, it is still possible to understand the Jeffersonian enthusiasm for the scene—the meeting place of three states, Maryland, Virginia, and West Virginia, then only two.

In 1858 Harpers Ferry was the important link connecting the Valley and the West by rail and water to the world of cities and of commerce. Along the Potomac and across a railroad bridge ran the Baltimore and Ohio Railroad, then as now; and the long low buildings of the United States Armory and Arsenal covered the flat beside the river. It was to vanish in exploding flames within a few short years and never to be replaced.

The young and slender Mr. Cook, with dreamy blue eyes behind his spectacles, spent a year in desultory bookselling around the countryside. Although he made long reports to his connections "at the North," he appeared to have private means and not to depend entirely on his commercial efforts. By the following summer there was little that he did not know about Jefferson County. He had traveled every "lane" to every "big house," retired from the road as a gentleman's house should be; he knew their owners and what slaves they kept. At Beall Air, home of Colonel Lewis Washington, he took a particular interest in the colonel's family heirlooms, a sword presented to his illustrious uncle by Frederick the Great and inscribed "From the oldest general in the world to the greatest," and a brace of pistols given by Lafayette. On the whole, this Connecticut Yankee passed a happy year along the Shenandoah, meeting the best people—if not entirely in a social way—and getting himself married, although the latter activity was not according to plan. He had charmed his bride by his nice quiet ways and idealistic talk, and if sometimes she felt that he did not tell her everything she forbore to question her Lohengrin.

In the summer of 1859 some other strangers came to the Valley, an elderly bearded man with piercing eyes who said that his name was Isaac Smith and that the three young men with him were his sons. They claimed to be prospecting for minerals in the mountains. They rented a remote farm five miles north of Harpers Ferry in the state of Maryland, and did not encourage visitors although they maintained a bowing acquaintance with Mr. Cook. By freight and by wagon they brought in a large number of cases filled with "mining instruments." Polite young Henry Douglas met the old stranger with such a load one day and lent his father's team to help him up a hill. The old man's dignified simplicity was impressive, but it later gave the youthful Samaritan small comfort to think that he had helped John Brown to haul his pikes and guns.

The three months at the secluded Kennedy farm must have been a strange time for the twenty-one men hidden there in the attic—a time of waiting and of preparation, of long days drowsing into autumn, illumined by an inner light fiercer than the summer sun. Their leader was a burning man, a man who saw apocalyptic portents in the clouds, who heard God's voice small and still in the night watches—a man as quiet and as dangerous as a sharpened ax. John Brown had been a farmer, a tanner, a preacher, who never succeeded in a worldly life but had been "called," as he reported it, into the work of Abolition. Months passed, years passed, God's vengeance tarried, and the messages which beat upon his fierce heart became ever more sanguinary. His inner ear heard the slaves groaning in the peace of the night, and in his mind's eye he became an instrument of the Almighty to avenge and to strike down.

He had a price on his head. In Kansas, on a night when the pro- and antislavery forces were rioting bloodily, he and his followers called a farmer named Doyle out of bed and murdered him with two of his sons. On that same night Brown killed two other men, Wilkinson and Sherman. Doyle had had no slaves, but he would not admit the Negro to be his equal. The others were connected with the proslavery party. Kansas must be free soil. Brown then camped like a soldier at Osawatomie, raided in Missouri, freed slaves, killed a man named Cruise. When the proslavery forces attacked his camp they killed his son Frederick, but Brown himself escaped to grow a beard and change to Isaac Smith, to seek new and steeper steps to celestial glory.

Now in the foothills of the Blue Ridge he slowly collected and concealed more than two hundred rifles and a thousand pikes. His men came in singly, by night, and were never seen about the farm in daylight. Nineteen of his followers were under thirty, five were northern Negroes, two were his sons, Watson and Oliver. His daughter Annie and his daughter-in-law did the housework so that no servants would be required.

As one reads the bald statements in the histories, there is something hard to understand. Fantastic and foredoomed as this attempt must be, it was no casual hurried plot, but a long-formulated and carefully worked-out plan. Eighteen months earlier, at Chatham, Canada, Brown and his friends had met in a convention and drawn up a new Constitution of the United States with himself as commander in chief, Kagi as secretary of war, with a Cabinet, a Congress, but no Senate. They admired their constitution enough to have it printed, copies were left at the Kennedy farm and are preserved. In the pockets of dead raiders were found officers' commissions, signed by the commander in chief and his secretary.

None of this is too strange. It follows a pattern set by a

long line of fanatics, breakers and remolders of the world. All over the North, people were ready to finance the plan. John Brown obviously did not suffer from a lack of money. Encouraging letters were found at his house from such prominent abolitionists as Gerrit Smith, Frederick Douglas, Dr. Howe. A bitterness had grown up in the North that would stop at nothing. An equal bitterness was growing in the deep moss-haunted South. Virginia lay between them.

But still there is something missing from the record. To no one had John Brown disclosed the full measure of his expectations. Even the young men with him did not know what they were to do until the night before they struck. Here are the facts. On the night of Sunday, October 16th, John Brown, after preaching at a Dunkard church, went with his well-armed followers to Harpers Ferry. They left three to guard their farmhouse, to which they evidently intended to return. Without firing a shot, they took prisoner the watchman at the armory, the watchman at the railroad bridge, the watchman at Hall's Rifle Works, half a mile up the river, and established themselves in those buildings. Then John Cook and others went to the home of Colonel Lewis Washington and took him out of bed for a hostage, with his sword, his pistols, and some slaves. In the same way another band took John Allstadt and others, and brought them in a wagon to their leader.

"I am Osawatomie Brown of Kansas," he told the hostages, and buckled on Washington's sword. He gave pikes to the slaves and told them to stand guard over their masters. John Cook went out again to deposit a large number of weapons in a schoolhouse between the Ferry and the farm. All the first steps had now been taken smoothly.

Within the limits of the burning belief which warped his whole life to its pattern, John Brown was a logical man. What could he have expected on this dark night for which he had prepared during two years? What could he have hoped when with twenty-two men he seized government property? Was it to be a general slave rising which would enthrone them while an aroused North rushed to their assistance?

HARPER'S FERRY

The answer is lost. Lost in the windowless darkness of the Negro cabins. Brown expected reinforcements, for he thought that the first band of attackers, appearing in Monday's dawn on the Maryland end of the bridge, was the advance guard of his rescue party. In all his wild apocalyptic dreaming, he had never dreamed the Negro unready to strike a blow for his own freedom. That may have been the dark link which gave way and left him holding only the fragments of his chain.

How much preparation had he made among the slaves themselves? No one knows, no one will ever know. Was the schoolhouse an appointed rendezvous? No one knows. At one plantation the hands brought two pikes to their masters, long sticks with a foot of sharpened steel on the end. They told no clear story as to how they had come by them, but merely turned them in as good children might bring in a suspicious find. The pikes were hung in the hallway of a Valley house with the swords and pistols of the family ancestors. Near Berryville a Mr. McCormick had been visited by an old clockmaker and had invited him to supper after the country custom. After the man left, one of the house servants advised the master to go down to the quarters, where he found the stranger talking to the Negroes. He recognized John Brown in the courthouse later, but what had been said he never knew. When it was over, the slaves were questioned, but not too strictly, for the white men who knew them best knew that they would not tell.

With the darkness of the jungle behind them, moving in the darkness of fear, the Negroes laughed and sang and kept their secrets. If white men talked to them, they listened to the answer in the white man's mind and gave it back to him. Perhaps that was the trait which misled John Brown. Perhaps he was so sure of understanding that he took everything for granted. No one knows. The Valley people knew that they could not find out, and let it rest.

Not one Negro rose. Not one voice or hand was raised against a master. There was a silence in the quarters, deep and impenetrable as night. The Washington slaves, the Allstadt slaves, took the pikes which John Brown gave them and stood around their owners awkwardly. They stood with the pikes in their hands, and their masters looked at them calmly, saying nothing. When Brown turned his attention elsewhere, they put down the pikes and huddled together talking in low mournful voices. Later, when the fight grew hotter, Brown ordered one of them to take a gun and stand guard on the armory wall, but the slave demurred: "O Lawdy, no! I might shoot Massa." One of them tried to get out and was drowned in swimming the river. One of them died three days later, "of fright and cold."

The raiders killed one man on Sunday night; ironically enough, he was a free Negro. The station porter, Shepherd Hayward, was nominally attached to Mayor Fontaine Beckham so that he might live on in Virginia, but was actually independent with his own money in the bank. He saw the raiders stop the Wheeling Express on the bridge at midnight, and walked out to see what had happened. He did not halt when they called to him and so they dropped him with a bullet in his belly and he lay twelve hours before death came.

After a short delay the raiders let the express go on, and when the news reached Washington a detachment of marines was promptly ordered to Harpers Ferry. It was Monday night before they got there. During Monday the raiders took more hostages, and failed to capture the relief watchman, Patrick Higgins, who was a good man with his fists. By nine-thirty in the morning the townspeople and the local militia had taken up the battle. The Jefferson Guards mustered in Charles Town marched to the scene, crossed the Potomac and seized the bridge, cutting off Brown's retreat. The Hamtramck Guards from Shepherdstown and the Jefferson Volunteers surrounded the armory but made no frontal attacks. They did dislodge the small group which occupied the rifle works, drove them into the river, and shot them down.

Before the militia arrived, John Brown amazingly negotiated through two paroled prisoners to have breakfast sent over from the hotel. The prisoners kept their parole and returned to him, and the hotel complied with his request although it resented his refusal to pay. Several of the hostages were paroled to go home and eat. They went and returned. As the day wore on, however, the hopelessness of the raiders' position became more and more obvious. All morning, while Kagi urged him to withdraw, Brown remained blindly, inscrutably fixed on his course like a comet timed to burst against the sun. When at last he sent two prisoners and two of his own men to ask for a truce it was too late. The bodies of four townsmen lay across the path to peace—Shepherd Hayward, George Boerly, Turner, and old Mayor Beckham shot as he went forward unarmed and alone to stop this bloodshed in his peaceful town, to "see what could be done." Blood calls for blood. There will be no truce now, John Brown.

The emissaries of the raiders were shot in spite of their white flag. One crawled back to the armory, the other was carried to the town hotel. When the respected and beloved old mayor died, two townsmen dragged this captive to the railroad trestle, shot him and threw him off. His white face stared up out of the shallow water all next day. The youngest raider, eighteen-year-old Leeman, lost his nerve, tried to get out of the armory by wading the river, and was shot as he begged for mercy. By late afternoon Brown selected the nine most prominent of his hostages and withdrew into the little red-brick engine house on the armory grounds. Kagi was dead, Dangerfield Newby, the freed slave, was dead, Taylor the young Canadian was dead, Oliver and Watson Brown were both mortally wounded, only five of the party were uninjured. The prisoners kept quiet and as much out of sniping range as possible. The herded slaves moaned faintly. John Cook, no last-ditcher, had seen the position from a hilltop after his trip to the schoolhouse, and had escaped to Pennsylvania.

Night fell. There was no light inside the engine house. At eleven o'clock Brown again sent one of his prisoners to ask that he be allowed to withdraw across the bridge into Maryland. No truce. No terms. Oliver Brown cried in the darkness, "Kill me and put me out of this suffering."

"If you must die," said John Brown, "die like a man."

After a while in the eyeless dark the voice grew fainter, ceased.

"I guess he's dead." said Brown.

It was a long black, seemingly endless night. Between eleven and twelve the marines arrived under command of Colonel Robert E. Lee and replaced the militia around the armory. The little town lapsed thankfully into order. Dawn came, a streak of light no wider than a bayonet, and Colonel Lee prepared to take the necessary steps. Thoroughly professional, courteous always, he offered the honor of attack to the colonel of militia.

"You go ahead," said the militiaman. "My men have their wives and children."

Lee made no comment. He ordered Lieutenant J. E. B. Stuart to take twelve men to the door of the engine house and demand surrender, with a promise of protection from the mob. Brown offered the counterproposition that the raiders be allowed the length of the bridge as a start for escape. Then Stuart ordered the marines to break down the door. With a ladder for a battering ram they soon made a jagged hole and Lieutenant Israel Green jumped through it, followed by the rest. Out of the dim interior came the voice of Colonel Lewis Washington.

"That one is John Brown."

Green struck the old man down with his saber. A second thrust might have killed him had not the weapon been deflected by the buckle of George Washington's sword. All the fighting was over in three minutes. One marine had been killed, one wounded. Two more raiders were dead. The rest were taken outside, still unconscious, and their wounds dressed. The hostages came out, dazed, hungry, recovering from their fright and breathing deep drafts of the sparkling October morning. On the threshold Colonel Washington paused long enough to draw on a pair of green kid gloves. Lightly and straight he crossed the courtyard and walked into the welcome of his friends.

"Won't you come to the Wager House and take a little something, colonel?"

The colonel bowed politely. "Thank you, I believe I will. It seems months since I have had one."

John Brown and the survivors were taken to the Charles Town jail to await trial. Of his twenty-two men, ten had been killed and five had escaped. Only seven remained, five whites and two Negroes. It took the countryside a few days to subside. Strangers were likely to be arrested first and questioned afterward. A delegate to the Presbyterian synod was netted in this way and then released. But there were no more acts of violence.

After the violence, the curling streams of blood in the river, the sacklike bodies used as targets, came the slow and dusty process of the trial, the re-establishment of a civil order badly shattered by the event. During that sanguinary day at Harpers Ferry, the entire fabric of Valley life had been torn asunder and through the gaping rents showed an unimaginable terror. If there was fear in the quarters, thick, inarticulate, unexpressed, there was no less fear in the plantation houses—fear mastered, ridden lightly, unacknowledged but implicit in the thin steel underneath the usual paternal kindness. John Brown had brought that fear into the daylight, let it gibber in the quiet streets, touch every forehead with its clammy fingers. The Valley people, whether they owned slaves or not, thought of the pikes with the sharp steel points, thought of the isolated houses, thought of their wives and daughters, and they hated him. They feared and hated him.

John Brown may have hoped by his seizure of Federal property to precipitate a national issue, to involve the central government, to start a war. His northern backers were loud in their disavowals of such a plan. Few protested when he was tried in a Virginia court.

They held a fair trial in Charles Town, as even he admitted in his last speech. He had not expected a fair trial. It is plain that he knew nothing of Southerners, black or white, understood only his vision, his conviction. He was a man with no gray in his character. Only the black of murder and the great white light of faith.

Eighty armed men protected the prisoners as they moved from jail to courthouse. The wide, dusty, shaded streets were crowded to capacity, but quiet. Everything moved with the strictest attention to formality, to precedent and procedure —and that correctness outlawed and underlined the crime.

At first defiant, John Brown asked to be spared "the mockery of a trial" as his health was insufficient. The court had him examined by a doctor who pronounced him able to appear. When the court appointed two attorneys he asked for another, Thomas C. Green, member of the legislature and mayor of the town. The court appointed him. A couch was brought for Brown to lie on in the courtroom. Nonslaveholders were selected for the jury. When on the second day Brown indignantly rejected a plea of insanity and protested a lack of confidence in his attorneys, they withdrew and were replaced by a young Bostonian, George Hoyt, who obtained a day's adjournment for study of the case and was then joined by two more northern lawyers. Nothing but courtesy and consideration was shown the prisoners during the five days of the trial. They were going to hang John Brown and they were going to do it right.

The raiders were indicted for treason against the commonwealth of Virginia, for conspiring with slaves and others to rebel, for the first-degree murder of five citizens, for the murder of three of them separately. The facts spoke for themselves and the verdict could not be in doubt. When he had been convicted the court asked John Brown if he desired to speak.

I have, may it please the Court, a few words to say. In the first place I deny everything but what I have all along admitted,— the design on my part to free slaves. I intended certainly to have made a clean thing of that matter as I did last winter when I went into Missouri and there took slaves without the snapping of a gun on either side. . . .

Had I interfered . . . in behalf of the rich, the intelligent, the so-called great . . . and suffered and sacrificed what I have done, it would have been all right. . . .

I see a book kissed here which I suppose to be the Bible . . . That teaches me that all things whatsoever I would men should do to me I should do even so to them. It teaches me further "to remember them that are in bonds as bound with them". I endeavoured to act up to these instructions . . .

Let me say one word further. I feel entirely satisfied with the treatment I have received on my trial. Considering all the circumstances it has been more generous than I expected, but I feel no consciousness of guilt . . .

I hear it has been stated by some of those connected with me that I have induced them to join me. But the contrary is true. I do not say this to injure them, but as regretting their weakness. There is not one of them but joined me of his own accord, and the greater part at their own expense. . . .

Now I have done.

It was a fine speech, but it ignored some facts. It ignored two hundred guns and more than a thousand pikes. It ignored Shepherd Hayward and Fontaine Beckham, who died with no weapons in their hands. It ignored the proposed and printed constitution. The court sentenced Brown to hang on December 2nd.

The trials of the six others were briefer, but reached the same conclusion. Daniel Voorhees came from Indiana to plead for John Cook, who had been captured in Pennsylvania, and described the misguided youth so feelingly that rumor says even the judge was moved to tears. The judge wept, and sentenced him to hang.

The barns of several jurors burned mysteriously. From the governor of Virginia to the clerk of the court, public officials were anonymously threatened by writers who would see the South in

FLAMES ! ! !

All of us at the North sympathize with

THE MARTYRS OF HARPERS FERRY ! ! ! !

But not all of the letters received were in favor of the raiders. One came from a woman named Doyle who had lived in Kansas.

John Brown,—Sir;
     Although vengeance is not mine, I confess that I do feel gratified to hear that you were stopped in your fiendish career at Harpers Ferry with the loss of your two sons. You can now appreciate my distress in Kansas when you then and there entered my house at midnight and arrested my husband and two boys and took them out of the yard and in cold blood shot them dead in my hearing. You can't say you done it to free our slaves; we had none and never expected to own one, but has only made me a poor disconsolate widow with helpless children. . . .
                              Mahala Doyle.

John Brown passed his last month quietly, writing letters full of allusions to the sword of the Lord and of Gideon, which fell like sparks on the tinder of the North. He had a lively appreciation of his value as a martyr, and refused all offers of rescue. "I am worth infinitely more now to die than to live," he said. "I can regain all of the ground lost by merely hanging a few minutes by the neck."

On December 1st he was visited by his wife, the mother of the four sons who had all been killed in following him. It is not known what they said to each other, but it is known that they wept together, and that to her John Brown gave his last written message, which rang like a trumpet call from Maine to Kansas.

I, John Brown, am now quite *certain* that the crimes of *this guilty land:* will never be purged *away:* but with Blood. I had *as I now think: vainly* flattered myself that without *very much* bloodshed; it might be done.

The morning of December 2nd dawned misty sweet. John Brown in a rusty black frock coat and red carpet slippers, stood for a moment on the threshold of the jail, with his face turned up to the sunshine. He did not kiss a Negro child, as has so often been stated and pictured, for six com-

JOHN BROWN

panies of infantry and horse kept all beholders at a distance, and no Negroes were abroad that day. Seated on his coffin, Brown rode with the sheriff, the jailer, and the undertaker, out to the scaffold on the edge of town. The checkered fields, still green in the lingering southern autumn, rolled sweetly down to the hazy Blue Ridge.

"This is a beautiful country," said Brown to the undertaker. "I never had the pleasure of seeing it before."

He ascended the platform with unflinching firmness, and stood for fifteen minutes with the cap on his head and the rope around his neck, while the troops deployed in silence to their positions. Then the trap fell. His knees and his arms, tied at the elbow, drew up, his hands clenched. The movements grew feebler until at last he hung limp and straight, swaying slightly in the wind. It was thirty-five minutes before the doctor pronounced life extinct.

Colonel Preston and Major Jackson watched with the V. M. I. cadets.

"I hope he was prepared to die, but I doubt it." Jackson said.

Colonel Preston turned solemnly to those around him.

"So perish all enemies of Virginia!

All such enemies of the Union!

All such foes of the human race!"

Now it was over. The Four Horsemen had begun their ride, and though they paused they were to ride again. John Brown's body had swung into eternity, and into a marching song.

13. The Swift Sword

I see before me now a travelling army halting,
Below, a fertile Valley spaced with barns and the orchards of
  summer.
Behind, the terraced sides of a mountain, abrupt, in places rising
  high,
Broken with rocks, with clinging cedars, with tall shapes dingily
  seen.
The numerous camp-fires scattered near and far, some away up on
  the mountain,
The shadowy forms of men and horses, looming, large sized,
  flickering,
And over all the sky—the sky! far, far out of reach, studded,
  breaking out, the eternal stars.

—WALT WHITMAN

THE CAUSES of our War Between the States are not within the scope of this narrative. Here should be recorded only the fact that it was desperately fought on both sides by devoted, honest men who themselves held conflicting opinions. On both sides there were those who thought slavery should be abolished, and on both sides men believed it a defensible institution. There were Federals who supported the constitutional right to secede, and Confederates devoted to the Union. Looking back, it seems that the conflict could have been avoided; yet there were wise and just men living in that day, between the fire-eaters and the fanatics, and they could not prevent it. They could not check the gathering calamity any more than they could have checked a tidal wave once the waters had been profoundly set in motion by the remote invisible winds.

The people of the Shenandoah Valley did not want war,

could not believe that it would come, watched it approach
with dread. Over the Valley as a whole the slaves were
nowhere more than ten per cent of the population, usually
not so much, and they were in the hands of a very few.
Decidedly, the Valley would not fight for slavery, an institution from which it derived little benefit—which was indeed
a positive detriment, for young slaves were tax-free property
and this gave the Tidewater which bred them an enormous
fiscal advantage.

As for the Union, when delegates were elected for the
Virginia Convention in February, 1861, every county in the
Valley sent only Union delegates, by majorities of four to
one. In Jefferson the vote was 2,783 pro-Union, and 897
against, in Rockingham, 2,499 to 593, in Augusta, 3,647 to
218. Union feelings grew stronger up the Valley to the south.

There was some incendiary talk, of course. A Mrs. Angus
McDonald of Winchester kept a diary in which she recorded
the conversations of her husband and his friends, Senator
James Mason and Randolph Tucker. Sooner or later at every
gathering someone felt obliged to defend the "peculiar institution," and Colonel McDonald, who owned only two
slaves and rented five others, cited both Old and New Testa-
ment in its support. Senator Mason went so far as to declare
that it was the restrictions on the trade which had caused the
sufferings on slave vessels, and that when Virginia took her
proper stand with the Confederacy he intended to use his influence (which he expected to be considerable) toward re-
viving the trade in its most unrestricted form. They declared
that the North was jealous of the comfort, leisure, and good
breeding in the South and meant to destroy it, but that secession would bring prosperity. The North would not dare to
move, for England would support the South. The world must
have cotton.

Why cotton? Why that strictly inedible commodity for
which there could be many substitutes? The faith in cotton
proves again that men believe only what they wish to believe.
In her old age, Mrs. McDonald looked down the dwindling
vista of the years and dryly remarked: "The gods must have

meant to destroy us, as the old Pagan said, for they made us mad."

Senators and congressmen of the seceding states were feted in the Valley on their way home from Washington. Enthusiastic hostesses, determined to buy nothing of the North, presided charmingly in gowns of linsey-woolsey. But the Valley went on electing union delegates. When some ladies at Winchester tried to make a Confederate flag, they were asked to desist for fear a mob would attack the building where they worked. When some little girls at Lexington started to wear the blue cockade, they were laughed out of it. "Now, girls, Tad Lincoln will be coming down here to marry you."

On April 4th, the Virginia Convention rejected secession by a vote of 85 to 45. On April 12th, Fort Sumter was fired upon. On April 15th, President Lincoln called for seventy-five thousand volunteers. Virginia could not be exempted from raising her quota, and troops were to be sent across her to hold the deep South in check. On April 17th, her convention adopted the Ordinance of Secession by a majority slightly larger than the one which had rejected it two weeks earlier.

And now the state showed no more hesitation. The people ratified the action of the convention three to one; the Confederate flags, which had been made in secrecy, came out and lined the streets; in every hamlet of the Valley, companies of volunteers began to form.

To understand these apparent inconsistencies, one thing should be remembered. Within the memories of the fathers of these men, there had been no Union. A united country was a new thing, a fine thing, a dream not three-quarters of a century old. But before the Union, there had been Virginia. There had been Virginia, surrounded by colonies which she regarded sometimes with dislike and almost always with suspicion. There had been Virginia when the Union-loving western states were only a hope in the mind of a Virginian, Thomas Jefferson. For nearly two hundred and fifty years there had been Virginia. She could not be coerced, she could not be invaded with impunity. From California, from Ohio, from Missouri, from Kentucky, from West Point itself, Virginia's sons came home to fight.

A few remained Union sympathizers to the end, and most of them left the Valley, turned their backs on home and friends to join the northern army. One of these was David Strother of Martinsburg, who wrote and illustrated for *Harper's Weekly* under the name of "Porte Crayon."

No one at home, except my father, knew that I was actually connected with the army. I had concealed it lest it should bring trouble on those I had left behind. I hid it from some who should have known it because I had not the heart to declare it . . . I was an exile indeed, poor, weary, and dispirited.

To the great majority, the question was no longer at issue. "The President has forced Virginia to secede," they said, and therewith abandoned all further consideration of the causes of the struggle. Logan Osburn, the most staunchly Union of Jefferson County's delegates, published an open letter reviewing his opposition to secession: "I regarded it as mischievous in its tendency and destructive in its consequences . . . But my opinions have been overruled by a large majority of the freemen of my state . . . I am a son of Virginia, and her destiny shall be mine."

At V. M. I. that angular professor of mathematics, Major Jackson, summed it up with his usual terseness: "I am in favor of making a thorough trial for peace, and if we fail in this and the state is invaded, to defend it with a terrific resistance . . . If I know myself, all I am and all I have is at the service of my country." By his country he meant Virginia.

Now all was action. At the Harpers Ferry Armory, the forty-two United States soldiers did not wait to make a Sumter of it, but fired the buildings, and retired across the Potomac into Maryland. In Lexington, with its two educational institutions, its population of young men of fighting age, the demonstrations were what might have been expected. When Lincoln called for volunteers, a Confederate flag was promptly raised on the statue of George Washington which topped the college cupola. President Junkin, a Northerner and a Union man, rushed out in dressing gown and slippers to order it hauled down, and the war might have begun there and then had not Willie Preston, a freshman, appeared on the roof of the colonade.

"He's right, boys. Virginia is still in the Union, and he is still our president. We must wait a few days."

While the students threw rocks at him, Willie scaled the cupola, took down the flag and folded it, tucked it safely into his coat—and called for three rousing cheers for the Confederacy! No trouble about getting those!

Willie Preston was just seventeen—one of the golden boys, eager for living, eager for action, with a heart to throw into a cause, and a life to throw away. Down the centuries in every tongue we hear them singing, the young, the inexhaustible army, the ripe harvest of war. Willie Preston was brave, and he was young, too young, his father thought, to march away with the first corps, the "Liberty Hall Volunteers." He waited and fumed for a long interminable year before he joined them, then within six months he was dead.

> They shall not grow old, as we who are left grow old.
> Age cannot wither them, nor the years condemn.
> At the rising of the sun and in the eventide,
> We shall remember them.

At V.M.I., "the West Point of the South," Major Jackson was ordered to bring the cadet corps to the army in Richmond. He set the hour of their departure at one o'clock, then for a last time held prayers at home with his wife. "For we know that if our earthly house of this tabernacle be dissolved, we have a building of God, an house not made with hands, eternal in the heavens." Shortly before one, the cadets formed on the drill ground. They were ready, and more than ready. They stood rigid in their trig uniforms of scarlet and light blue, and turned their pink young faces toward the chaplain. His brief prayers ended at ten minutes to one. Major Jackson waited with one eye on the clock. He had given his orders for one o'clock, and at one o'clock he would move and not before. The impatient boys had to stand like statues. When the clock struck he called out clearly:

"Forward. March!"

Perhaps now it is time to look more closely at this Major Jackson, for he and the Valley were to achieve their immortality together. He had not been born there, but he had adopted it. He loved it enough to fight for it, and when he spoke of a "terrific resistance," he meant exactly that.

A trans-Allegheny boy, an orphan, from the rough-and-ready foothills between the mountains and the Ohio, he had gone to West Point late and self-educated, and had crawled by hard study from the foot of his class to graduate the seventeenth. He piled coal on his fire to study at night, he sweated with nervousness when he stood up to recite, he bought a book on etiquette and studied it as if it had been tactics, but he stuck it out. "You may be whatever you resolve to be," he said. "I am determined to make a man of myself if I live."

George B. McClellan was the whiteheaded boy of that year, who won all the laurels, but someone noticed the lanky mountaineer, and remarked: "If we had to stay here another year, Old Jack would be head of the class."

Already Old Jack at twenty-two, he graduated into a war, and at first was assigned to garrison duty, where he paced under the great low stars of Mexico, and exclaimed to a slightly older officer, Daniel Hill, "Oh, how I envy you men who have been in a battle! If I could only be in *one* battle!"

His wish was richly to be gratified.

He did well enough at Chapultepec to become a major within eighteen months of graduation ("My health is better than it has been for some time," he wrote his sister.) After the war came three years of garrison duty, and then through his friend Daniel Hill he was offered the post of professor of natural and experimental philosophy at V.M.I. He was to teach optics, mechanics, astronomy, and artillery tactics, and about the first three he knew nothing, but he felt that he could keep a day or two ahead of the class. "I can do whatever I will to do," said Major Jackson, putting his old maxim into a more positive form.

From the age of twenty-six to thirty-six, he lived quietly at Lexington, walked the shaded streets, fenced with the students at Judge Brockenbrough's law school, made a few close friends, and taught his classes with the strictest regard for discipline and the letter of the law. The rigidities of the strongly Presbyterian community were congenial to him, and he was happy there. He joined the Presbyterian Church, and resigned his soul completely to God as his commander, nor did he permit his excessive nervousness to turn him from the duty of leading in prayer after he had been made a deacon. He married Miss Eleanor Junkin, daughter of the president of Washington College, and lost her in childbirth after a year. Four years later he married again, Anna Morrison, sister-in-law of his old friend Daniel Hill.

As a teacher, Old Jack was not an unqualified success. His students found his eccentricities amusing, his punctiliousness funny. He would walk an hour in the rain before the superintendent's office, waiting for the precise moment when he had been asked to present his report. On one occasion the superintendent asked him to wait, then went home and forgot him, and he sat bolt upright all night in the outer office. He expected no less attention to duty from his students, for since the major had never blanched before self-discipline it was hard for him to understand the widespread human aversion to it. He organized a large Negro Sunday school, called it "my militia," and if the scholars came late he would not let them in. They learned to come on time. On the other hand, he once walked several miles in a snowstorm and woke a cadet in the middle of the night to offer a stiff apology, when reflection had convinced him that he had been wrong in an argument. "Tom Fool Jackson," said the boys.

In his home life, however, he laid aside the caution with which he faced the world, and his wife has left a biography of a gentle tender husband, whose strongest rebuke was, "Ah, that is not the way to be happy," and who called her "my little sunshine." Needless to say, the household ran with military precision. Up at six, a cold bath winter and summer, a walk, and family prayers at seven, "waiting for nobody, not even his wife." Classes for three hours, then study from eleven to one, standing upright at a high desk because the position was better for his stomach. Half an hour after lunch for conversation, then work in his garden, or on the little farm he had bought outside the town. Still a country boy, the major liked to work with his hands, and although he owned two or three slaves who had asked him to buy them, they did not help him out of doors. Dyspeptic spots before his eyes prevented his using them at night, but after supper he would turn his chair to the wall, and sitting bolt upright with his hands on his knees and both feet on the floor, would mentally review his studies. No one was to speak to him while this was going on, but when he completed his task he would emerge "with a bright and cheerful face into social enjoyment again."

So passed ten tranquil years at Lexington, in teaching, in scholastic and religious duties rigidly performed, in domestic happiness. Major Jackson could safely feel that he had fulfilled his boyhood determination to make a man of himself, and that ambition which had been "excessive" in Mexico had been tamed by resignation to the will of God. His country and his heart had been at peace.

Now this was war.

The government at Richmond, with the proverbial perspicacity of civilian governments in military matters, first set Major Jackson to doing desk work, but within a week or two he was rescued and sent to command the garrison at Harpers Ferry as colonel of Virginia Volunteers. "The post I prefer above all others," he wrote his wife. "Little one, you must not expect to hear from me often, as I expect to have more work than I ever had in the same length of time."

Colonel Jackson replaced some dashing officers of militia, and he was not dashing, but he was resolved by discipline and drill to make an army out of the eight thousand motley volunteers who had poured in from the surrounding countryside. Men were arriving from every county in the Valley, eager, amateurish, without arms, willing to try their luck with rocks if they could not get rifles. Colonel Jackson was a professional, and this was not an army, but he meant to make it one.

Over the Baltimore and Ohio Railroad, then the only link between Washington and the pro-Union western Virginia, an unprecedented number of coal cars were rolling to the capital. Jackson informed John W. Garrett, president of the road, that the traffic disturbed his camp at night and must stop. The railroad complied, since he was astraddle of it, and ran their trains by day. Then Jackson said that the daylight traffic interfered with military routine, and that all freights must run exclusively between the hours of eleven A.M. and one P.M. Again the railroad complied. When he had thus got the trains nicely concentrated, Colonel Jackson sent Captain Imboden of Staunton across the Potomac at Harpers Ferry to stop the east-bound freights and let the west-bound go through. The officer in charge at Martinsburg was ordered to act on the opposite principle. The trap closed, and in an hour the Virginians scooped up fifty-six locomotives and more than three hundred cars.

Jackson had reason to feel satisfied with the success of the small operation, but he had no time for more, since next day, May 24th, he was relieved of his command and superseded by General Joseph E. Johnston. President Davis wished to place a more experienced officer at this important post.

Jackson at first refused to surrender his command without written orders, but when they were produced he gave up without comment, except to write his wife that he hoped "now to have time for longer letters to my little pet." He was retained at Harpers Ferry, promoted to brigadier general, and given the First Brigade of Virginians in Johnston's army, a brigade largely composed of Valley men. General Johnston viewed these untrained enthusiasts with dry misgiving. "I would trade the whole lot of them for a company of regulars," he said. Jackson, however, had a brighter idea of the possibilities. "Did he say that? And of these splendid men?"

Within three weeks General Patterson arrived from

Washington with a considerable force, and as Harpers Ferry was untenable, the Confederates fell back to Winchester—at which Jackson remarked only that he "had hoped to have engaged the enemy." When Patterson went to Martinsburg, Jackson was there before him to burn forty-two of the locomotives he had bottled up, with about three hundred cars, and to haul the rest by horses down the Valley Pike to the branch lines where they became very useful. This set the northern press to howling "vandalism!"—"As villanous almost as the crime of murder . . . a movement every step of which has been taken in fraud, treachery, violence, bloodshed, wanton destruction." General Jackson took a different view.

"If the cost of the property could only have been expended in disseminating the gospel of the Prince of Peace!—But my duty was to obey."

May and June were gay in Winchester—apple blossoms and uniforms, roses and swords. This was the romantic, the traditional Virginia, the legend they deeply believed, and all the girls were beautiful and all the men were brave.

The war could not last long, for Yankees did not like fighting. The newborn nation would be rich and free. What they lacked in ammunition they made up, they thought, in dash and spirit. Everywhere there were young laughing soldiers, volunteers and eager. They slept in the orchards, they slept on the porches, they slept on mattresses on the parlor floors. The first regiment to arrive from the far South did not need to make a camp, for they were entirely taken care of in private houses. In the camps life went gaily, and when a youth was twitted for carrying slops, he had a ready answer. "Hell, this isn't slops. This is patriotism." Colonel McDonald, intractable grandson of that intractable Angus who had been too proud to fight in the Revolution, raised a regiment of cavalry, and the Ashby brothers, Turner and Richard, brought their Black Horse Troop to join it. If some of the deep South soldiers "took sick" in the treacherous Virginia spring, there were plenty of loving hands to nurse them.

Hostesses set three or four supper tables every night, and

even the house servants joined in the general festivity and produced mountains of beaten biscuit, hot rolls, batter bread, slivers of dark red ham, and caldrons of chicken stew. Young and old, the ladies sewed night and day, without machines to help them, making havelocks—which turned out to be perfectly useless—and haversacks, jackets, trousers, even tents.

As for the young girls, they were in Paradise. A flounce caught on a spur, a button for a keepsake, a rosebud with the dew on it—no one dreamed the flounce bedraggled, or the button tarnished, or the roses dead. It was so gay that fifty years later one Emma Reilly Macon, remembering everything, remembering the end, could look back at her sixteen-year-old self flirting there in the moonlight, and still say, "The girls of this generation will never know the good times we had then." Down the long road to the inevitable conclusion, the Valley took the first steps dancing.

A beautiful regiment arrived from Georgia under Colonel Francis Bartow, in uniforms of dark green and gold, with a gold-fringed silk banner, red, white, and red. Their drill was wonderful to watch, and they put on a show which left the more staid Valley people gasping. When they concluded their maneuvers, the boys fell out and went to playing leap-frog and prisoner's base. Their colonel watched them with an awful sadness.

"They are so young," he said. "They are so young."

The new conglomerate army had time to laugh, for there was still no fighting, still the great battle did not come. In a small skirmish, to which the generals referred as "that little affair at Falling Waters," Colonel J. E. B. Stuart captured a scouting company of Federals. It gave the Confederate trooper a good opinion of himself, and only one of them got hurt. The Parks boy had his head carried off by a cannon ball, and when they brought his body back to Winchester, his father lost his reason, and never recovered sanity again.

Now there were Yankees at Martinsburg, and Yankees at Harpers Ferry. When the Union General Patterson occupied Martinsburg on July 3rd, there were many northern sympathizers in the town, but one of them was emphatically not, a young lady of sixteen named Belle Boyd. Miss Belle, who was allegedly pretty, on her record fascinating, and one who thrived upon the stir of war, saw herself as the beautiful female spy of the Confederacy. She got a running start toward her career on that hot Fourth of July when her town was invaded, by shooting one of the soldiers dead—a gesture which caused her no regret, either then or later, nor, so gentle were the usages of that far-off war, any real inconvenience. She wrote her own story afterward, in a style as infectious as an epidemic disease, from London where her circumstances threatened to become reduced.

There she was, living in the two-storied house of her childhood overgrown with roses and honeysuckle, "petted by her parents, loved by and loving of her brothers and sisters." Her father had gone off as a private in the Confederate Army, unselfishly leaving the glories of leadership to others, and her mother, never alone since she had married him at fifteen, was suitably prostrated. Miss Belle's first contact with the invaders was an unfortunate one, for she and her Negro maid were in the hospital nursing two fever-ridden soldiers when an officer of the North entered and referred to the patients as damn Rebels. Belle could not let that go in silence.

"These men, sir, are as helpless as babies, with no power to reply to your insults."

"And who are you?"

"A Rebel lady," answered the Negro maid.

"A damned independent one," remarked the officer, and let them alone.

With her delicate ears ringing from this rough talk, Miss Belle went home, but worse was to follow. The Irish troops began to celebrate Independence Day with benefit of whisky, by breaking into houses, and throwing furniture out of windows. They came to the Boyd home to confiscate the Rebel flags with which Miss Belle was said to have decorated her room. The devoted little Negro maid, who never achieved the dignity of a name in the narrative, but who evidently had far better judgment than her mistress, ran upstairs, tore down the flags, and burned them while the Yankees were still arguing below. The soldiers found nothing, but nevertheless insisted that they were going to raise a Union flag over the house, and Mrs. Boyd, with her little children clinging to her skirts in the classic pose, retorted that she and every member of her family would die first. One of the soldiers then spoke to her insultingly, and Belle drew a pistol from her bosom (of course) and shot him dead.

This, not unnaturally, created a sensation, and the comrades of the dead man would have burned the house had not Miss Belle sent a message to the commanding officer. He came in person to investigate the circumstances, told Belle that she had done "just right," and placed sentries around the house to see that the family were not molested further. This was war in the American style, fought by our unenlightened ancestors without the psychological advantages of terrorism.

Miss Belle made friends with the sentries, and with the young officers who came to inquire for "the little Rebel with the chestnut curls"—and stole their pistols, swords, and bullets, which she smuggled through the lines together with such information as she could gather. One dispatch was interrupted, her handwriting identified, and General Patterson summoned her to his headquarters.

The general was displeased if not disillusioned. He remonstrated with her, he spoke severely to her, he went so far as to read her the Articles of War: "Whosoever shall give food, ammunition, or information . . . to the enemy . . . shall suffer death, or whatever punishment the honorable members of the court-martial shall see fit to inflict."

"Miss Boyd," said the general, "I positively forbid you to do anything of this sort again. You really *must not* do it."

Belle went home somewhat subdued, to be consoled by the praises of her mother, and her spirits might have remained chastened for a time had not the victory at Bull Run revived them . . .

For now there was a battle. By midsummer, the wheat, yellow as sunlight in the fields, flowed like a golden sea under the wind. It was warmly ripened for the scythe, for the harvest that would end its dancing. A courier on a dying horse galloped into the camp at Winchester with a dispatch from General Beauregard. "If you want to help me, now is the time."

At dawn on July 18th the people of Winchester heard the tramping, and came out with pale and wondering faces to see their army deserting them. The Valley men did not know where they were going, they knew only that they were abandoning their homes to the Yankees, their waving cornfields, fat pastures, harvested grain. The line stretched for seven miles down the pike, and at its head rode General Jackson in the faded uniform he had brought from V.M.I., mounted on his close-coupled, uninspiring, tireless horse, Little Sorrel, whose real name was Fancy. After an hour and a half, the men were halted to hear an order: "Our gallant army under General Beauregard is now attacked by overwhelming numbers. The Commanding General hopes that his troops will step out like men and make a forced march to save the country."

The cheers rolled back down the line like the wind passing over the fields. This was what they had been waiting for, and they marched all day on the strength of it, under the baking sun. The dust rolled up and powdered the new uniforms, gritted their eyes, choked their throats. The generals thought the recruits moved too slowly, the men thought someone had forgotten to order a halt. They saw no reason why they should not stop at the brooks, sweet with water cress, take off their shoes, and bathe their swollen feet.

At dusk they forded the Shenandoah, with the cool water curling about their waists, and climbed the Blue Ridge in the twilight, shoulders rubbed sore under the haversacks, dust caked into mud, muskets growing heavier no matter how they were carried. Now it was dark. Nothing to see but silent stars, silent trees looming suddenly out of the black, silent men shuffling on and on.

"I'll make a bargain with you," said nineteen-year-old Willie Blue to nineteen-year-old John Casler. "I'll bury you if you'll bury me."

John did not like this way of talking. "Mebbe you'll just be wounded."

"I don't want to be wounded. If I'm shot, I want to be shot right through the heart," said Willie Blue.

And now the column reached the crest and wound through Ashby's Gap and down the other side. The Valley was behind them. At the foot of the mountain they would find trains (with some of General Jackson's cars and engines) to take them to Manassas. It was two in the morning when they stopped at last near a mountain village called Paris. The two-month soldiers, accustomed only to drilling, had marched twenty miles. They threw their muskets on the ground and fell beside them without even bothering to unroll their blankets. An officer came up to General Jackson.

"The men are all asleep. Shall I rouse someone for picket duty?"

"Let the poor fellows sleep. I will watch the camp myself."

Back in the Valley, suddenly empty and quiet, the people waited. Friday and Saturday and Sunday passed without news. Near Winchester the little boys roved over the trampled grass where there had been an army, and dreamed themselves soldiers too. Then on Monday all the bells were ringing, ringing for victory.

It had been glorious. It had been wonderful. It had been just as they expected. The Yankees had run all the way to Washington, they were the "Bull Runners" sure enough, and the war was nearly over before it had started. In that day of joy and exultation everyone stood at a doorway or a gate, to pick up good tidings from the passers-by.

But on Tuesday the wagons began rolling back, bearing the fruits of victory—"the first fruits of that bitter tree which our people had helped to plant and nourish." Here were the bloody groaning wounded, the stiff and livid figures under the motionless tarpaulins. The list was long, as long as the Valley, and every county bore a share.

Now Willie Preston mourned for Willie Page, his dearest

friend; and Willie Blue had been shot through the heart as
he had imagined. John Casler sat down and cried when he
found him, until he remembered that a soldier must not cry.
"Last Sunday was such a day as I had never seen," he wrote
his mother, "and I hope to God I never will see another such
a time. . . . You must not be surprised to hear of me getting killed, for we don't know when we will be killed." A
wagon came to Powell's with the body of their son who had
come home from the West in time to fight once and once
only; and to Glaize the plasterer, who had never owned or
hoped to own a slave. When the wagon came to Mr. Conrad's he went out and looked under the canvas, returned in
silence, and said to his waiting wife and daughters, "Let us
pray." They knelt without a question while the teamsters
carried in the bodies of his two sons and his nephew, killed
by the same shell. Some of the highest officers also were missing. General Bee was gone, after giving a new name to Jackson and his Virginians; and Colonel Bartow, he who had
thought his soldiers were too young.

They would never be so young again, the boyish soldiers. They had discovered, each one for himself, the iron
in the soul which stiffens the knees and drives the body forward when all the instincts clamor to go back. They knew
the incommunicable secrets of the vast fraternity of fighters.
They were men.

The people of the Valley were also changed forever.
They would never again talk with the same glibness and assurance of the future, for they had learned the first lesson of
the many lessons.

War is not drill and flags, cheering and gallantry. War
is death.

14. Marching On

There is Jackson, standing like a stone wall. Rally behind the Virginians.

—GENERAL BEE at Manassas

GENERAL JACKSON and his brigade won a new name at Manassas. The official records of the battle made him a hero to a nation thirsty for heroes, and by the time he returned to his beloved Valley in November there were few who had not heard of the order given by dead General Bee. Jackson did not comment on the events which rendered him famous. A day or two after the battle, his pastor in Lexington received a letter from him, and tore it open eagerly, crying: "Now we shall have news!"

My dear pastor:—In my tent last night, after a fatiguing days service, I remembered that I had failed to send you my contribution to our colored Sunday School. Enclosed you will find my check for that object, which please acknowledge at your earliest convenience and oblige

yours faithfully,
T. J. Jackson.

With his wife, after reminding her that all the glory was due to *God alone,* the general permitted himself to be more expansive:

He made my brigade more instrumental than any other in repulsing the main attack. This is for your information only, let others speak praise, not myself . . . And so you think the papers ought to say more about your husband! My brigade is not a brigade of newspaper correspondents.

168

STONEWALL JACKSON

The rest of the army might relax and rejoice after the battle, but not General Jackson's command. His men lay on their arms, furloughs were refused even to those who wished to see dying relatives, rations were issued three days in advance, and everything was kept in marching order, waiting for the command to proceed to Washington. The orders never came. August passed. September passed. In October, Jackson was promoted to major general, and ordered to the Valley in charge of the new Shenandoah district. To his mind this had only one defect. He must leave his Stonewall Brigade behind.

Jackson and his soldiers knew each other now, for they had been baptized together. Critical voices in the army might declare that "they had exchanged their best brigadier for a third rate major general," but the complaints did not come from the men whom Old Jack had led into battle—for they had witnessed his transfiguration. They had seen the awkward silent professor blazing with inner fire, transformed into the "very God of War." So he appeared to them, so they remembered and spoke of him, even when they were old men.

On November 4th he rode out to tell them good-bye. They stood in silence at attention, with their newly stained and tattered banners floating against the lingering autumn leaves. The regiments were proud of their torn flags, proud of their nicknames. They were veterans.

The Innocent 2nd (because they never stole anything)
The Harmless 4th (because they never fought in camp)
The Fighting 5th (because they always did)
The Bloody 27th (Irish)
The Lousy 33rd (because they were the first to have them)

General Jackson delivered some brief and formal sentences with the awkwardness which no amount of practice or preparation ever enabled him to overcome. It was soon finished, and it was not enough. He sat his horse and looked at them in silence, then for once his emotions broke through the iron shell of self-control. He flung his reins on Little Sorrel's neck, he stood in his stirrups, spread his arms, and shouted:

In the Army of the Shenandoah you were the First Brigade!
In the Army of the Potomac you were the First Brigade!
In the Second Corps of the army you are the First Brigade!
You are the First Brigade in the affections of your general, and I hope by your future deeds and bearing you will be handed down to posterity as the First Brigade in this our second War of Independence!
Farewell!!

When the men began to cheer their hearts out, Jackson could not stand it. He blushed crimson, tore off his cap and waved it, then galloped away. It is pleasant to record that within a month brigade and general were together in the Valley, never again to separate while he lived.

When General Jackson took up his command at Winchester, he found himself back at his old task of turning a disorganized skeleton force into an army. In spite of Manassas, in spite of more than three thousand dead, this was still in most respects a highly informal and indeed an amateurish war. Histories incline to treat of armies as though they sprang up overnight, composed of ordinary men miraculously transformed into heroes; but that did not happen in our Revolution, nor in our Civil War, nor in our World War I or II. It is true that when the exasperated South at last instituted conscription of all able-bodied whites between eighteen and thirty-five, in the spring of '62, the act made little change in the Valley, where everyone except the Dunkards and the Quakers had volunteered. Yet the records and the memoirs of old soldiers make it clear that even the Stonewall Brigade had its share of grafters, slackers, stragglers, and cowards. Do not be deceived by the quaint clothing, the butternut suits, the hats of different cut, the beards. These men were G I's, and the gold-brick was not invented in 1942.

In the North, after Manassas, they stopped talking about "thirty days of concerted effort" and men poured into the Federal army at the rate of 40,000 a month; but in the South a tenth of the troops went home on leave, sure now that they could lick twice their weight in Yankees. Most of the volunteers had enlisted for twelve months and had no intention of serving longer. The civilian government at Richmond offered them a bounty of $50 and a furlough of sixty days if they would re-enlist for the duration, and allowed them to change commands and elect new officers when they did so. As a result, infantry with some experience might change overnight into artillery with none, nor did the elections take place without political intrigue. One North Carolina regiment balloted for seven days before they chose their colonel. Many young men of good families thought it distinguished to serve as privates, and one wrote complacently, "our major is the plainest man in the regiment, but a very good officer." When the appalled generals complained of such policies, the bland Mr. Benjamin insisted that they "should be carried out to the extreme verge of prudence." It was the most democratic and independent army ever assembled to fight for an aristocratic ideal.

Take the career of Edward Allen, a son of the Valley who fought from Manassas to Appomattox. At the outbreak of war he was on his way to join the militia regiment of which he was the colonel, when he saw a volunteer taking tearful leave of his wife. Ever a man who found only sentimental reasons valid, he at once offered to take the man's place, and so enlisted as a private in the 10th Virginia. While a private he was sent with a detachment to burn a bridge, and on the mission his lieutenant cheerfully resigned to him both sword and horse. He continued in command with the rank of private, until asked to call out his militia regiment, but before he could comply the army went off to Manassas, and he hesitated to assemble the militia to defend the deserted border because most of those left were Union men. In this dilemma, Edward decided to join the cavalry, and hurried to the field, but arrived just too late for the battle. Afterward he made another effort to call out his regiment, but when he found that only forty of them were available, he received permission to make them a troop of cavalry instead, and was duly commissioned their captain, and later their major when they were recruited up to full strength and became the 11th Virginia.

If the reader is confused by this little history, the effect of such irregularity on the mind of a professional soldier may easily be imagined. General Jackson was a professional, but he told no one what he was thinking. Later, when his men had proved themselves, he referred to the months after Manassas as the darkest period of the war. In General Jackson's army discipline would not be lax.

A soldier who broke into a house and talked roughly to the women was court-martialed and shot within twenty minutes of his arrest. Another soldier struck his captain. The Presbyterian minister of Winchester called in person to plead extenuating circumstances, and ask that the man be allowed to die at the hands of the enemy. General Jackson listened with tears in his eyes. "I will review the case, and no man will be happier than myself if I can reach the same conclusion you have done." The soldier was shot.

The higher the rank of the offender, the more merciless the discipline. An officer reduced to the rear of his regiment was no uncommon sight, riding without arms in punishment for something he had allowed his men to do. Some of them resigned, while others refused to stand for re-election. Even Ashby was at times the target of Old Jack's criticism—even Ashby, the cavalryman's ideal, and the idol of the army.

When that stouthearted old Indian fighter, Colonel Mc-
Donald, was driven from the field by rheumatism, he turned
his cavalry regiment over to Turner Ashby, and within a year
it had become a legend. To a people naturally romantic and
individualistic, reared on knightly stories and fiercely sentimental, Ashby had every quality. He was silent and darkly
fascinating, with deep hazel eyes and full black beard. He
was not particularly young at thirty-eight, but he was dashing. He wore white gauntlets and a white plume in his hat,
rode a white stallion as fearless as himself. Legend said that he
had vowed vengeance for the death of his younger brother
who had been bayoneted as he lay wounded on the ground;
that Turner had broken a sword and dropped the pieces into
Richard's grave; that he never laughed again, and that he
swore to fight the Yankees every day for a year, and well he
kept his promise. This is rumor, but his courage is no
rumor, for he was ever first to enter a fight and last to leave
it, and if the tales of his daring are halved there is still enough
to satisfy. His discipline was irregular, he never knew just
how many he had in his command; but his young men would
follow him to hell and back.

"We thought no more of riding through the enemy's
bivouacs than of riding around our father's farm," wrote a
veteran of four years, who was nineteen when Richmond
fell.

"I can't catch them, sir," a Federal cavalry commander
reported to General Banks. "They leap fences and walls like
deer; neither our men nor our horses are so trained."

The Confederates claimed that the Yankees had to have
their feet tied together under an animal's belly in order to
stay on at all. The Yankees complained that even the Rebel
guns could jump—and so they could, for attached to Ashby's
command was an early experiment in mobile artillery:
Chew's Flying Battery, mounted on light wagons, drawn by
riding horses, operating on the simple principle that the guns
would go where the cavalry did. It was commanded by three
young men of Jefferson County, Captain Chew, nineteen,
Lieutenant Rouse, seventeen, and Second Lieutenant Thom-

son, eighteen—all graduates of V.M.I. Their former professor inquired of them sternly: "Young men, now that you have your company, what are you going to do with it?"

Actually both the general and the colonel knew very well what they could expect from their men, for frequently they demanded the impossible, and frequently they got it. These soldiers were, it is true, only average men, waiting there in the Valley for the guns to announce the arrival of spring, making their jokes, grumbling and complaining, discovering that war is a long stretch of boredom punctuated by unpleasant intervals of fright. But there was nothing average about their leaders. That was a formidable pair as they rode through the dawn mists: the praying shabby general with the inner fire, on his strictly utilitarian little horse, and the magnificent colonel on the magnificent steed, plume floating, beard floating, speaking as gently as a woman, with the softness in his eyes hiding the killer's gleam.

In spite of his organizational difficulties, General Jackson found life so comfortable in Winchester that ever after he called it his "war home." He sent for his wife and installed her in the most congenial surroundings, at the home of the Presbyterian minister, Dr. Graham. They saved money to buy Confederate bonds. She found the Winchester ladies "among the most famous of Virginia housekeepers, and lived in a good deal of old fashioned elegance and profusion. . . . Under the rose colored light in which I viewed everything that winter, it seemed to me that no people could have been more cultivated, attractive, and noblehearted."

It is true that the townspeople were beginning to find some drawbacks to having an army camp at their doors, but they did not complain so long as it was the right army. Mrs. McDonald's eight children, all under fourteen, contracted the itch, which they cured with poke roots, sulphur, and molasses. Typhoid caused no more comment than dysentery, and almost every household had a touch of scarlet fever. In Winchester four of Emma Reilly's family, including her mother, died in a single week. In Lexington, thirteen-year-old Elizabeth Preston, who had recovered, was roused in the night to nurse her baby brother, and kept him quiet by reciting "Cowper's Grave," "He Giveth His Beloved Sleep," and "The Burial of Moses."

In spite of everything, for this little while there was still plenty and prosperity in the Valley, if there could not be peace. The Negroes were quiet and faithful as always, suppers were plentiful and tempting, doors stayed unlocked at night, and silver still gleamed on the old mahogany and walnut sideboards. Although the rains of November and December took some of the merriment out of camp life, the soldiers had a favorite song:

> Let the world wag as it will,
> We'll be gay and happy still.
> Gay and happy, gay and happy,
> We'll be gay and happy still.

If they fell ill, there were ladies to nurse them, for although such behavior was considered somewhat unladylike if not downright unwomanly, the women could not be kept out of the hospitals. One of them gave calomel to a typhoid sufferer, and another soldier reported that seven had washed his face in a single morning, until he was perfectly clean, or very tired of it—but these were minor errors.

Miss Belle Boyd tried six weeks of nursing, but found it undermining to her health, and returned to the sort of exploit better suited to her temperament. One day when riding with some Confederate officers, her horse ran away and carried her into the Federal lines. She meekly declared herself prisoner, and the Yankees replied as gentlemen should, that they would escort her home.

"I suppose those damn cowardly Rebels would not catch us, would they?"

"Don't you be afraid of the Rebels," laughed Belle.

So they rode along in a merry party until her former escort came out of the woods and took her new friends prisoner.

"Who are you?" asked the Federals, too late.

"Belle Boyd."

"Good God."

The Yankees were furious at what they considered Miss Belle's treachery, but she retorted that they had started the whole thing by making her blood boil with their jokes about cowardly Rebels. In any case they were released after an hour's detention and returned to their own camp. The war was still conducted on the most sporting principles.

Sporting or not, comfortable and happy or not, General Jackson had no intention of wasting the winter. Since his government would not support him in an expedition to western Virginia, he determined to take Romney, a town just over the first range of the Alleghenies, and thereby to secure the Valley, the B. & O. Railroad, and to cut off the Federals in the west from General Banks' new Blue army north of the Potomac. Reinforced by seven thousand men under General Loring, he started west on New Year's Day.

It had been an open Christmas in the Valley, the sort of mild and sunny December which keeps the grass green and brings the spears of the daffodils an inch or so out of the ground. Dust flew in the roads, and the cheerfully improvident soldiers tossed their coats and blankets into the wagons. Then as they reached the mountains in the afternoon, the skies hung slate-gray and the snow began to fall. They bivouacked that night in an icy wind with the spitting snow stinging their faces, and an officer who allowed his men to take down a rail fence for a fire was promptly court-martialed and sent to ride without his sword in the rear. The stiffened soldiers combed the woods for fuel, and in complete disgust one cried: "I wish the Yankees were in hell!"

"I don't," said William Wintermeyer, the camp wag, "because Old Jack would have us there by morning, with this brigade in front."

Next day the snow turned to ice, and the wagons skidded so that four men with ropes had to hold each one in the roads. The horses plunged and fell, and one German driver burst into tears when he saw icicles of blood hanging from the knees of his team. A tall officer who happened to ride by, dismounted, put his shoulder under the wagon, and helped to push it up the hill. Only after they reached the top did the straining men recognize their general. When the Stonewall Brigade halted, Jackson rode up to ask the meaning of the stop.

"I halted to let the men cook their rations, sir," said General Garnett, their commander.

"There is no time for that."

"But it is impossible for the men to go on without it."

"I never found anything impossible with that brigade."

By night the snow fell soft and thick, resting like wool on the blankets of the exhausted men. A group of them, in a shivering huddle, kept themselves warm by cursing their commander. Old Jack was crazy, he was trying to kill them, nobody could be expected to stand this kind of thing. At dawn an angular soldier rose from beside them, brushed off the snow, bade them a courteous good morning, and strode away. It was Jackson himself. William Wintermeyer looked at the men as they broke out from under the white blanket and shouted: "Jumping Jehosaphat!! It's the Resurrection!!!"

For ten days the Army of the Valley toiled on across the mountains. It rained, and the rain froze on them. It snowed, and they slept in it. Men and horses broke their legs on the ice, many died from cold and exposure—and they never saw the enemy. The Federals kept retreating in front of them, and Romney was empty when they reached it. After a day or two, Jackson left General Loring in charge, and took the rest of his army back to the Valley.

On January 24th he reached Winchester. When he arrived his wife and all the family were in the sitting room around a crackling wood fire, the lamps lit, the icy darkness excluded and forgotten. Jackson's face glowed at their welcome. He crossed to the fire, held out his hands to it, looked about him with beaming delight, and exclaimed: "This is the very essence of comfort!"

His satisfaction, however, was not to endure for a week. General Loring did not like his position, complained to Richmond over Jackson's head, and without consulting Jackson,

Richmond ordered Romney evacuated. This meant the loss of all the advantages gained by the expedition, meant that all the soldiers who had coughed themselves to death had died in vain. General Jackson took his pen and wrote to Secretary Benjamin.

Sir:

Your order requiring me to direct General Loring to return with his command to Winchester immediately, has been received and promptly complied with.

With such interference in my command, I cannot expect to be of much service in the field, and accordingly respectfully request to be ordered to report for duty to the Superintendent of the Virginia Military Institute, as has been done in the case of other professors. Should this application not be granted, I respectfully request that the President will accept my resignation from the army.

I am, sir, very respectfully your obedient servant,

T. J. Jackson, Major General, P.A.C.S.

The resignation was not passed over in silence. General Johnston protested, Governor Letcher of Virginia protested. Congressman Boteler protested, delegations of citizens protested. In the end, after a solemn assurance that the government would never again interfere with his military plans, Mr. Benjamin's obedient servant was preserved for the army.

And now it was March, and green spring in Virginia. Around the houses the forsythia shook out its golden bells and the violets pushed through the succulent new grass. In a few weeks, or possibly days, the fruit trees would begin to blossom. The spring breeze fanned and dried the roads. In a few weeks, or possibly days, the Federal Army would begin to move.

General Johnston, Confederate commander in chief, took stock of his position, and decided to evacuate Manassas and fall back nearer to Richmond, which he did during four days of the greatest waste and disorder. At the packing plant in Thoroughfare Gap, he burned or distributed to the countryside a million pounds of meat. Now General Jackson was unsupported. His army numbered 4,600. Across the Po-

tomac, Banks waited with 37,000. Frémont at Romney had
12,000 more, and Jackson looked like a small mouse in a
closing trap. President Davis, who had no reinforcements to
send him, hoped gloomily that at best he might so divert
Banks as to prevent his joining McClellan in front of Richmond. The situation looked hopeless to everyone except Jackson. "I do not feel discouraged . . ." he wrote. "Send me
what men you can. . . . *If this Valley is lost, Virginia is
lost.*"

For ten years Stonewall Jackson had labored sincerely
to make himself a man of peace, in conformity with what appeared to be God's plan for him. Now it seemed that God
had other work for him to do. Isolated and outnumbered,
confronted by the possibility of immediate action, his twin
plagues of nervousness and cold feet left him entirely. During the first week in March he moved his stores down the
Valley to Mount Jackson, and sent his wife back to her father
in North Carolina. "My darling, you made a timely retreat
from here, for on Friday the Yankees came within five miles
of this place . . . How God does bless us wherever we
are! . . . I do not remember having been in such good
health for years!"

The general began his retreat by marching in the direction of the enemy, in the hope of tempting Banks to give
battle. But Banks was cautious. He was one of Mr. Lincoln's
political generals, who had begun life as a hand in a Massachusetts cotton factory, had risen to the governorship, and
then to be speaker of the House of Representatives. It seemed
only just to reward so ardent an abolitionist and so useful
a politician with command of an army. Sobered by responsibility, Banks confined fire-eating to his dispatches, which
were models of flamboyance and optimistic promise. His
splendid soldiers, from Ohio, Indiana, West Virginia, could
not go where he did not send them, and his cavalry was
deficient, for they had been assembled in the belief that to
make a horseman it is only necesary to place a man and a
horse in proximity. Thanks to the activity of Ashby, Banks

believed Jackson stronger than he was, and so remained inactive.

On March 12th, Jackson ordered his army to move southward, and summoned a council of his regimental officers. While it was gathering he called at Dr. Graham's, and buoyantly told the family that he would take dinner with them on the following night. To the council he disclosed his plans. He intended to bring his troops back through Winchester under cover of darkness, and to make a surprise attack on the Federals four miles to the north. But the council found that someone had blundered. Instead of halting just outside the town the men had been sent eight miles down the pike to join the wagons. The regimental officers felt that they could not be brought back in time, so voted solidly to give up the attempt.

With a retreat before overwhelming forces, Stonewall Jackson began the Valley Campaign which made him famous, and which has become a classic in the art of war. Technicians have written textbooks on it for the British cadets at Sandhurst, showing how it illustrates each vital military principle: maintenance of aim, economy of force, surprise, mobility, co-operation, concentration, security, offensive action. There is hardly a military academy in the world which has not studied it. In the summer of 1936, the German General Rommel spent some time as a civilian in the Shenandoah Valley, tramping the grassgrown battlefields.

Before Jackson left Winchester, he rode again past Dr. Graham's and told them the bad news, for he was unwilling to leave them (or anyone else except the enemy) under a misapprehension. Accompanied by his surgeon, Dr. McGuire, he went on slowly and halted on the southern ridge for one last look.

The town lay quiet under the newly feathered branches of its trees. No one stirred in the quiet streets, and the warmly lighted windows spoke of peace. But behind them old men imprisoned in their years paced rooms which had become cages, and women knelt by sleeping children, and smothered sobs against the pillows. Dr. McGuire was leaving behind his home, his family, everything that he loved, and his heart was bursting, but when he turned to the general "my emotion was arrested by one look. Jackson's face was fairly blazing with the fire of wrath that was burning in him, and I felt awed before him. Presently he cried out, in a tone almost savage:

'*That is the last council of war I will ever hold!*' "

15. The Invaded

A defensive campaign can only be made successful by taking the offensive at the proper time.

—T. J. JACKSON

THE ANGRY GENERAL on the rise below Winchester did not come to his great trial unprepared. Now he was to reap the benefit of the concentration he had taught himself facing the wall in Lexington. Shortly after his retirement from Winchester an unusual young officer named Jedediah Hotchkiss joined his command as adjutant of Augusta militia. Hotchkiss was a New Englander who had fallen in love with the Shenandoah Valley while on a visit, settled there, and took up arms in what they all referred to as "The Cause." He had an engineer's training, a New Englander's thoroughness, and a marked natural gift for making maps. When Jackson heard of him he sent for him and announced with customary abruptness:

"I want you to make me a map of the Valley from Harpers Ferry to Lexington, showing all the points of offense and defense between those points. Mr. Pendleton will give you orders for whatever outfit you want. Good morning, sir."

The accurate maps soon materialized, for Hotchkiss was as indefatigable as his commander. Jackson studied them night and day, and among his papers are found more carefully compiled tables of distances than in the papers of any other Confederate officer. The country boy who had made a man of himself by hard work and determination was not neglecting any advantage that hard work could provide.

He made the countryside itself his ally, the rolling fields edged with woodland, the streams swollen with spring, the hidden roads, the retired friendly houses, and above all the great shaggy bulk of Massanutten, splitting the Valley in two and crossed by secret paths. It was a fair valley, made for peace, hemmed in and bulwarked by mountains for security. It was, the soldiers said, *"a lovely Valley to fight for."* Now the Yankees had arrived in it, and the Valley people, men, women, children, even the slaves, even the trees and stones, were going to teach them that they were not wanted.

From the old diaries comes the story, from the letters yellowing in attic trunks beside the Confederate notes and bonds, from the family tales repeated to successive generations until the grandchildren think that they lived through it too. They may pretend that they are tired of it, but it is in their blood like the limestone and the river. All of it is there, the false pride which burned away and the true pride which lasted, the folly, the weakness, and the rocklike strength. And because in the flow of time history repeats itself always, the story is fresher today than it may have been forty years ago to a generation not then preoccupied with war and with invasion.

In justice one thing must be stated. In spite of the ruin which this war brought upon the Valley, in spite of a percentage of casualties in battle which has never been surpassed, it was by modern standards a gentle war. The soldiers themselves were the first to discover it as they swapped tobacco for coffee across the river, as they picked berries together in warm fields until the bugle told them to kill each other. The soldiers remembered afterward, and were the first to let the quarrel rest. But the Valley people did not think it was gentle. They saw themselves invaded and forcibly possessed by a horde of strangers. That the strangers were their own breed, speaking their language, only made the situation more intolerable, the insults more pungent. That the strangers might have some right on their side no one dreamed. In the rage of war no one could see so clearly, for once battle has been joined the causes of it are forgotten.

Let the story stand then, true to the records, and let the
knowledge that its bitterness has faded be a reminder that
the newer bitterness will fade. This is how it feels to be
invaded, how it felt then, how it will always feel. To be surrounded by strangers who can take from you what they like,
to have no weapons against them except your angry eyes and
tongue. To be separated from your husbands, from your
sons, to know that they are in danger and not know when
or how, to be unable to reach them or hear from them. To
see the men who mean to kill them under your roof, eating
at your table, eating their food while you and they go hungry, while the young children sicken and die for lack of
nourishment. To be a tenant in your own house at a strange
landlord's mercy, to wake at night weeping with dread of
what may come. To see crumbling around you all that the
years have brought, wasted and spent all you have labored
for and saved—and to do nothing, nothing but hate. No, the
women could not be expected to forget the bitterness. But
let it be remembered that their children did.

On the morning after Jackson's men withdrew, the people of Winchester woke to sunlight and silence. With the day
they felt better able to face whatever might be coming. They
dressed carefully, assembled their families and servants for
prayers as was the universal custom, and sat down to good
breakfasts of hot cakes and chicken hash or fried ham, with
pitchers of cold milk for the children, and fragrant coffee
steaming in silver pots. Then in the distance they heard
martial music. The children jumped up shouting, "Our men
are coming back!" "Wait," said the mothers, "wait and lis-
ten." Yes, there was no mistaking it. It was "The Star-
Spangled Banner" that the bands were playing. And the
Yankees came over the hill and camped in the orchard.

When the Federals marched in, only Ashby's men were
there to meet them, waiting on the southern side of town.
Ashby himself tarried the longest, sitting on his fine white
stallion where a broad street merged into open fields. The
Yankees recognized his charger and his plume, and two of
their troopers spurred after him. History says they did not

catch him. Legend, which his men had no trouble in believing, says that he waited until they were almost upon him, shot one, swept the other off his horse, carried him a little way down the Valley Pike, and dropped him sprawling, waved the plumed hat and thundered off.

> If you want to have a good time
> Jine the cavalry!
> Bully boys, hey!

The newly arrived army wore crisp blue uniforms very different from the homespun and individualistic headgear which had just departed, but these too were American boys from no very distant states. Most of them had been raised on farms not unlike farms in the Valley. They were full of that general promiscuous good will which characterizes the American. One of them dropped his hand on the curly tow head of a three-year-old sitting on a doorstep.

"Howdy do, bub."

"Take your hand off my head. You are a Yankee."

The soldier frowned, but there was not much he could do about it. Nor could he do anything more than whistle when the girls swept their hoop skirts aside to avoid contamination as he passed.

"Why do southern ladies always look so sour?"

"Why should they look glad to see you when they wish you were drowned in the sea?"

In front of one encampment, three little boys were playing soldier. Two sided against one, but the one was always victorious. Finally a Federal asked the question for which the little boys were angling.

"Why do the two of you always let one boy make you run?"

"Oh, we *have* to run. We are the Yankees."

Well—it was a pity, but the troops were there with a job to do and they must stay, so they made themselves as comfortable as possible. Poor Mrs. Seever, that meticulous housekeeper, had to move out for General Banks and turn her home over to his bodyguard of Zouaves, offensively fine in red trousers, white gaiters, and red fezzes. Senator Mason's visitors were from Massachusetts, and a United States flag floated over him. Colonel Candee of the 66th Ohio, all gold lace and epaulets, presented his compliments to Mrs. Mc-Donald and hoped that she had no objections to his seeing her rooms. She replied that as she had eight children of whom three were ill, she had great objections but did not suppose she could prevent it. She meant to sound proud and unbending, but found that she was weeping tears of rage.

Colonel Candee tried to be agreeable. He had the kindness to remove the Stars and Stripes from the doorway at the family's request so that they might enter without walking under it. His soldiers were not really hard on anything except chickens, although they chopped down one of the best shade trees for firewood and milked the cows every morning before the Negroes could get to them. Colonel Candee set one of the milkers astride a barrel on the lawn until the kind-hearted Mrs. McDonald was forced to beg for his release. Major Wilkins, the second in command, offered to take letters down the Valley to her husband and five stepsons in Jackson's army and send them through under a flag of truce. She wrote them and he sealed them in her presence. She was obliged to thank him for the risk he ran of losing his commission through his kindness, but pride forced her to add condescendingly, "Don't hesitate to come to me if ever you need help."

The people of this occupied territory were still proud, unpacified, and indignant. Their houses were subject to search or seizure, their chickens disappeared, sometimes a horse was stolen. "When we had a closer acquaintance with war, we wondered how such things could have disturbed us so much." Their animosity displeased the Yankees, and a Union paper exulted: "The traitor Jackson is fleeing up the Valley with Banks in hot pursuit. The arch rebel suffers not the grass to grow under his flying feet. There is perfect confidence in his speedy downfall." Yet in spite of these attitudes of conqueror and unconquered, one fear gnawed every heart. The citizens and the northern army waited together, sharpening their tongues on each other, with one question unspoken in hostile company yet ever in the mind. "Where is Jackson? What is he doing?" It was not long before they had an answer.

When the cautious General Banks discovered in Winchester how few men Jackson had, he sent General Shields with 11,000 to catch him, and prepared to withdraw his main body to Washington. McClellan was transporting his forces by water to the Peninsula near Richmond, and Banks was to protect the capital. When Shields moved, Jackson fell back forty miles to Mount Jackson, where he made a stand, but the pursuit was not pressed. On March 21st Ashby reported that Banks had begun to send his wagons eastward and that Shields was withdrawing to take his place in Winchester. Then Jackson moved.

On the twenty-second the Army of the Valley marched twenty-two miles. On the morning of Sunday the 23rd they rose at dawn and marched fourteen more. This brought them to Kernstown, a village four miles south of Winchester, by one o'clock. Ashby was there before them, skirmishing with the Federals. Jackson ordered a bivouac while he surveyed the situation.

The Yankees stretched over the gently rolling ridges on either side of the Valley Pike. Between the enemies lay freshly plowed fields, wet from the spring thawing, fenced with rails and a few stone walls. They could see each other plainly, and Jackson believed that he had all the enemy in view - and that if he waited reinforcements might come up. At half past three he gave the order to attack. But for once Ashby had been mistaken in his information, and the main body of Shields' corps was lying concealed in the woods beyond the fields.

Jackson sent most of his weary little army around the Federal flank by a wagon track while Ashby kept charging at their front. Within fifteen minutes.. through the worst the guns could do, the gray soldiers had seized the ridge. Then suddenly a roar of musketry burst in their faces, and the hidden Union regiments leapt out of hiding.

The Confederates raced back to a stone wall, reached it in time, and stood fast behind it, mowing down the Federal ranks as they came up. Jackson hurried each of his companies into the firing line as soon as they arrived, but his men were fighting twice their number and their ammuntion was beginning to give out. One fifth of them fell dead or wounded. Jackson, galloping across the field like a battle cloud, trying to be everywhere at once, saw with astonishment his Stonewall Brigade in retreat. Their general, Garnett, had given the order on his own responsibility.

Jackson thundered over to Garnett and ordered him to stand his ground. He grasped a startled drummer boy by the shoulder and whirled him around. "Beat the rally! Beat the rally!" Frozen by the general's clutch in a hail of bullets, the boy rolled his drums as never before, but it was too late. The encouraged Federals pressed on in force, and the Confederates retired slowly, firing as they went. Jackson dashed back to hurry reinforcements but found that they had been halted ten miles in the rear. There was nothing for it but to count the day lost, and to retire in as good order as posible.

Twilight fell. The 5th Virginia made its last stand in a walled lane near the Pike and the pursuing cavalry dared not charge them in the darkness. In good order and without pursuit, the Army of the Valley withdrew three miles to Newtown, where the exhausted men dropped on the cold ground and slept without waiting to unroll their blankets or draw their rations.

Through the night lumbered the wagons of Dr. McGuire, carrying the wounded to the rear. Over the deserted battlefield a small chill rain began to fall. The little boys of Winchester, who had run away to watch the battle when they first heard the guns, would have lingered to help the wounded, but the Federal sentinels sent them home. The lanterns of the Union ambulance bearers wavered over the field all night, and the wind sighed through the sedge grass. At Newtown, one after another of Jackson's weary soldiers was wakened by a light hand on his shoulder and the soft voice of a Negro body servant, gentle, apologetic, persistent as the rain, wandering from one row to another, searching the darkness.

"Marse John, is you see Marse Charlie?—Excuse me, suh, but is you see Marse Charlie? Oh Lawd, Lawd! Isn't anybody seen Marse Charlie?"

Not until after the Federal casualties had been cared for could the people of Winchester make their pilgrimage to the bloodstained fields near Kernstown. The slow procession wound up the Pike on foot and in every conceivable conveyance. If a family had a man left at home, he undertook this duty; if not, the women went alone to find their dead and wounded.

The churches, the banks, the courthouse were turned into hospitals. On the courthouse porch lay rows of dead men with papers pinned to them telling who they had been. Like bundles of blue cloth they lay, with the capes of their overcoats turned back over their faces, and only their hands gave them identity. Workworn and calloused, smooth and frail, old and young, their mute and motionless hands spoke for them. "This we did, and now our work is done."

Inside, the floor of every high square room was covered with the groaning bloody wounded. Mrs. McDonald walked between them, followed by a servant with a pitcher of lemonade. She had meant to give it only to Confederates, but one pair of Federal eyes entreated her so pitifully that she stopped, and since he could not hold up his head, gave him some with a tablespoon. "It is a beautiful drink for a thirsty man," he said, and his eyes followed her as he moved on. By the time she passed again his head was thrown back in the rasping death struggle, and later still she saw them carry out his corpse.

In another room she found Confederates and asked the surgeon if she could help. Bloody, busy as a butcher, he motioned her to a man who had had both eyes and the bridge of his nose plowed out by a minie ball. "If you will wash that out I think I can save him. The brain is not touched." The boy heard them, and spoke out of his endless darkness, putting a finger to his temple. "Oh, if only they had hit me here, I should have troubled no one."

Mrs. McDonald tried to answer cheerfully, tried to begin work, but when she looked at the eyeless face she turned faint and had to stagger to the door. On the way her full skirt caught against a stack of arms and legs thrown together for disposal. Another neighbor finished where she had failed.

When she recovered and went back to the wounded, she found among them an acquaintance, a Mr. Townes. He informed her that he would never see his wife in Missouri again as he was going to die. The surgeon had warned him, as the custom was, so that he might have time to prepare himself. He would have liked to hear some church prayers read, but this was impossible because they had no prayerbook, and because at the end of the room on two deal tables covered with bloody sheets the surgeons without antisepsis or anesthetics continued their terrible work of hacking off arms and legs. The cries of the wounded, the hurried breathing, the saw grating through bone, the orderlies rushing past with a limb and running back for more, shattered an atmosphere of quiet piety. Instead the two friends talked cheerfully for a moment, in the formal phrases to which they had been educated.

"When you see your husband," said Mr. Townes, "do be good enough to remember me to him, and give him my warm regards."

By next afternoon the courthouse was empty, and a brightly painted banner over the door announced: "Theater Tonight!" Enough had died to make the extra accommodation unnecessary, the blood had been scoured from the floors. The soldiers must be amused. Secretary Seward arrived to celebrate the victory, and they held a great review during which the bands played both "Hail Columbia" and "Dixie." In spite of this gesture of conciliation, a Yankee who had letters to some of his father's friends was not received.

A long April and a long May passed over Winchester. The Blue soldiers came and went, the people waited for news and heard nothing. Where was Jackson? Where was the Army of the Shenandoah? Where were the Valley men? Colonel Candee was ordered up the Valley and his hostess, sarcastically gracious, invited him to stop on his way back "if you have time." The colonel flushed angrily. "Madam, Jackson is now pushed to extremity and three columns are converging to crush him." When he was out of sight Mrs. McDonald allowed herself to cry and to regret her impudence, but soon her spirits rose at being once more mistress in her own home.

And again spring came. What man had destroyed, grass and the rain made new. The soft blades laid a tender velvet over the scars, bloom frosted the mock orange and syringa, and the freshly trimmed drive shone under the dark cedars. One afternoon she stood at her window quietly enjoying it when the large gate opened and troop after troop of cavalry came in.

It was the last look of beauty that scene ever wore . . . Fifteen hundred horsemen camped before the house, tied their horses to trees, poured out corn for them to eat, tore off the ornamental railing from the stone wall to kindle their fires, drove in their wagons, and made themselves at home. In half an hour the green lawn was a sea of mud.

She locked her doors and forbade the servants to answer a knock, but when the pounding became too importunate she opened them herself. The Yankees brought in a young Captain Pratt whose horse had thrown him on the way to the stable and broken his leg. She directed them to lay him on a sofa in the dining room, "for fear he would be too comfortable upstairs." Once the Yankees were in they took possession. Since it was imposible to get supper, she gathered her children and retired, making sure that her two oldest boys, Harry and Allan, were in their room for fear they would talk themselves into trouble.

When she came down in the morning her house was unrecognizable, for coats, saddles, and equipment were drying everywhere and the colors on the carpets had disappeared under the mud. In the dining room Captain Pratt's lounge had been drawn close to the fire, and the men who were sitting with him neither moved nor spoke as she came in. One was drying a dripping greatcoat over a chair, and another was placidly scraping the mud from his boots onto her best rug. She took the coat, threw it out on the porch, turned the chair and sat down in it. One by one the men left the room, and Pratt murmured palely that he regretted the inconvenience.

Having cleared the dining room, she forced her way through a crowd of soldiers into the kitchen, where she found the cook, "Aunt Winnie," backed into a corner, scared almost white and ready to cry. She insisted that they make room for her, and in an hour or so had breakfast ready for her family, her eight children and her stepdaughter Mary who had come from Charles Town with three more, "to get away from the Yankees." Poor Mary moved many times during the war, and never found a place to which the Yankees did not come. She went to Winchester, and the Yankees came there. She went to Lexington, and the Yankees came there. She went to Richmond, and the Yankees came there too. She was like the gentleman who moved his family away from Manasssas in the July of 1861—moved them to a safe place called Appomattox.

But on this damp spring morning Mary did not know what was ahead of her, and when she poured the fragrant steaming coffee it seemed too cruel not to give some to poor pale Captain Pratt. Once the ice was broken, he made himself very agreeable and in a few days was quite a member of the family and especially fond of little Donald, who was four. When he showed Mrs. McDonald his gold-mounted pistols, Donald objected anxiously: "Be careful, mama. You might shoot Captain Pratt."

"Don't you think I ought to shoot him? He is a Yankee."

Donald gave his new idol a long sad glance of disillusionment, and breathed a heavy sigh. "Well, shoot him then."

But Captain Pratt got well and rode away as many had done and were to do. He offered his hostess a bank note, which she pointedly ignored although she graciously shook hands. "If I had known then how much more efficacious a

United States bank note was than a stock of lofty pride, I would have thrown away the latter, and accepted the former." That was a later wisdom, and these were early days, when pride still had a value, no matter how numerous or well equipped the Yankees. Still they kept pouring through the town, and still Jackson was lost in an impenetrable silence laced with terrifying rumors. How could he stand against so many? The people of the lower Valley had a high faith, but they began to feel as had John Casler when he looked down from Henry Hill at First Manassas and saw all the distant meadows blue with Union troops.

"My God, have we still got all them to fight?"

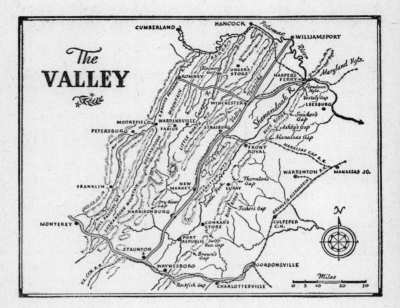

16. Valley Campaign 1

If I can deceive my friends I can be sure of deceiving the enemy.

—T. J. JACKSON

ON THE NIGHT after Kernstown, General Jackson, wrapped in his long coat, stood in the slow chill rain turning the embers of a campfire with the toe of his boot. His men had that day marched fourteen miles and fought a battle. The general himself had eaten nothing since "earliest dawn," and his aide went off to borrow bread and meat for him from the soldiers, and to make a bed of rails. One of Ashby's youngest and brashest troopers dared to disturb his reflections.

"General, the Yankees don't seem to want to leave Winchester."

"Winchester is a very pleasant place to stay in, sir."

"It was reported they are retreating, but it looks like they are retreating after us."

"I think I may say I am satisfied, sir."

The course of the war immediately after Kernstown showed that from a military point of view General Jackson had reason for his satisfaction. General Shields was convinced that Jackson would not have ventured so boldly if he had not had a large force ready to reinforce him. President Lincoln fell a prey to new fears for the safety of Washington. Banks hastily reversed his eastward march, and returned to the Valley. Thus McClellan, on the eve of attacking Richmond, found his army reduced by 50,000 men and his operations suspended. All this Stonewall Jackson had accomplished with an effective force of about 3,500, of whom he had lost a fourth.

The Confederate Congress passed a resolution thanking him. Jackson court-martialed Garnett for ordering a retreat without instructions and relieved him of command. Although his men had been out of ammunition they still had their bayonets, and there was no place in Jackson's army for generals who thought themselves defeated. General Banks dashed back to Winchester, and began writing dispatches.

March 24: Jackson's 15,000 have been cut up and demoralized.

March 25: Reported by Rebel Jackson's aide (a prisoner), that they were assured of reinforcements to the number of 30,000, but don't credit it.

March 26: The enemy is broken, but will rally.

March 27: No reinforcements yet. We will press them further and quickly.

By the twenty-ninth, McClellan grew weary of dispatches, and ordered Banks to drive Jackson from the Valley.

"Deficiency in ammunition detains us here," Banks replied. "Expect it hourly, when we shall push Jackson sharply." On April 2nd he actually moved as far as Woodstock, where he again came to rest. His troops were charmed with the scenery, the gently swelling fields, the budding trees, the high blue wall of mountains, the quiet flowing of the silver river. Early April was warm and sunny. The peach trees blossomed.

General Jackson, cut off from his "war home" by a wall of Yankees, rested on Rude's Hill, read the Bible, sucked at his favorite fruit, the lemon, and reorganized his army. The soldiers who had thought him crazy when he marched out of Winchester and then marched back to attack with a re- duced force, began to revise their opinion. General Winder replaced General Garnett in command of the Stonewall Brigade. The men had liked Garnett and did not like Winder, who introduced bucking and gagging, stringing up by the thumbs, and other unpopular punishments. The Brigade sulked, and for as much as three weeks Jackson was allowed to ride past it without a cheer. Nevertheless, recruits poured in, and the army increased to 6,000. The militia, that curse of early American wars, were mustered into the regular forces, at which some of them ran away, thinking it certain death to belong to the Stonewall Brigade. In the midst of great activity, General Jackson found time to write to Deacon Jackson's wife.

You appear greatly concerned at my attacking on Sunday. I am greatly concerned too; but I felt it my duty to do it, in consideration of the ruinous effects that might result from postpon- ing the battle until the morning . . . Arms is a profession that, if its principles are adhered to, requires an officer to do what he fears may be wrong, and the fact of its being necessary to success . . . suggests that it must be right.

The General spoke hopefully of a return to civil life, and hoped that his Heavenly Father would not place him in such a position again. But from then on if he needed another Sunday battle he fought it without hesitation. He might be a casuistical reasoner when it came to making peace with his wife and his conscience, but he was an excellent general.

When Banks at last advanced on April 17th, Jackson fell back twenty-six miles farther, to the mountains near Harrisonburg. Ashby as usual screened his retreat, and Henry Douglas of his staff was left behind to maintain communications. Douglas looked down from Rude's Hill at the lush bottoms and the curving river, and presently saw a column of Federal cavalry led by a galloping officer on a white charger. While he was admiring the horsemanship of the leader the pistols of the men began to spit white clouds, and he realized that he was watching Ashby head his pursuit as usual. At the bridge Ashby reined in to set fire to the combustibles which had been placed there, but two of the Union troopers reached him before he could succeed. One of them fired at close quarters and wounded the horse. Ashby cut him down with a sword stroke, the white stallion bounded up the hill, and the Federals saw the battery on the top and forbore to follow. The great white horse plunged on as though it understood the danger, and did not fall until it reached the Confederates. Then Ashby knelt beside it stroking its mane and looking into its eyes until it died. "Thus the most splendid horseman I ever knew lost the most beautiful warhorse I ever saw."

The new camp at Conrad's Store, a crossroads near Swift Run Gap, was a bad camp and the soldiers cursed it during the two weeks they spent there. It snowed and rained and snowed again, their shelters were flooded, and they slept half covered with water. A staff officer, resting his feet on a log to keep them out of the mud, wrote home despairingly: "As sure as you and I live, Jackson is a cracked man, and the sequel will show it." A shivering soldier, cursing the general and all his works, was startled to hear a deep and gentle voice behind him.

"It's for your own good, sir," said Jackson, and passed on.

At this camp Jackson completed the reorganization of his army under the new Conscription Act, and drove a small party of deserters who had not wanted to reënlist out of the mountains by gunfire. Officers were elected for a last time, after which they were to be appointed for merit only. Discipline was tightened, and even Ashby fell under Jackson's displeasure—even Ashby, the darling of the Valley, whose bright young men were like the ace pilots of later wars.

Ashby had twenty-two companies by this time, bound to him by their worship of his daring rather than by regulations. They had fought the enemy twenty-eight times in the month past, they had been unsurpassable as scouts, screen, and rearguard, but they were badly out of hand. When some of them got drunk instead of fighting, when others took French leave in the mountains for ten days, General Jackson divided them up and apportioned them among his other brigades. Ashby, virtually deprived of command, prepared to resign. The subordinate generals hastened to mediate and Jackson at last became convinced that "if I persisted in my attempt to increase the efficiency of the cavalry it would produce the opposite effect, as Colonel Ashby's influence, who is very popular with his men, would be thrown against me." Ashby got his troopers back.

Ashby was a star, glittering, intractable, not to be swung into any orbit but his own. The irresistible force had almost met the immovable body, but now the parabolas of the planet and the star interlocked without colliding, and gave new luster to each other by their independent shining.

If Jackson had a plan, he confided it to no one. His uncomfortable position was strategically sound, for from Conrad's Store he might cross the Blue Ridge and join Ewell in eastern Virginia or he might re-enter the Valley by one of three roads—at the southern end of Massanutten, over the pass from Luray to Newmarket, or down the Luray valley and around the northern end. Aware of Frémont across the Alleghenies, and slowly coming down on Staunton, aware of Banks strung out between Harrisonburg and Strasburg, aware of Shields at Front Royal, he waited to see what the three of them intended to do next.

On the day he had reached Harrisonburg, at about sundown in a driving rain, Jackson had sent for Henry Douglas and calmly ordered him to take a message to General Ewell one hundred miles away on the other side of the Blue Ridge. Douglas, who had already ridden twenty-five miles that day, replied that he would start as soon as he could borrow a fresh horse from another officer. "Good night," said the general politely in the dripping darkness, "and a pleasant ride."

Twenty hours later, Douglas handed his water-soaked and crumpled papers to General Ewell, and collapsed. He had skirted Massanutten, crossed the Blue Ridge, worn out three horses, and rushed like a calvary charge for one hundred and five miles through rain and mud and impenetrable night. After twenty-four hours in bed he did it all over again, picking up each horse where he had left it. He found Jackson asleep on the floor in an empty room near Swift Run Gap, aroused him, and reported.

"Very good," said the laconic general. "You got there in time. Good night."

The young officer went away inconsolable at so cool a reception of a considerable effort, and began to see what life was on the staff of a general who "never found anything impossible." But a promotion next day comforted him. Small, bald, brave, testy General Ewell also began to discover what it meant to serve with Stonewall. On the seventeenth he was ordered to Swift Run Gap, on the eighteenth to Fisher's Gap twenty miles north, on the nineteenth to Harrisonburg, on the twentieth to remain east of the Blue Ridge. As each time he prepared uncomplainingly to obey, he began to doubt Jackson's sanity.

General Banks also was bewildered. Unable to penetrate Ashby's screen of patrols, for two weeks he reported to Washington only "Ashby is here." On April 30th he sent word that Jackson had crossed the Blue Ridge and abandoned the Valley, and that since he had nothing more to do, he would like to go and support McClellan. "Such an order would electrify my force."

It was, however, General Jackson who electrified the force. On April 30th he ordered Ewell to come through

Swift Run Gap and occupy the camp at Conrad's Store so long as Banks was in the Valley. He sent Ashby to annoy Banks as if reconnoitering as usual rather than screening a move. Then for no reason that anyone could see, he dragged the remainder of his army over sixteen miles of the most bottomless road in Virginia, to the village of Port Republic. The road was so abysmal after two solid weeks of rain that it took even Jackson's army two days to cover sixteen miles, and every man from the general down had to lift and push and pull the wagons through the mud. As soon as they arrived, they promptly swung back toward the mountains and went through Brown's Gap. Now the army knew that their general was crazy, for they had camped only twelve miles from this spot three days before, near a good hard road which would have taken them there.

"Always mystify, mislead, and surprise the enemy," Jackson said.

At the eastern foot of the mountains the soldiers climbed aboard trains. Now they knew that they were going to defend Richmond. *But the trains went back to Staunton.*

The unprotected citizens of Staunton, fearfully waiting for the invader to attack them from north or west, were overjoyed when their unexpected defenders rolled into town on Sunday, May 4th. Jackson picketed the roads in the direction of Harrisonburg so strictly that even the country people who had come in to church could not go home. The town could not understand all this, but it gave itself up to feasting the footsore and dirty veterans, and the veterans enjoyed it, although they grumbled a little when the ladies petted the spruce and pink-cheeked V.M.I. cadets who joined them there. "Most of the starch was taken out of them a few days later," said the veterans. But now a disturbing rumor began to circulate that Jackson did not intend to remain and defend the town. A deputation of prominent citizens waited upon him to discover the truth of it. Jackson called their leader into private conference.

"Judge Baldwin, can you keep a secret?"

"Certainly, general. Certainly."

"Well, so can I."

On Tuesday the Army of the Valley marched out of Staunton to the west. Again they climbed a mountain range, this time the Alleghenies. When they had carried their knapsacks for twenty miles they were ordered to pile them in a village street and to advance on the double. Now they knew that Old Jack had work for them to do, and the knowledge stimulated them. After a march of twenty-six miles, they found a small Confederate force under "Allegheny Johnson" engaging the troops of Milroy, one of Frémont's generals, on the craggy mountain slopes around the village of McDowell.

This was the battle where they set the woods on fire, where even the dark laurel thickets burst into sheets of flame. Both sides fought without artillery support. The Rebels held the mountaintops, and the Yankees from Ohio and West Virginia clambered up like wildcats, were thrown back, clambered up again. They had an unfavorable position and they were outnumbered. Jackson marched each weary brigade straight into the battle as soon as it arrived, and the constant reinforcements proved overwhelming. Night fell, and under cover of darkness the Union army withdrew in perfect order.

Jackson remained on the field until the stretcher bearers finished sliding down the mountain with the wounded, then went to a near-by farmhouse and flung himself down without removing his sword or his boots. His Negro Jim tried to feed him. "I want nothing. Nothing but sleep."

Next day and for three days more he pursued the Federals through the burning woods, then rested his army half a day and held a service of thanksgiving to the God of Battles. Whenever his men missed a Sunday at church due to military necessity, "Old Bluelight" tried to make it up during the week, and in this manner during a busy season he sometimes celebrated three Sundays in a row. The victory justified his strategy. Of the three columns opposing him he had selected and overcome the weakest. He took time to write a terse report. "God blessed our arms with victory at McDowell yesterday."

General Ewell, left with the barest of orders, left without a sight of the general whom he had come to support, sat in the dripping camp at Swift Run Gap and fumed—and did not care who knew it. He wrote his cousin:

> I have spent two weeks here of the most unhappy I ever remember. I was ordered here to support General Jackson, pressed by Banks. But he immediately upon my arrival, started on a long chase after a body of the enemy far above Staunton. I have been keeping one eye on Banks, one on Jackson, all the time jogged up from Richmond, until I am sick and worn down.

To a Colonel Walker who had once been a cadet under Jackson at V.M.I. he stormed: "I tell you, sir, he is as crazy as a March hare. He has gone away, I don't know where, and left me with instructions to stay until he returns, but Banks' whole army is advancing on me, and I have not the most remote idea where to communicate with General Jackson. I tell you, sir, he is crazy, and I will just march my division away from here. I do not intend to have it cut to pieces at the behest of a crazy man." A little later Ewell called Ashby away from his harassing of the Yankees at Harrisonburg. "I've been in hell for three days, in hell for three days, Colonel Ashby! What's the news from Jackson?"

On April 14th, however, a courier brought encouragement. Jackson had started back to the Valley and Ewell might attack Banks. This was welcome news, but before Ewell could act, the supreme command suddenly ordered him to return to Richmond. He got in the saddle and rode a day and a night to tell Jackson what had happened. It was a heavy disappointment.

"Then Providence denies me the privilege of striking a decisive blow for my country," Jackson said, "and I must be satisfied with the humble task of hiding my little army among these mountains to watch a superior force."

Ewell, who in an age of faith made no secret of his agnosticism, did not see what Providence had to do with it, but as he listened to the man whom he had called "that enthusiastic fanatic" he began to see something in him. He agreed that a blow at Winchester and a threat to Washington would disturb President Lincoln more than a few additional thousands in the vastly outnumbered garrison at Richmond, and he bravely decided to risk his military career by delaying until Jackson could telegraph Lee and receive a reply. When a favorable reply came back the two generals began a working partnership which was to prove eminently successful.

In military matters, Ewell suited Stonewall perfectly. A brisk small birdlike man with a weak stomach, he had the same courage, the same love of action, the same coolness under fire. He arrived at his positions on time. "The road to glory cannot be travelled with much baggage," he said, and he marched his troops without equipment save for food and ammunition. When he had been with the "Bluelight Elder" in several engagements he was heard to remark: "If that be religion, I must have it."

His command joined Jackson's at Harrisonburg on the evening of May twentieth after three long marches. General Taylor's Louisianians, French Creoles who marched to waltz time, wheeled into camp as jauntily as if they were on parade, and Taylor found his new commander sitting on a fence sucking a lemon. "How far have you come today?" asked Jackson in a low and gentle voice. "Six and twenty miles." "You seem to have no stragglers." "I never allow straggling, general." "You must teach my men, they straggle badly." Taylor bowed. Just then a regimental band started another waltz, and the men began to dance. Jackson took a contemplative suck at his lemon.

"Thoughtless fellows for serious work," he said.

Next day in the gray of morning, General Jackson's "earliest dawn," the Army of the Valley moved north, seventeen thousand strong. For the first time Stonewall commanded a considerable force, and at once he put their faith in him to a severe test. Instead of going up the Pike to attack Banks at Strasburg, they swung right, crossed Massanutten, and vanished without a word of explanation into the Luray valley. Taylor's men had made three forced marches to come from that very region, and they saw no sense in the maneuver.

If Jackson's friends were confused, the enemy was more notably so. McDowell reported from the Rappahannock that Jackson was in front of him. Schenck in the Alleghenies said that Jackson was in his rear. Frémont, from West Virginia, reported that Jackson was going west. Banks felt comfortably sure that he was still in Harrisonburg. President Lincoln dryly remarked that when a force got that badly strung out, it should be possible to hit it somewhere in the middle and cut it in two.

On May twenty-second, Banks wrote a placid dispatch to the President. "I regard it as certain that Jackson will move north as far as New Market . . . He is obstinate in his intention to defend the Valley, but I see no cause for immediate alarm." In the light of this conclusion, Banks decided that Shields should leave a garrison of only two thousand at Front Royal, and with the rest of his men join McDowell at Fredericksburg in time for a grand review, the prelude to the springing of the trap which was to crush the Confederacy.

On that night, ten miles from Front Royal, within striking distance of the Valley Pike, Jackson was camping in the Federal rear.

17. Valley Campaign II

By the blessing of Providence and the vigorous use of the bayonet.

—T. J. JACKSON

BEHIND the Federal lines in the little village of Front Royal, the citizens had adjusted themselves as best they could to the occupation. Young Tommy Ashby, cousin of the colonel, made such friends with the officers that one of them gave him a silver watch, and the family cook, "Aunt Susan," sold so many cakes and pies that after the war she bought herself a house.

Young Emma Cassandra Reilly, whose mother had died in the scarlet fever epidemic, spent an exciting summer with Front Royal relatives, dressed throughout in the black wool serge, coal-scuttle bonnet, and congress gaiters which she had procured as mourning. Fourteen-year-olds are resilient, and it must not be supposed that "our boys" did not come home to visit just because the Yankees were in town. Emma Cassandra and her cousin hid John Lionberger in the attic until the servants reported the trays they carried up. Then John put on his sister's clothes, crossed a street filled with guards, reached his own house, and there crawled under the mattress of his sister's bed, piling pillows around himself to level it off, while she climbed on top with a calico wrapper over her underwear and wet cabbage leaves tied round her head, playing sick. The Yankees did not find him that time, for the girls smuggled word to Gilmore's cavalry to come and make a diversion, and John escaped in the confusion. When Emma Cassandra bragged about it afterward, the Yankees threatened to burn Mr. Lionberger's house, but he pleaded ignorance and begged off.

Emma Cassandra in her hot black serge was not the only young lady to find Front Royal exciting, for here we have our friend Belle Boyd again. Reminiscing neighbors have scoffed at Miss Belle's achievements and called her "an unreliable flirt," but there is no doubt that this was Miss Belle's war and that she made the most of it.

As spring activity approached, Mr. Boyd, who felt that his little Belle attracted too much attention, sent her away from the Yankees in Martinsburg to her aunt at Front Royal. It was a joke on the old gentleman (of forty-one) that Front Royal was captured a week after she arrived there. General Shields himself took her aunt's house as his headquarters while the family moved into a cottage in the yard. Before long Belle made friends with the general, whose Irish wit she enjoyed, and at least one of his staff tried to marry her. Belle says she did not care much for this officer's flowers and pretty speeches, but she did like the information he sometimes let slip, and this she smuggled out by her regular "underground" —an old Negro with a silver watch out of which the works had been taken to make room for messages written on tissue paper.

According to Belle's story, it was she who told Ashby that Shields was going to Kernstown. She listened to a council of war by laying her ear to a hole which opportunely happened to be in the closet floor of a room above. In the darkness of midnight, she saddled a horse by herself, and galloped off to the mountains where she knew that Ashby was staying with a friend. Twice she was stopped by sentries, but she had thoughtfully provided herself with passes issued to exchanged Confederate soldiers, and she got through. Why the sentries thought a soldier's pass fitted a young lady riding alone at night—a circumstance which might well have attracted attention in that part of the world—only Miss Belle could have explained, and she has not done so.

When she arrived at her friend's home, she pounded on the door until the friend came down and admitted her with the inevitable reaction: "Good God, Belle! What are you doing here?"

Then Ashby himself made his appearance, fully clothed. An hour away from the Federals, Ashby did not remove anything except his boots.

"Good God, Miss Belle! You here?"

Belle delivered her information, and galloped back to her aunt's "before Aurora peeped over the horizon."

After the battle, it took only a few weeks of inactivity to convince Belle that she and her cousin Alice ought to visit Winchester, chaperoned by the little Negro maid whom we have met before (still nameless). Young ladies did not travel without their servants in those times, unless between two and six in the morning. It cost Belle little effort to get a pass out of young Lieutenant Hamilton, who happened to be in charge because a superior officer had gone hunting, and when he offered himself as an escort, that was better still.

They spent a happy evening with friends in Winchester, and started back next morning, not without having picked up some letters to smuggle through. There was an important packet which Belle hid on her maid, who as "intelligent contraband" was assumed to be on the Federal side, and so would not be searched. There was a vital note for General Jackson, which Belle carried in her own hand. There was a less important packet which she placed in a little basket, and inscribed "Kindness of Lt. Hamilton." What girlish whimsey induced her to put that on it, she could not say.

A bunch of flowers to Colonel Fillebrowne, in charge of Winchester, procured a pass and some pretty compliments, and off they set, still under the gallant guard of Lieutenant Hamilton. But a servant had reported seeing Belle accept the letters, and much to her dismay she was suddenly placed under arrest and brought into the not very cordial presence of the commanding general. Asked if she had any letters, she thought it best to hand over the basket immediately.

The general was considerably startled to see Lieutenant Hamilton's name on the wrapping, and still more startled when another package, similarly inscribed, was found in the lieutenant's coat pocket, which proved to be a red-hot southern newspaper, banned behind the northern lines. The general roared at the lieutenant, while Miss Belle, a picture of pretty confusion, protested vainly that it was just a girlish prank and the officer had not had a thing to do with it, indeed he had not. The general was so furious with Hamilton that he let the young ladies go without further inquiry, and the important messages were safe. Belle felt a sincere regret when she later heard that the lieutenant had been dismissed from the service, for the unfair old general should not have blamed him for what was really her fault.

She slept sweetly in Front Royal that night, and woke next morning to real excitement, for Jackson was coming, and the Yankees were getting ready to leave. She decided at once to take her message to the general in person, and ran out, tarrying only long enough to lock the correspondent of the New York *Herald* in his room where he was packing hastily. (Definitely not a gentleman, he had plagued her with his attentions for a month.)

Most of the women of Front Royal were down on their knees, sobbing with joy and calling down blessings on their deliverers. But Miss Boyd (in a dark-blue dress with a white apron) was running past the Federal pickets who fired at her, running past the hospital where the wounded took a few shots, throwing herself on the ground when a shell burst near her, jumping up and running on.

She waved her sunbonnet at the first Confederate troops she saw, and told them to hurry and keep the Yankees from burning the bridges. Taylor's Louisianians did not need to be told twice. They charged, and General Jackson, riding not far behind, was surprised to see his soldiers running forward without orders. Henry Douglas at his side recognized the lady.

"Good God, Belle!" he cried inevitably. "You here?"

Belle gave her information, cautioned him not to mention her in the town, stood while the army rushed past her, then went back the way she had come. Next day the general sent her a letter saying that she had been "of inestimable service" to her country.

The Yankees ran, but they did not run fast enough. The Rebels killed or captured 904 out of the town's garrison of 1,063, and this with a loss of only fifty men.

At about noon that day, Charles Greenleaf of the 5th New York Cavalry was coming with his company and others to reinforce Front Royal, when they heard cannon, and dashed forward to find a few companies of their infantry "engaged with thousands of the enemy." Greenleaf's colonel ordered him to take a fast horse and carry the news back to General Banks. He found the main road already closed behind him, and had to make a detour of seventeen miles, which he covered in fifty-five minutes.

General Banks did not take the information seriously. Merely another cavalry raid. He had lately felt himself out of favor, and he would now show that he could not be stampeded into retreat. He ordered a regiment and battery to the scene, gave Greenleaf a fresh horse, and told him to rejoin his company. One of his subordinate generals, Gordon, urged that the stores and wounded be sent to Winchester.

"No," said Banks. "I must develop the strength of the enemy."

This phrase doubtless came out of a good military text-book, but it did not satisfy General Gordon, who continued to urge his point. Then Banks banged the table with his fist and shouted: "By God, sir, I will not retreat! We have more to fear, sir, from the opinions of our friends than from the bayonets of our enemies."

"That, sir, is not a military reason for occupying a false position," replied the professional soldier, and took his leave.

By then it was night, and the brightly lighted camp teemed with sutlers, strolling players, musicians. Gordon ordered the supplies of his own battalion to leave at once for Winchester, but the rest of the army continued to be gay. Charles Greenleaf, galloping back to his company on a fine fresh horse, found two men standing in the road about four miles on the Union side of Front Royal. Since they did not stop him, he asked if they were Federal pickets.

"No," said the soldiers, grinning.

"Who are you then?"

"Part of General Jackson's staff."

Greenleaf took this for a joke, and rode on until he met another quietly strolling soldier and asked him to what regiment he belonged. "Eighth Louisiania."

That was enough for Greenleaf. He turned, and with his heart in his mouth, rode as quietly as possible past the first two, who did not bother to stop him. By good luck he met no pickets. "When I got out of the enemy lines I rode as fast as my horse could carry me to General Banks and reported what I had seen. He said I had saved the army."

At seven on the morning of the twenty-fourth, Banks reported that Jackson was still in front of him on the Valley Pike, but by nine he had seen the light. He began to move, and in a hurry. The Rebels were actually two miles nearer Winchester than he, on their way from Front Royal, but they were advancing slowly. They had marched twenty-four miles the day before, and had fought a battle, and for once they had not started at dawn. Their general rode ahead of them. If he spoke at all it was to give the order which they came to associate with him above all others. "Press on, men. Press on. Close up, men. Close up." Skirmishing interrupted their progress, but by afternoon they came in view of the Valley Pike, and found it full of the dust of wagons and of marching men. The army of General Banks was falling back to Winchester.

Chew's Flying Battery poured shells into the wagon train. The Louisiana Tigers formed at the double behind a wall and fired into the Union cavalry until, in the words of Jackson's official report, "the road was literally obstructed with the mingled and confused mass of struggling and dying horses and riders." Ashby leapt a gate, charged the rear of the demoralized and flying cavalry, brought back a squad of prisoners singlehanded. Jackson reproved his rashness, but without heat. The Federal army had been cut in two. What next?

"Press on, men. Press on. Press the pursuit to Winchester."

But now the lack of discipline in Ashby's command made itself felt. His men, who should have driven the retreating enemy, scattered so widely that when assembly sounded barely fifty troopers gathered to the call. The rich temptation of the wagon train lured them to plunder instead of pursuit.

Still Jackson led his army down the Pike. Without lunch, without dinner. Darkness fell and brought no bivouac. Again the soldiers grumblingly thought that someone had forgotten to halt them. The general and his staff ignored the fire of the Federal rearguard. When a stone wall blossomed in the night with a crest of fire, some near-by cavalry broke and ran, and the general expressed himself.

"Shameful! Did you see anybody struck, sir? Did you see anybody struck? Surely they need not have run, at least until they were hurt."

The quartermaster found him and reported that the supply wagons had stuck in the mud on the Luray road.

"And the ammunition wagons?"

"We doubled teams on them and brought them through."

"Ah—" a sigh of relief.

"Never mind," said General Taylor, who liked jokes and did not share Jackson's indifference to food, "there are plenty of stores in Winchester, and the general has invited me to breakfast there tomorrow."

Jackson reached out in the darkness and touched him warningly on the arm. Never mention your objective.

On and on through the black spring night, scuffling, dragging, heads down, shoulders bowed. At about two o'clock an officer rode up to report that his men were falling beside the road, and that unless he could rest them they would be ineffective for the inevitable battle in the morning.

"I am obliged to sweat them tonight that I may save

their blood tomorrow. The line of hills below Winchester must not be occupied by the enemy."

But even Stonewall was at last obliged to order two hours of rest, two miles outside the town. The men dropped where they stood in the road, and slept. Jackson and Ashby tied their horses to a fence and paced to and fro, passing each other like silent sentinels, absorbed in their own thoughts. Before two hours had passed a faint gray tinged the black pool of the sky, and Jackson mounted to begin the day. He observed that in spite of every effort the Federal guns had had time to take up a position on the hill.

"General Taylor, can your brigade charge a battery?"

"It can try."

"Very good. Move it forward."

Five terse words of command to General Winder and the Stonewall Brigade.

"You must occupy that hill."

This was the battle, the screaming bloody conclusion toward which they had plodded through the warm and secret night. Here were the sloping fields, the dew-drenched meadows where blood must wash away the dew. General Jackson covered the field in the blazing absorption which consumed him during an engagement, ignoring the bullets as if they had been raindrops. The disposition of his troops was planned and executed with a mathematical clarity. The Louisianians stepped out briskly across a meadow sweet with clover, as the first rays of the morning sun reddened the points of their bayonets. They walked as quickly and easily as if they were on parade, and General Taylor rode ahead of them, sword in hand, turning now and then in his saddle to make sure that the line followed closely. And so they moved straight into the firing guns.

Charge and fire, fall and charge. Until at last the Yankees around the batteries wavered, then ran in panic down the hill. "Forward after the enemy!" shouted Jackson. "Tell the whole army to press forward to the Potomac!"

On Little Sorrel he bounded up to the ridge. Over the crest lay Winchester, and the general tore off his hat and

yelled like any private. "Very good!" he shouted, then re-
verting to his native idiom, "Let's holler!!"

The guns had brought the people to their doors and
windows. They saw the Federal batteries on the hill and the
slopes blue with Yankees. They saw a line of gray caps reach
the crest, with the battle flag floating over them. They saw
the Yankees break and run. They heard the Rebel yell, wide-
mouthed, exultant, tearing out of ten thousand throats.
Yai-ai-ai! Yai-ai-ai! Yai-ai-ai! They rushed out into the
streets, sobbing, cheering, tears streaming down their faces,
and saw their own army rushing past them!

The Yankees ran in complete confusion. "Never was
there such a chance for cavalry!" cried Jackson. "Oh, that
my cavalry were in place!" But the cavalry were missing. He
ordered the artillery to unhitch their horses and pursue bare-
back with the harness flapping around them, but it was soon
plain that the half-dead animals had nothing left. About five
miles north of Winchester Jackson ended the chase with bitter
regret.

It was a sunny quiet Sabbath evening, another Sunday
battle, but this time "Old Bluelight" did not apologize, for
Winchester was free. In three May weeks the Army of the
Valley had marched 170 miles, routed three armies, seized
supplies worth $125,185, accounted for a third of the enemy,
and had driven the Yankees across the Potomac—had driven
them *out of the Valley.*

General Jackson spent a quiet evening at Dr. Graham's
manse, ordered services to be held on Monday, wrote his wife,
and complained of his cavalry in his official report. Across
the Potomac, General Banks put the best possible face on
what he described as "a premeditated march of near sixty
miles in the face of the enemy, defeating his plans and giving
him battle wherever he was found . . . There were never
more grateful hearts in the same number of men than when
we stood on the opposite shore." Anything is right if you put
it right, thought Banks, but Washington did not share his
satisfaction in this strategic retreat. McDowell was immobi-
lized by an order to send half his force to the lower Valley,

Frémont and Shields were ordered to the upper Valley. Mc-Clellan was crippled again, and the militia of thirteen states was called to the defense of Washington. Banks' own soldiers wryly remarked that he was worth more to the Confederates alive than dead.

Only the ragged hungry Rebels had a good word for the defeated general, only they spoke praise of him. Affectionately they called him "Commissary Banks." They feasted in Winchester with unwonted richness on cake and pickled lobsters, cheese, canned peaches, piccolomini and candy, coffee, ale, and milk, and lauded his bountiful if somewhat exotic table. It would be a pity to have any of these good things recaptured, and the soldiers did their best, in spite of orders, to prevent such an accident. The whole army started turning blue in fine Union garments until an order from headquarters transposed it back to gray.

Five days they rested at Winchester, and only the more thoughtful among them wondered what would happen next. They were still surrounded by three Federal armies, all of which were being reinforced at top speed, each one of which outnumbered them. General Jackson's diversion had again saved Richmond, but what and who would save General Jackson?

The men did not find these reflections too depressing. They were learning what every soldier learns—that in war everything which is done has to be done over, for no battle is decisive except the final battle. Now, although they were surrounded by 60,000 troops, they talked less about the "crazy" general. A new spirit pervaded the Army of the Valley.

"Old Jack got us into this fix, and with the blessing of God he will get us out of it."

18. Valley Campaign III

Never take counsel of your fears.

—T. J. JACKSON

WINCHESTER, which was to change hands between sixty-eight and seventy-two times before the war ended, had a brief respite, a brief and busy interlude, when General Jackson took it from General Banks.

On the night of the twenty-fourth, Major Wilkins had "time to stop on the way back," and see Mrs. McDonald. He arrived in the darkness, weary and spent, with the news that his army was routed. Even though he risked capture, he could go no farther until he had rested, and as a regular army man he was disgusted with the management. Mrs. McDonald gave him a room upstairs, but with the dawn he heard the guns and left.

The suspense was brief. Dew had not dried before the bluecoats came pouring back over the ridge. Now they were really running, and that high wavering screech which split the air behind them was the Rebel yell. The laughing, weeping population of the town actually impeded the progress of their deliverers in the uncontrollable manifestation of their joy. It was a wild and glorious day, a day of triumph, of reunion, and of laying out the dead.

Mrs. Barton was handing food to the soldiers, like all the other housewives, when they brought in her oldest son, Marshall, a descendant of the chief justice. "Take him upstairs," she said. "He was born in that room, and there he shall lie." She gave away the rest of her provisions before she went up to sit beside his body.

Happy as most people were, they had to curb their hospitality; in the first place, food was not so plentiful as it had been and, in the second place, many of the "servants" had gone off with the Yankees. The McGuires' coachman, Nat, came back a few weeks later complaining that the Yankees made him work too hard, and cheerfully certain that his white folks would be glad to see him. Mrs. McDonald's Manuel disappeared with his wife Catherine and their two babies. After several days someone brought word that he was ill in a shack on the outskirts of town, and his mistress—who had been reared in a tradition of responsibility for her "people"—went to bring him home. When he recovered from his fright at seeing her, he begged her to look for Catherine, which she did, and found the girl sitting with her babies on the road to Harpers Ferry. They had not been able to keep up with their new protectors, and none of them had eaten for three days. With good meals and careful nursing from their mistress, they soon recovered, and Manuel was grateful, so grateful that the next time he had a chance to run off with the Yankees he and Catherine took the family horses and carriage along.

Far different was the case of Lethea, the children's nurse. She had proved her loyalty through successive occupations, she had nursed the youngest baby while it slowly died, she and her little girl were the constant companions of the two-year-old. But she was only rented, and her real owner decided to sell her South to prevent her going off with the Yankees when they came again.

For a week Mrs. McDonald protested in vain. She had not enough money to buy her, she could not reach her husband, and poor Lethea had to go, taking her little Margaret, and leaving another child behind. It was hard to tell her, to watch her humble submission, to see the slow and silent tears falling on her work-worn hands. And all the next day little Hunter called her from his cradle. "Edy, where are you? Margie, come here!"

General Jackson did not waste time resting in Winchester, but sent the Stonewall Brigade and others to make a demonstration toward Harpers Ferry in the teeth of the

Federal guns mounted on Maryland Heights—this by way of assuring President Lincoln that Washington was far from safe. "Quem Deus vult perdere primus dementat," murmured Colonel Crutchfield of Jackson's staff, but this time he smiled affectionately while he said it.

On the way back from Harpers Ferry, Jackson heard that Front Royal had been retaken. Colonel Conner, whom he had left in command, had evacuated without a fight, and would have lost his troops except that the men themselves had refused to obey his order to surrender, and evacuated under one of their captains. This meant that Shields and Frémont might be able to unite at Strasburg before Jackson could get there, for the Yankees had only eleven miles to go, and the Rebels, forty-four. Across the Potomac, Banks organized another attack. Jackson reached Winchester and sent for Colonel Conner.

"Colonel, how many men did you have killed?"

"None, sir."

"How many wounded?"

"None, general."

"Do you call that a fight? You are under arrest."

In this crisis, Jackson asked his friend A. R. Boteler to go to Richmond with a request for additional troops. With forty thousand men, he said, he could carry the war to the Susquehanna.

"What will you do, general, if they cut you off here?"

"Fall back on Maryland for reinforcements."

The retreat began. Before dawn the supply wagons started on another creaking and rumbling journey down the Valley Pike. Four thousand prisoners followed under guard, and then the army. Jackson sent word to the Stonewall Brigade at Harpers Ferry that he would try to wait for them, but if they could not come up in time they must take to the mountains and join him later. He himself did not leave Winchester until the last soldier had gone. On the march one of Ashby's young lieutenants rode up to him.

"General, are the troops going back?"

"Don't you see them going?"

"Are they *all* going?"

Jackson looked at him narrowly, and snapped: "Arrest that man as a spy!"

The poor young lieutenant almost fell from his horse, but Ashby got him off by explaining that he did not have much sense.

The army marched on, with a ten-minute rest every hour, and every man urged to lie down flat while he was resting. When they reached Strasburg, Frémont was only three miles to the west, and Ewell went to hold him back with skirmishing while the wagon train proceeded. At Strasburg the Stonewall Brigade caught up, after an all-night march of thirty-six miles—Jackson's foot cavalry indeed.

"Press on, men. Press on. Close up, men. Close up."

Through a hailstorm, with hailstones as big as walnuts, through a sudden bitter cold and driving rain. When one command was halted in exhaustion General Jackson arrived almost at once to ask the reason for it.

"It's impossible, general. The men can't do any more."

"Don't say it's impossible. Turn your command over to the next officer and let him try. If he can't do it, I'll get someone from the ranks."

Throughout another blustery night Taylor, Winder, and Ashby kept the enemy at bay behind them. Jackson burned the bridges below New Market so that Shields could not surprise him by coming across Massanutten. He burned the bridges behind him at Meem's Bottom, and the Shenandoah itself rose to his assistance, flooded twelve feet in four hours, and washed away the pontoons on which Frémont hoped to cross. It also flooded the Confederate camp, but this time the men did not curse the water as they lay in it, for it had stopped the enemy. The general had refused to take shelter in a house that night, and his staff considered him well punished for his obstinacy when they saw his hat and his belongings floating like boats on the stream which rushed through his tent. For the moment, The Army of the Valley had escaped. Jackson sent the sick to Staunton and established the rest of the force on high ground below Massanutten where they could watch both sides of the Valley between the vanished village of Cross Keys and Port Republic. He wrote to his wife:

The Federals endeavoured to get in my rear by moving on both flanks of my gallant army, but our God has been my guide and saved me from their grasp. . . . You must not expect long letters from me in such busy times, but always believe that your husband never forgets his little darling.

And now the soldiers had a respite of a day or two, while on the broad spreading meadows near Harrisonburg Ashby and his men kept the vanguard of the Federals "amused" and from time to time brought prisoners back to the main camp. Roberdeau Wheat of the Louisiana Tigers, perching on a rail fence, saw an old friend pass under guard. "Hello there, Percy!"—"Why, Bob!" It was the golden curled Sir Percy Wyndham, English gentleman adventurer, with whom Wheat had served under Garibaldi in Italy. That morning Wyndham had set out with the avowed intention of capturing Ashby, and had rashly invited a newspaperman to come along and see it done. He had sighted the gray cavalry, and was impetuously leading a charge when a company hidden behind a stone wall fired on him, his men fled, and it was not Ashby, but Sir Percy who gave up his sword.

Yes, Ashby was still fighting the Yankees every day, and sometimes more than once. "Look at Ashby enjoying himself," the generals said. They promoted him to brigadier, and Sandy Pendleton handed him his commission. "I hope that it will make you more careful." Ashby smiled. "I'm not afraid of the shots aimed at me. It's the bullets going nowhere that are dangerous." Even the Yankees admired him, even the prisoners repeated stories which added to his legend. Lieutenant Kane of the Pennsylvania Buckskins told how he had struck up the rifle of one of his own men, "for Ashby is too brave to die that way."

So many hazards sought for, so many dangers passed, he seemed immortal. Death did not want him. The bullet had not been molded that could kill him. He must ride forever nearest to the Yankees, the first to charge them, the last to withdraw.

That night Sir Percy Wyndham sat talking to General Jackson, comparing the wars he had experienced around the world, blaming the cowardice of his men, discussing the architecture of continental cathedrals, when a courier brought a message. Jackson read it, dismissed his guest with an apology rather than an explanation, and shut himself up alone. He had received a heavy blow, and his soul needed to wrestle in silence with his God. Ashby was dead.

It had been the last skirmish of the day, an unimportant little engagement without a name, a gallop at sunset through a field of golden wheat with Ashby at the head of it. And all the future of that bit of earth lay in the claim: "Ashby fell here." When his stallion was shot under him, he leapt up and ran forward, waving his sword, calling his men to follow. A bullet struck his heart, one of his comrades caught him, and he died. His troopers fought wildly, drove off the enemy, and carried him back to camp sobbing like children. One of them tried to make a speech. "We will miss you in camp," he said. "We will miss you in the field. We will miss you . . ." but he could say nothing more.

The troopers wept. Jackson wept and wrote a eulogy in his official report: "His daring was proverbial, his powers of endurance almost incredible, his character heroic, and his sagacity almost intuitive." All of Virginia burst into tears and verse.

There through the coming ages
　When his sword is rust
And his deeds in classic pages,
　Mindful of her trust,　　　　or
Shall Virginia, bending lowly,
　Still a ceaseless vigil holy
Keep above his dust.

Saw ye the veterans—
Hearts that had known
Never a quail of fear,
Never a groan—
Sob mid the fight they win
Tears their stern eyes within
Ashby, our Paladin,
Ashby is gone!

Ashby was gone, and with him passed the last glory and romance of the war, leaving the long road of blood to be

TURNER ASHBY

traveled to the end under a burning sky. Others would follow him. The long roll of the lost generation would stretch on and on.

Meanwhile, the morning of June 8th dawned blue and cloudless, and brought another Sunday battle.

General Jackson had his headquarters on a hill outside of Port Republic. He knew by now that Shields was coming after him down the Luray valley, and Frémont down the main valley, and that there could be no more dodging around Massanutten. But he still hoped to prevent a junction. On his way to devotional exercises, he heard firing in the town below him and had barely time to mount and cross the North

River ahead of the Yankees. Two of his staff were caught, but escaped in the later confusion of the day.

Almost immediately after, sounds of cannonading to the west announced that Ewell had already engaged Frémont at Cross Keys. Jackson waited, anticipating an attack from Shields. With his eyes beaming like a child's on Christmas Eve, he said to the Presbyterian minister for whom he had found a place on his staff: "Major, wouldn't it be a blessed thing if God would give us a glorious victory today?" "Delightful excitement!" he said to General Taylor.

With or without the assistance of that Providence in which he did not believe, General Ewell repulsed the Federals, because Frémont threw in his numerically superior troops too cautiously. Ewell rested on the field, where Jackson joined him. By two o'clock in the morning, Stonewall had his plans prepared, and made ready to move again. He ordered Colonel Patton to take his brigade and hold Frémont in check while the rest of the army disposed of Shields. Since Frémont still had nearly 13,000 men, the gallant colonel made bold to ask how long his one thousand would be expected to hold out.

"By the blessing of Providence, I expect to be back by ten o'clock."

But across the river at Port Republic, Jackson found Shields a more formidable opponent than he had expected. These men had whipped him once in the Valley, and they had set their hearts on whipping him again. This time it was the Union troops who held the wooded hills which steeply framed the battleground. The Stonewall Brigade charged first, and a Federal battery on a hill proved almost too much for them. The Louisianians went around to take the battery from the rear, and did so—with a loss of fifty per cent. Then they were so hard pressed that "there seemed nothing to do but to set our backs to the mountain and die hard."

General Jackson began to see that he could not make his schedule. Reluctantly he ordered Colonel Patton to join him, and to burn the bridge when he had crossed it. This was done, and the fresh reinforcements made the Federals waver. After the hardest fought and bloodiest battle of the entire campaign, the Northerners finally retreated around twelve o'clock—two hours late.

Because of this unforeseen delay, General Jackson had to abandon his plan of going back after Frémont, but at least he had the satisfaction of seeing him blocked on the other side of the river, and unable to do more than send a few shells onto the battlefield, which by that time was full of ambulances picking up the wounded of both sides. This firing enraged the Confederates, and when a shell passed through a wagon carrying a Yankee and a Rebel, killed the Yankee and left the Rebel untouched, they felt poetic justice had been done.

Jackson had dealt with the two armies that were pursuing him, his wagon train was already safe in the mountains at Brown's Gap, his prisoners had been sent south, his losses were comparatively few. With an army which had never exceeded 16,000 he had disposed of 30,000. In six weeks his men had marched 400 miles, defeated four armies, fought five battles (with skirmishes almost every day), captured 4,000 prisoners and compendious stores, and held 175,000 men in two great armies immobile before Richmond and Petersburg. Rarely in the history of war has so much been accomplished by so few. After the battle of Port Republic, General Jackson laid his hand gently on the arm of the godless General Ewell.

"He who does not see the hand of God in this, is blind, sir. Blind!"

The army got a day off on the tenth, and held their belated Sunday services, camping in the lush and beautiful country around Weyers Cave. John Casler, veteran of twenty-one, rested with the others, but when he suggested to a friend that they should visit this natural wonder, the friend replied: "Oh, what's the use? We'll be underground soon enough."

No one doubted John's courage any more, least of all himself. "High private in the rear rank," and contented to stay there, he had nevertheless a good opinion of himself, and he had earned it. "We could break down any cavalry brigade on a long march," he said modestly. He was not trying to be a hero like Ashby, and he had retained his cheerful disregard for regulations, but he could take it if he had to, and take it he did, without rest, without pay, without clothes, without shoes, often without food.

It was well that he could take it, for now he faced the summer of the Seven Days, the long hot July slaughter around Richmond, when Americans celebrated their day of independence by killing one another. Cold Harbour, Gaines Mill, Savage Station, Frayser's Farm, Malvern Hill, ordinary names of ordinary places, soon rang like knells in the hearts of North and South alike, for twenty-seven thousand men, proud of their strength and warm with life, there met the inescapable adventure.

The Army of the Valley rested for five days, only five days. Then in such secrecy that even his staff did not know where he had gone, Jackson visited Richmond, consulted Lee, returned, and led his army east across the mountains. "If my coat knew my plans," he said, "I would take it off and burn it."

On the night after Malvern Hill a new soldier was on picket duty next to Johnny Casler, and saw him sitting on a stump.

"Soldier, you must not sit down on your post. It is against orders."

"I know the orders," yawned John.

A little later— "Soldier, indeed you must not sit down. The officer will punish you, and if you go to sleep you will be shot."

"What regiment you belong to?"

"Forty-seventh Alabama."

"How many fights you been in?"

" 'Nary fight yet. We just got to Richmond and was assigned to General Jackson's division."

"Well—" a silence pregnant with meaning, "you walk your beat as much as you please, and I'll attend to mine."

19. The Long Year

All quiet along the Potomac tonight,
Except here and there a stray picket
Is shot, as he walks on his beat to and fro,
By a rifleman hid in the thicket.
It is nothing. A private or two, now and then,
Will not count in the news of the battle.
Not an officer lost, only one of the men,
Going out on a long death rattle.

AND NOW the Valley was again without its army.
The two weeks of joy in Winchester fled like a dream, a
confused time of troops passing and repassing, a chance to
hear something of husbands, sons, or sweethearts, a time of
wildly optimistic rumors. Then General Jackson withdrew,
mysterious as ever, then the Yankees came back, in a worse
and more uncivil form.

This was Blenker's Brigade, the German division, many
of whom hardly spoke English, officered by Germans, and
with a German manner toward the inhabitants of occupied
territory. The Valley people called them Dutchmen, as was
their custom, although Colonel D'Utassy protested redly that
he was Hungarian. They stole the raspberries and pulled
up the sprouting potatoes, they tore down the outhouses and
killed the pigs. They took the stone walls for fortifications,
the shade trees for firewood, and the women with them hung
their washing to dry on the old front porches. They walked
through the houses as if they owned them, and rifled bureau
drawers.

"Don't you know God is watching you steal my things?"
cried one girl in helpless fury.

"Ach, Gott is played oudt," replied the Dutchman.

News filtered back dimly to the Valley. The people did not trust the Federal reports, and they could hear nothing from their own side. They could be sure of but one thing—Richmond had not yet fallen.

During July and August, only one body of Confederate troops stayed near at hand—a company of Ashby's cavalry, now the Laurel Brigade, left on scouting duty. They hid out in the mountains between Harrisonburg and Luray and, oh, did they have fun! Most of them were Jefferson County boys, Baylor and Chew, Yates and Crane, Stryder and Rouss and Washington, who knew the country like their own places, who had cousins or sweethearts or friends in every house. Under a lieutenant of twenty, they rode rings around the Yankees for two happy months, laughing to hear themselves called "guerrillas" or "bushwackers," laughing to see their strength estimated in Federal reports as "a squadron of cavalry" or even "three brigades."

They raided Front Royal with twenty-five men, and took three hundred prisoners, but they could not take them far, for the Yankees counterattacked and freed them. When Front Royal was evacuated, they dashed down on Woodstock. No one knew how they managed it, for their routes and their helpers were their secret. Best of all was the attack in late August on the Winchester train between Summit Point and Wades Depot, which netted $4,000 in good United States money, bags of important papers and dispatches, cases of champagne and fine food intended for the overfed blue bellies. They fired the boiler and let the engine racket off alone under a full head of steam, they burnt the cars—not without regret, for they had sentimental memories of riding to parties or visits on that train, and it was a harsh good-bye to an old friend. To their satisfaction, this resulted in the evacuation of Winchester by the then commander, General Julius White. Menaced, as he said, by three brigades, he blew up his magazines, burnt his stores, and left the town. Company B had the additional pleasure of hearing that he was court-martialed for it afterward. Yes, they were tough, these wellborn young guerrillas. Six of them could look like sixty to the enemy, or felt sure they could. They made themselves a terrible reputation—and there was no one to see when one of them lay in the high brush beside the road with his arm around his wounded mare, sobbing his heart out because she was dying.

The news of two great battles interrupted their pleasures. East of the Blue Ridge, Lee and Jackson licked General Pope in the second battle of Manassas on August 26th. Commissary Pope joined Commissary Banks in the Confederate esteem, and "everything was branded U.S.A. except ourselves."

> The race is not to him that's got
> The longest legs to run,
> Nor the battle to the people
> That shoot the biggest gun.
>
> When I can fire my rifle clear
> At Yankees on the roads,
> I'll say goodby to rags and tags,
> And live on sutler's loads.

So sang the Rebels, impudently, for although unequipped and underfed, outnumbered three to two, they had done it again. But the more sober among them had some unsettling afterthoughts. It was after this battle that John Casler noticed how the lean and sun-cured Confederates did not rot so quickly as the plump Yankees, whose black and swollen bodies showed where their lines had been. He also noticed that they captured two hundred civilians who had come out merely to see the fight, and he doubted whether there were that many able-bodied men left in the South outside of the army.

And now the homesick Valley men, the foot cavalry, waded the Potomac and entered Maryland through country which reminded them of the Valley. Ragged, barefoot, dirty, they marched through Frederick, where General Jackson did not see a bedridden old lady named Barbara Frietchie. The Confederates marched singing:

I hear the distant thunder hum,
     Maryland!
The old line bugle, fife and drum,
     Maryland!
She is not dead, nor deaf, nor dumb!
Huzza! She spurns the Northern scum!
She breathes, she burns,—she'll come! She'll come!
     Maryland, my Maryland!

She did not burn, she did not come. Slaveholding state with many southern sympathizers, she looked with kindness on the "dirty darlings" and fed them well, but her young men did not join them.

The tide was high at Antietam, where, with the Potomac at his back, General Lee and forty thousand men gave battle to twice as many Federals, where the reddened waters of the river rolled three thousand bodies toward the sea. Where twenty thousand Americans fell at the hands of their brothers. All the next day both armies waited, lying on their arms. McClellan did not attack, Lee could not. On the night of September 18th, under a fine warm rain which thickened the darkness, the Confederates fell back into Virginia.

The summer campaign of 1862 had ended. It had begun on the Chickahominy thirty miles from Richmond, it ended on the Potomac sixty miles from Washington. For a month the armies lay inactive, looking at each other, and it was all quiet along the river. There was not a Yankee left in Virginia. But this was not enough.

The patient Mr. Lincoln, who had been disappointed in so many generals, said that the South must have a million men, for every time his troops engaged the Rebel army it was reported that they had encountered twice their strength—and he knew the North had half a million. The South did not have half a million, and had no source from which they could be drawn.

On his way back from Maryland, General Jackson was mobbed by the liberated ladies of Martinsburg, who strewed his path with roses, cut the buttons from his coat, and threatened to have his hair. He escaped from them, and brought his army into winter quarters near Winchester.

And what of John Casler and the other GIs who had walked and fought, shivered, grumbled, sweated and fought, during a long two years? They were no longer the hopeful boys who had gone singing to first Manassas. They had explored the utmost limits of weariness or hunger, and had survived. They had known the ultimate in danger, and had survived that too. Death in its most gruesome aspects no longer shocked them, and when they went back to the battlefields after a fight it was to rob as well as to bury the dead. When asked to do the impossible they had responded nobly, but they reserved the immemorial American right to complain and criticize, and no orders could prevent their making themselves comfortable along the way. They would not steal. No. Who ever heard of a soldier stealing? But if attacked by a belligerent pullet or piglet, they did not tamely fly. Their grandsons met similar dangers on Anzio beachhead.

Anzio, February 15 1944 (AP)
"Yes sir," said the platoon leader, as the men squatted around the little field stove eating pork chops, "you'd never believe it, but there's hardly a day goes by that one of these hogs doesn't attack some of the men, and has to be killed in self defense, and sometimes the only way you can keep a chicken from scratching your eyes out, is to wring its neck."

On the long dark march from Harpers Ferry to Strasburg, when no one knew whether the Stonewall Brigade would be able to rejoin Jackson, John Casler and about five hundred others were invited to spend the night comfortably with friends, and accepted without the formality of leave. By morning the Yankees had cut them off from the army, so they went into the mountains in little squads of three or four, and took a week trying to get back to their commands and living off the mountain people. They missed some of the battles, but brought in a few prisoners on their own, to keep their captains happy, and these defections lay like feathers on their consciences.

Now in the winter camp, without the Yankees to engage their attention, they turned their mordant wit upon each other. "Get out of here!" yelled the infantry as the jingling cavalry dashed by. "Who ever saw a dead cavalryman?" The North Carolinians declared that they made the backs of the Virginians sore, climbing over them to get into battle. An officer who tried to be a dandy with waxed mustachios was advised: "Take them mice outa yore mouth! I see their tails a-hanging out! Climb down outa that hat! I see your feet a-swingin'." Even Old Jack, in the fine new uniform which Beauty Stuart gave him, was not immune. "God Amighty!" shouted the soldiers. "Old Jack has drawed his bounty money and got hisse'f some clo'se."

They did not have long to admire their general in his finery. The bright gold braid oppressed him, so he cut the cord off his hat and gave it to a little girl. By the time he had worn his new coat for a month it was as muddy and unpressed as the old one. A soldier wrote a song about him, and the army took it up.

> Come men, stack arms, pile on the rails;
>   Stir up the camp fires bright;
> No matter if the canteen fails,
>   We'll make a roaring night.
> Here Shenandoah brawls along,
> Here lofty Blue Ridge echoes strong,
> To swell the brigade's roaring song
>   Of Stonewall Jackson's way.
>
> We see him now,—the old slouched hat
>   Cocked o'er his eye askew;
> The shrewd dry smile,—the speech so pat,
>   So calm, so blunt, so true.
> The Bluelight Elder knows them well,
>   Says he, "that's Banks,—he's fond of shell;
> Lord save his soul! We'll give him—," well,
>   That's Stonewall Jackson's way.
>
> He's in the saddle now! Fall in!
>   Steady, the whole brigade!

Hill's at the ford, cut off. We'll win
　　His way out, ball and blade.
What matter if our shoes are worn?
What matter if our feet are torn?
Quick step! We're with him before morn!
　　That's Stonewall Jackson's way.

Silence! Ground arms! Kneel all! Caps off!
　　Old Bluelight's going to pray.
Strangle the fool that dares to scoff!
　　Attention! It's his way!
Appealing from his native sod
In forma pauperis to God,
"Lay bare thine arm. Stretch forth thy rod.
　　Amen." That's Stonewall's way.

It was good in the Valley during that quiet winter. Across the Potomac the pickets taunted one another, and on warm days swam to the middle of the river and swapped coffee for tobacco. Young Henry Douglas rode to Shepheardstown with a courier and watered his horse in the Potomac while he looked over at his home, the house still standing, the barn burned, Federal soldiers lounging in the yard, and light artillery behind the stone wall. He saw his father come out and walk toward the barn. The Yankees invited him over. He offered to meet them at midstream in a boat, and when they found out who he was they insisted that he should pay his family a visit. They said their officers were in town, and they would guarantee his safety.

"I wouldn't give a damn for a Union," roared one, "which could be broken up by a man seeing his mother!"

Douglas could not resist letting them lift him into their boat. They sent up the hill for her, and mother and son had a few moments together on the riverbank while she kissed him and wept, fearing that it might be a trap. His father could not come down to him, for he had given a parole not to leave the yard. Douglas told General Jackson about it later, and was reprimanded for taking the risk, but not too severely.

It was indeed good in the Valley during those lingering

autumnal days, when the blue haze intensified the color of the mountains, and the sun still had a caressing heat although the leaves burned red and gold. After all the marching and the fighting the soldiers found it good just to be alive, to sleep at night in the firm expectation of dawn, to rise confident of the sunset. Their feet had time to heal. They supplemented their rations with wild onions to prevent scurvy, and although they did not fatten on their meager flour and bacon, at least their stomachs were filled.

The happy respite could not last. The South had won the battles, but it had not won the war. On November 22nd Jackson again led his command over the familiar trail across the Blue Ridge, to join Lee at Fredericksburg. The column wound up the well-known road, where the dark green of the pines mingled with the russet of the last clinging leaves, and over Fisher's Gap. This time the men knew well what to expect. They knew that they were going back to the dead-dog weariness of all-night marches, to the hungry waiting for the wagons which were almost empty, to the hideous din of conflict, the fierce and always unexpected stare of death. One must be either an Ashby or a very inexperienced soldier to look forward to a battle, yet these ordinary men with an ordinary man's repugnance to pain, to dying, marched willingly enough. They did not know where they were going, but Old Jack did. Their trust was in Old Jack.

From the top of the mountains they took a last look at their Valley, mistily lying below them, brown and green, threaded with a shining river. "It is a lovely Valley to fight for," their hearts said silently. "When shall we see it again?" This was the answer: *never*, for one quarter of the men, and for the leader, *never*.

An unspeakable sadness settled on the Valley when the troops had gone. The low moon cast long black shadows, and the whippoorwill saddened the nights with his haunting call. The autumn winds whirled the leaves away in thin and chilly sunshine, and the November rains fell bleakly on the barren earth like the hopeless tears of old age, shed when there is nothing to renew.

The women wore black. Widows, mothers, sisters, sweethearts, scarcely a family was without a loss. It was not only the soldiers whom they mourned, for the camps with their ignorance of sanitation had brought epidemics particularly hard upon the very old and very young. Almost everyone with little children saw at least one die.

The women were tired. Those who had owned no slaves, and they were the majority, missed their men and struggled with the heavy chores. The others learned to bake and clean and cook, to work the dough with aching unaccustomed wrists, to make up the heavy tester beds which had formerly required the services of two maids and a man. They discovered the infinite patience needed for the care of little children when there were no warm black arms to hold them, no soft husky voices to admonish, "Come now, let your mamma 'lone."

The Valley people could not hope to have the winter to

themselves after their army went across the Blue Ridge. It was said that the citizens of Winchester did not know in the morning which side possessed them until they went downtown. General Milroy arrived on Jackson's heels, and made a protracted visit. All through that winter the people groaned under him.

A change had come in the temper of the conflict, "not the civil, but the *un*civil war." The North was growing angry, slowly and thoroughly as American anger grows. The rebellion proved too hard to put down, the war was lasting too long. It was absurd that this outnumbered people should still delude themselves with hopes of victory, should still stubbornly defy "the best government in the world." General Milroy raged at the civilians who would rather go hungry than take an oath of allegiance, raged at the women who made their very suffering an insult to the conquerors. The North would beat them, he said, if it had to send every Rebel soul to hell. He was expecting orders to send all the damn Rebel sympathizers out of his lines, and by God he would do it.

He began with Mrs. Logan, whose handsome white house on the corner was suitable for headquarters. When she demurred, he shut her up with her two daughters in a bedroom and gave them no food all day. In the evening he had them driven six miles in a wagon, and left by the roadside. As Mrs. Logan went out she passed Mrs. Milroy coming in, jangling the household keys.

The "Jessie Scouts," Northerners dressed in Confederate uniforms, went among the people and trapped the unwary into disastrous expressions of opinion. A young schoolteacher who wrote an indiscreet note was sent down the road to find what shelter she could. Miss Mary McGill wrote a criticism of Milroy to the wife of a Union officer whom she had been nursing, and found herself sitting beside the Valley Pike "without baggage and without a house or a human being in sight." When the leader of these scouts was captured, George and Julius Ward, aged fourteen and ten, were taken to prison and held as hostages.

Now the problem was not to keep the Yankees out of the house, but to find the least obnoxious and invite them to occupy. If horses were stabled in the cellar of a dwelling, the owners merely thanked God that it had not been taken for a smallpox hospital. "I feel as if I must give out," the women said—but they did not do so. Because Senator Mason was in London as special commissioner for the Confederacy, the Yankees razed his home to the ground, stone by stone. Next door, Mrs. McDonald had the good fortune to secure as her guest a mild old quartermaster who gave little trouble, and who brought with him the additional advantage of a supply tent from which her boys could steal.

For it was food, food, food, the lack of food, that preoccupied everyone that winter. When General Milroy proclaimed that food would be sold only to those who took the Federal oath, some capitulated, but most preferred semi-starvation. Occasionally the general would allow the Rebels to stand in line for an oversupply of some commodity, and so to secure a jug of molasses or a pound of bacon. The dried fruits and vegetables usually laid by for the winter had been destroyed or eaten as they ripened. By good luck the McDonalds had hidden several barrels of flour in their attic from which they made bread to trade with the soldiers for coffee, sugar, and meat—a traffic strictly forbidden. Better still, although the chickens were gone, the pigs were gone, the sheep were gone, the cattle were gone, *they had a cow in the cellar.* She never emerged into the light of day, but the Yankee teamsters knew about her and sometimes threw off a forkful of hay as they drove by on the road which now ran across the lawn under the parlor window. Once a whole bale of hay rolled from a wagon and vanished almost before it struck the ground. That teamster had children of his own, and knew that in this house there were six under twelve. The little boys stole what they could—a barrel of crackers was the largest single haul—but it seemed strange to them that their mother never mentioned it, never reproved them for stealing, never commended them for bringing in food. "Oh, it was so hard to live! So hard to keep alive!"

Only the very young girls still had the spirit to be gay, still adorned themselves with necklaces of popcorn and tied bright worsted in their hair instead of ribbons, referred to their drink of parched rye and chicory simply as "beverage," talked saucily to the young Yankees, and considered that they were making a sacrifice for The Cause when they refused to ride in some of the smart carriages with which rich boys from New York City decorated the scene.

During this time the irrepressible Miss Boyd had the misfortune to spend some time in the Old Capitol Prison in Washington. She had attempted to send a message to General Jackson by a man in Confederate uniform who posed as an exchanged prisoner of war—despite the protest of her little maid, still intermittently appearing as the voice of wisdom.

" 'Fore God, Miss Belle, he ain' no Revel. I seed him in town wid de Yankees."

The treacherous fellow, who was indeed a spy, carried her missive to Washington, and a Major Sherman came to get her, accompanied by a man whose evil and lowering aspect readily identified him as a member of the secret service. In vain her aunt protested, in vain her mother swooned, in vain the Negro maid (who had had the wit to burn her papers) flung herself on the floor, embracing Belle's knees. Belle had to go, and go alone, and take only one trunk! She expected to be hanged, but even this fear paled beside the horrid discovery that she would have to spend the night in the midst of the army, *in a tent!* It mollified her little when the commanding general turned out and gave her his.

The prison was not too bad. It was not unpleasant to be a martyr for The Cause while the other prisoners cheered her, made her walnut-shell baskets filled with Confederate flags, while the crowds gathered under her window to catch a glimpse of her. After a few weeks she was exchanged and went unrepentantly back to her activities in the Valley. Later she was again arrested, and this time sent to a more disagreeable prison, made gloomier still by the fact that she nearly died there of typhoid fever. She was tried and sentenced to hard labor in the Fitchburg jail, but again her father managed to get her out, and this time removed her as far from the Yankees as possible—to Richmond.

While in Richmond he unfortunately died, and after a time Belle set off by sea with dispatches for London, only to have her vessel captured and sent to Boston under guard of a Lieutenant Hardinge of the United States Navy. That is the end of her, one might say. Oh, no. Before they docked in Boston she was engaged to the lieutenant, who helped her escape to Canada and then to London, resigned his commission, followed, and married her. Nice going, Belle. In one of those anticlimaxes with which history closes the most romantic stories, Belle divorced him in 1868, went on to have several other husbands, and to die at last in her sixties, on a lecture tour in the Middle West.

But that is far ahead, and sad, and somewhat sordid, and it is best to leave Miss Belle in a last gallop down a Valley road, her chestnut curls flying, her youth and courage high. She was a joyous girl, and joy will not be plentiful in the Valley much longer. Too many of the characters are passing from the story, and their places cannot be filled.

To all the brave young men who will not sing again under the Valley moonlight, add Ashby, the embodiment of their dream. To the lost riders, the lost marchers, the lost fighting men, add Jackson, greatest fighter of them all. Add General Stonewall Jackson, pressing on into the long darkness after Chancellorsville, and the last river crossing.

They buried General Jackson in his Valley, at Lexington on May 15, 1863. His old brigade could not have the privilege of escorting him to his last rest. They had shivered with him in the snow around Fredericksburg, without him they had carried through his plans to drive the enemy from Chancellorsville. Now Lee prepared a new offensive and could not spare them even for a few days.

The men reluctantly acquiesced in this decision, for there was no need to explain to Old Jack's veterans the duties of a soldier. Their commanding general, Winder, had been killed at Cedar Run, their General Baylor at Second Manassas, their General Paxton at Chancellorsville. None of this had perturbed them greatly, for they had always looked beyond their brigadiers to Stonewall himself.

Now he was gone. They would never again see him slouch past on his uninspiring little horse, blushing at their cheers; never again would they hear the crisp voice at unexpected moments in the deadened weariness of a forced march, "Press on, men. Press on. Close up, men. Close up." They would never again see his flaming presence ride through the smoke of battle. "Steady, men, all's well. You must stand it an hour longer, men. You must hold out another hour." Never again would they have the same confidence in their ability to outflank any number of Yankees, "to find their rear if they had a rear." They felt his spirit with them as they fought on, but alas, they soon found that the spirit did not issue orders or plan strategy.

"You have lost your left arm," Lee wrote him when he was wounded, "but I have lost my right." As Henry Douglas saw it, "It took the battle of Gettysburg to convince General Lee that Jackson was really dead."

"I am badly hurt," said Jackson in amazement, lying in the dark woods near Chancellorsville, "and all my wounds are from my own men." When pneumonia set in to finish what the bullets had begun, he said to his wife: "You are too frightened, my child. I think God still has work for me to do and will raise me up to do it." Later, much later, "Doctor, Anna tells me I am to die today. Is that correct?" On confirmation, he lay a long time silent, digesting and accepting the reality. At last he spoke. "Very good. It is all right."—Jackson, the good soldier, under orders from God.

The body lay in state in Richmond, then was sent on to Lexington. The V.M.I. cadets escorted it, followed by Negro Jim who sobbed as he led Little Sorrel with the empty saddle and the reversed boots. With the cortege went the sorrow-stricken hearts of the entire Confederacy. He had said that he did not desire to outlive the independence of his country, that life was nothing without honor, that degradation was worse than death. Now for him and for two hundred thousand other Americans had come the silence, the

unbreakable rest—but the living would have to struggle two
years longer.

On June 14th the Confederates came back to Winchester, and Milroy left with flying coattails. The liberators were
Jackson's old corps, now fighting under Jubal Early.

Mrs. McDonald and a friend sat in rocking chairs by
the dining-room window and watched the onset of the battle
and the shells flying directly overhead. As the firing increased,
they moved with the five younger children into the shelter
afforded by an angle of the house. Little Hunter and Donald
sobbed with their faces hidden in their mother's skirt. Old
Aunt Winnie kept moaning, "Miss Cornelia, you gwine all
be kill'," and Tuss, her feeble-minded son, was a picture of
terror.

During an early afternoon lull in the firing, the little
boys began to play in the sunshine, grabbing the Federal soldiers who passed, shouting: "I take you prisoner." But in a
short while the shelling grew hotter than ever.

The Yankees also discovered the comparative safety of
the angle, and their wounded and their fugitives poured into
it. On the bench beside Mrs. McDonald sat a man with a
ball in his throat, gasping as he slowly drowned in his own
blood. The ambulances backed up to discharge their ghastly
loads, and the frantic horses, streaming blood, reared and
screamed with distended eyes. The soldiers packed in until
they overflowed the angle and had scarcely room to breathe.
And the sweet June sun lingered interminably in the sky.

At last it set. The cannonading slowly died away. The
soldiers released from death began to joke with one another
and to walk around the yard. Mrs. McDonald boiled some
milk for the poor man beside her, but he could not take it.
Her floors were covered with prostrate men in all stages of
wounds and exhaustion. She saw the impossibility of getting
anything to eat for the children and herself, so gathered them
together and took them upstairs without even closing a door.
What was the use? She had, as she wrote with some humor, a

strong guard downstairs, and she slept soundly that night with her house unlocked.

When the cannon roused her at dawn, she went down to find the floors still hidden under sleeping soldiers. She stirred one of them with her toe, and told him to rouse the rest and go, so that she could get breakfast for her children. When they lingered, she went to the front door, and there saw the Confederates filing into the ravaged yard. It was no small pleasure to tell them about the Yankees, to see the bluecoats lay down their muskets and file out to surrender. For the first time since it had been built with her stone walls, she dared to run up to the fort on the hill behind her. It was empty, but the Stars and Stripes still floated over it. Her triumph did not long endure. After two days of rejoicing, the Army of Northern Virginia crossed the Potomac and marched on—to Gettysburg.

The inimitable John Casler was dissatisfied, and lonely for Old Jack. He thought they should have captured more booty in Winchester, and Milroy with it. They had not been pushed hard enough in getting there, for their new general had actually allowed them to go into camp instead of marching all night. They would never surprise anybody that way. Then in the town, their quartermasters gobbled up everything that was good, and the Johnny Rebs, used to eking out a meager living by personal efforts, never got a smell of it. The march through Pennsylvania was a worse disappointment, for General Lee had a theory about not making war on civilians, and they must obey—at least when the officers were looking. Horses had to be impressed, of course, although the Dutchmen tried to hide their Clydesdales in their parlors. The cherries hung temptingly ripe over the highway, and hungry soldiers could not be expected to starve in the first land of plenty they had seen in two years, especially when surrounded by infuriated hens.

They went to Gettysburg, John Casler and the others. They went, and fewer than three-quarters of them returned. On July 13th, Major Edward McDonald drew rein for the last time in front of Hawthorne, and called to his stepmother without taking time to dismount: "If you don't want to spend another winter with the Yankees, you had better leave."

The news did not find the family wholly unprepared, for though the mother was a loyal Southerner, she was not a blind optimist, and she had been packing. Edward arranged to have an army wagon come that night, and the beds, the silver, such household treasures as could be hastily assembled, were sent to Staunton in charge of fifteen-year-old Harry. The children slept on the floor after the beds had gone, and next morning they climbed into a spring wagon which a neighbor let them have, "rather than have it taken by the Yankees."

Six children in a wagon, thirteen-year-old Allan driving, his mother on the seat beside him, the four little ones on stools in the wagon bed, and Kenneth mounted on the old horse, they set out down the Valley Pike in the early morning, with no idea where they were going or how they should find shelter or the means of existence. Old Aunt Winnie told them good-bye in tears, shook hands with each one at the door, cut off a curl from each child's head, held a little shoe of Nelly's, which she said she would keep forever.

They did not know it then, but they had seen the end, the high-water mark of Confederate hopes and illusions, the end of life as they had known it. From then on, though the gray army was still to come back several times, the war in the Valley would be the Yankees' war.

20. The Burning

THE CONFEDERATE ARMY fell back through eastern Virginia, back to Brandy Station, back to the bridge over the Rappahannock, back to winter quarters on the Rapidan, back to the Wilderness. As 1864 began they had a new general opposed to them, Ulysses S. Grant, in temper as dogged and indestructible as Stonewall Jackson himself, and backed by a numerical preponderance of two to one. If one hundred and forty thousand men oppose sixty thousand, and can take all the killing the sixty thousand can inflict, the larger number must inevitably win, Grant thought—and he was right.

The gray soldiers, with the instinct of old campaigners, sensed the difference, and some of the mirth went out of Lee's army. The stronger spirits were more determinedly sacrificial, and the fainter-hearted, or perhaps more rational, deserted more freely. In the spring of '64 Lee proclaimed that deserters would be pardoned if they came back of their own accord in thirty days.

In the Valley, two new stars were rising, and both wore blue. Where Ashby had ridden, now George Custer rode, and bluff Phil Sheridan was to be crowned with the ultimate success. The southern reminiscences grow reticent about this period, and the Northerners take up the pen, for it is pleasanter to remember victory than defeat. The new crop of military memoirs has a different flavor. They are saltier, less impressed by their commanders, less given to the heroic gesture, the garlanded phrase. They have a realistic factuality only matched on the southern side by that cheerful reprobate John Casler.

As 1864 opened, General Siegel, German born and

trained in the German Army, took command of the Department of West Virginia, and threatened the Valley from the west. It was another political appointment, a sop to the German vote.

> I've come shust now to tell you how
> I goes mit regimentals
> To Schlauch dem voes of Liberty
> Like dem old Continentals
> Vot fights mit England long ago
> To save der Yankee Eagle,
> Und now I gets my soldier clothes,
> I'm going to fight mit Siegel.

To the east, a new sort of soldier garrisoned Harpers Ferry—the 19th Regiment, colored, made up of Negroes from Maryland. Their specific and optimistic purpose was to recruit among the ex-slaves in the lower Valley.

A large number of colored troops fought for the Union during the Civil War. Captain James H. Rickard of the 19th, a Rhode Islander who admired his men and wrote a memoir of his service with them, gives the total number engaged as 186,097, of whom 36,847 died. Neither Lincoln, Grant, nor Sherman favored their use as soldiers. Their white officers were afraid to admit when captured that they had been connected with the colored troops, until one stouthearted lieutenant announced himself as "Lemuel D. Dobbs of the 19th niggers, by God!" and received special consideration for his courage. General David Hunter used them first, amid a storm of abuse from North and South, and one of his subordinate generals, Charles Graham Halpine, whose book of war memoirs bears the sinister title *Baked Meats of the Funeral*, wrote a song about them salted with his own peculiar humor.

> Some tell us tis a burnin' shame
> To make the naygers fight;
> An' that the thrade of bein' kilt
> Belongs but to the white:
> But as for me, upon my sowl,
> So liberal are we here

I'll let Sambo be murthered instid of meself
On every day of the year.

On every day of the year, bhoys,
An' every hour of the day,
The right to be kilt I'll divide wid him,
And divil a word I'll say.

It is a long road, a long and slippery road, up which the colored race has climbed. In spite of the mistrust that surrounded them, they fought well at Petersburg and Richmond, and it was they who made the last charge at Appomattox.

Here they were then, 750 of them, in the chilly early spring of '64, learning to be soldiers, and starting on March 12th their recruiting march across the lower Valley. It was considered expedient to issue only five rounds of ammunition to each man. On the first night's march, the blackness around them suddenly blossomed with the red fire of a surprise attack, and one of them was mortally wounded. The dark astonished inarticulate soldiers probably never knew what their officers later discovered—that their Colonel Perkins had arranged to have their courage tested by a party of Federal scouts in gray. In this macabre encounter, they acquitted themselves well, one died, and the rest marched on to a night's quarters in the church at Charles Town. Later, at Winchester, they found the town so hostile that it was deemed prudent to take them directly to Martinsburg, where they remained a few days, and then returned to Harpers Ferry.

Not a single recruit joined them during their two weeks' expedition. Not one of the local Negroes availed himself of the opportunity to strike a blow for his own freedom. On the contrary, they hid themselves when the colored troops went through, for it had been rumored that the regiment was impressing men. If the ghost of old John Brown had walked the riverbank at Harpers Ferry, it might have told Colonel Perkins something which would have spared him the trip.

The Negro soldiers exercised their instinct for avoiding trouble and were quiet in their stay at Harpers Ferry. The citizens ignored them. A Mrs. Brown came back from a trip to Baltimore with her daughter's doll stuffed with quinine, and was marched under military guard to headquarters for questioning. She reduced her dark escort to a musical comedy status by refusing to walk either behind or in the midst of them, and made them follow her down the street. The quinine was not found.

Now spring again brought the new green wheat thrusting through the freshly worked earth, brought the young lambs, brought the renewed necessity for killing. Toward the end of April, General Siegel was ordered to destroy the Virginia Central Railroad at Staunton. He was a general notorious for the deliberation of his movements. From Winchester he announced that he could go no farther without reinforcements; then, moving much more slowly than his soldiers wished, he passed through Woodstock and Mount Jackson to Newmarket, where he fought a battle, and was completely routed by a smaller force.

The battle at Newmarket on May 15th, was neither large nor decisive. Another sleepy Valley town looked to the hills and found them full of smoking cannon, but discovered that the noise of battle does not kill. Little Leila Zirkle, sent to a neighbor's where she might have the advantage of a cellar, escaped and ran home to her mother—surely the safest refuge for a little girl. She said the bullets sang "Oh, Lordy!" as they passed her. Again after the battle the Federal tide ebbed back, only to rise higher at the flow. But Newmarket has an especial claim upon the memory of the Valley, for it was there that the thinning southern lines were strengthened by the V.M.I. cadets.

No reinforcements could be spared from the desperate defense of Richmond, so the lads closed their schoolbooks, stepped out in their light blue and scarlet, and marched into the guns as smartly as they had maneuvered on the drill ground. During four years past, youths of seventeen or more had graduated from the institute as officers, until at this time many of the corps were barely adolescent. Frank Preston, who had lost an arm at First Manassas, captained them. In perfect formation behind a one-armed leader the boys swung sharply forward over the tender blades of the new wheat. For many of them there was no return. The townspeople and the gray soldiers found them afterward, with their young heads pillowed on their muskets, eternally asleep. Some were so small that the women could lift them in their arms and carry them from the field.

The boys are dead, and those who wept for them also are beyond sorrow. Their cause is dead, and no one living would have it otherwise. Nevertheless, now after eighty years they still are not forgotten, and this is right and just. They are forever in attendance at their old institute.

On May 15th each year at Lexington the V.M.I. cadets assemble. The roll is called, and as each name is read, a first classman steps forward and replies to it:

"Dead on the field of honor."

Still, say the Federal reports, "the Shenandoah Valley was for us the Valley of Humiliation." Halleck wired to Grant after the battle: "Siegel will do nothing but run. He never did anything else." Then General David Hunter was put in command of West Virginia. He was sixty-two, a West Pointer, born of a Virginia family, son of a Presbyterian minister, and he fought against his relatives with all the fury of a convert.

In Georgia, in 1862, he had freed all the slaves under his jurisdiction by a proclamation which President Lincoln made haste to repudiate. In 1863 he advocated "a general arming of the negroes and a general destruction of all the property of the slaveholders." His chief of artillery, Colonel H. A. Dupont, and others of his officers and men have left accounts of his expedition down the Valley. Among them, that wag General Halpine, writing under the name of his alter ego "Private Miles O'Reilly,"

Indeed it was often ludicrously, though painfully, amusing, to hear Colonel David Hunter Strother, "Porte Crayon", or the old

General himself, inquiring anxiously after the health of "Cousin
Kitty", "Aunt Sallie", "Cousin Joe," or "Uncle Bob", from some
nice old Virginia lady in smoothed apron, silver spectacles, and in
tears, or some pretty young rebel beauty in homespun, without
hoops and in a towering passion,—our soldiers meanwhile cleaning
out the smoke houses and graneries by wholesale; and the end of the
conversation, as the affectionate but politically sundered relatives
parted, usually finding those of the rebel side without a week's
food in the house, without a single slave to do their bidding, and
with horses, cattle, sheep, bacon, pigs, poultry, and so forth, only
to be recalled in ecstatic dreams.

Indeed, the Yankees had much to laugh at now, but the
Valley people laughed only when Mosby's men harassed Hunter's supply lines. "Bushwackers," Hunter called them,
although they had been officially incorporated into the Confederate Army. They hid out in the mountains and swooped
down on the Valley, carrying on the merry work of Company B, appearing, disappearing, and with them a large stock
of Federal supplies usually vanished also. Small detachments
could never be safe from them, it was unhealthy for Federals
to wander alone through the countryside, wagon trains had
to be heavily guarded. Hunter insisted, quite rightly, that
they were sometimes aided, fed, and hidden by the civilians;
but he also arrived at the "absolutely untenable conclusion"
that Mosby's command was composed of the men of military
age in the villages down the Pike. He therefore announced a
system of reprisals which seems strikingly modern. He would
burn any town near which an attack took place.

The attack came soon enough near Newtown eight miles
south of Winchester, and Hunter sent the 1st New York
Cavalry to burn "every house, store, and outbuilding in that
place except the churches. . . . You will also burn the
houses, etc., of all the rebels between Newtown and Middletown."

When the detachment arrived in Newtown the women,
children, and old men came out in tears. They were simple
people, hard-working people. They proved that they had

nursed the Union soldiers who had been wounded in the attack on the wagon train, they proved that their young men were with Lee across the mountains, and not with Mosby. Major Stearns listened carefully, and listened also to his own men, who grumbled that "it was no part of a soldier's duty to burn the houses of noncombatants." In the end he decided to take the responsibility of disobedience, left the town intact, and reported all the circumstances to General Hunter, who let the matter drop.

At Lexington, however, the commanding general was on the scene in person, and the flames roared as he ordered. The Federal troops entered the town on Saturday, June 11th, with two Negro women riding at the head of Averill's column. On Sunday Hunter burned the V.M.I., the houses of the professors, the house of Governor Letcher. The statue of George Washington on the cupola of Washington College was taken down and removed to Wheeling to save it from the "degenerate sons of worthy sires." Captain William McKinley, Colonel Rutherford B. Hayes, with their own hands helped some of the people carry out their belongings. Professor Gilham's wife sat all night alone on her little heap of furniture, to protect it from looting, for what the flames had spared the looters now devoured. The Negroes were encouraged to take what they could, and the riffraff of the town boiled to the surface as hell's caldron stirred. At the mansion on a hill, which General Crook had taken for his headquarters, the lights blazed all night, the military band kept playing, and the local Negresses strolled languidly to and fro, dressed in the silks and satins of their former owners, fanning themselves against a background of flame-pierced smoke.

Mrs. Letcher had to take in two Federal officers, who ate with the family. After a chatty and agreeable breakfast, they rose and announced that they would have to burn the house. Captain Berry took a bottle of benzine from his pocket, poured it over the sofa and the curtains, put a match to them, and went upstairs. Mrs. Letcher had barely time to snatch her baby out of the cradle and run from the house. Elizabeth, the oldest daughter, was attempting to save some clothes when

Captain Berry met her in the hall and set fire to them as they hung on her arm, then piled the bedding and garments in the middle of the floor and lit them.

Mrs. Letcher, tearless and calm, sat on a stone in the street with her baby asleep in her lap, her other children around her, and watched her home burn. The first person who came to her there was the intrepid Mrs. McDonald, formerly of Winchester, and now of Lexington, whither she had gone to get away from Yankees.

By this time Mrs. McDonald had seen too much to be afraid of anything. The problem of finding shelter for seven young children had been no easier than might have been expected. When she at last rejoined her stalwart and fire-eating colonel, she found him changed into an elderly invalid with snow-white hair. They had no money except what she could raise by selling her jewelry and a brocade dress, un-worn, which he had brought her from London just before the war. At last he had been appointed commander of the post at Lexington, and she set up their home on a necessitous and meager scale, in a bleak little rented house.

Her former occupations no longer fitted her circum-stances, for she could not sew without material, nor cook without food. She took long walks and made sketches, "so as to learn well what I might afterwards be able to teach." She patched the children's garments, and kept them clean, forever haunted by the time when there would be nothing left to patch. Some old red curtains at the windows and over a deal table made the parlor bright and comfortable, and there they entertained their friends with unsweetened tea and butterless bread. "I actually used to find myself for-getting everything but that I was pouring tea for agreeable people again, and never felt once humiliated because I had nothing better to offer."

Even this degree of comfort could not last. When the Yankees came to Lexington the small garrison had to with-draw, and Colonel McDonald, unable to walk or to ride, left in an ambulance which his son Harry drove. He spoke cheer-fully of coming back, but told his wife privately that if it was not to be, she must teach the boys to be brave and true, and the little girl to be gentle and modest. Then he was gone, and the blue troops poured in.

The northern soldiers laughed when they found only a barrel of flour and some tea in the McDonald pantry, and a few hens running around the attic. Mrs. McDonald, veteran of occupations, smiled when she heard that some ladies had to be revived by blackberry wine during the shelling. On the evening of the burning, when the air was acrid with smoke, when the ashes fell like snow and the looters whooped, she saw a file of soldiers lead out Captain Matthew White of the 1st Virginia Cavalry. The children said that they were taking him out to shoot him, but what could children know? The officers who slept at Mrs. White's and ate her food said that he was still in the jail across the street. But when the Yankees left on Tuesday, the country people found his body in the woods and brought it in.

After his funeral on Wednesday, Mrs. McDonald was sitting alone on her porch in the twilight, when a little boy climbed the railing and whispered to her: "Did you know that Colonel McDonald and Harry were killed and are lying in the woods fifteen miles from here?" It was not true. They had merely been taken prisoners. Nevertheless, she never saw her husband alive again.

Hunter went on to Lynchburg, which he did not take, and then across the mountains into western Virginia. In the barren and sparsely settled mountains the Federals themselves knew for six days what it was to go without food or fodder. How the Confederate Army would have enjoyed watching them!

As Hunter withdrew from Lexington, Early's men were on their way from eastern Virginia. They marched one hundred miles to Charlottesville in the old foot-cavalry style. On the night they arrived there, John Casler's bare feet were so sore that he had to crawl around the fire on his hands and knees in order to cook his rations. Only three soldiers and the captain were left in Company A of the Stonewall Brigade. Of the original seventy-five, twenty-six had died, twenty-

three had "gone home" (deserted). The rest had been
wounded or captured. Five generals had been killed while
leading them. All through Early's corps, regiments were
down to a strength of about one hundred. In the Stonewall
Brigade two hundred were officially reported without shoes.
General Lee had rejected the new breech-loading rifle because
it made the men waste their fire, and he could not provide
them with so much ammunition. Lice devoured the army,
"as big as wheat and branded C.S.A.," the Yankees said.
Hunger was a habit of long standing. For a year they had
fought on no more than a pint of cornmeal and a quarter
pound of bacon daily, and several times had voted to go
empty and send their food to the starving civilians in Richmond. Still they had their bands, and as they marched
through Staunton the bands were playing:

> We're the boys that's gay and happy,
> Gay and happy still.

They were still fighting, they could hold or drive an
enemy who outnumbered them three to one, and even the
Federals found their courage "beyond all wonder and beyond
all praise." What were they fighting for, these ragged hungry
filthy men? Not for the slaves which four-fifths of them
never hoped to have. Not for their civil government, for
which they had little respect. Not because they clung to hopes
of winning. They were fighting primarily for their leader.
Ashby was dead, Jackson was dead, Stuart was dead, but Lee
remained, and the army found no irreverence in bracketing
him with God. They were fighting for "Old Marse," and
also they were fighting because they were Americans and had
forgotten how to quit.

These were the men who came back to the Valley and
were appalled at its devastation, who pursued Hunter to the
west along a road lined with abandoned loot and smoking
ruins, with women's dresses, broken china, children's toys,
trampled in the mud. Then they left the chase, and turned
northward. Jackson's division filed past his unmarked grave

in silence, and dipped their tattered flags in homage to his dust. The long Gray Trail throbbed under their feet again, as they marched back over the well-remembered miles, past old House Mountain, past Betsey Bell and Mary Gray, past John Craig's Old Stone Church, and the Willow Spout, over the Narrow Passage, and for a long time in the shadow of their bulwark, Massanutten. The houses were utterly familiar, utterly familiar the faces that smiled at them and the hands that waved. Filthy, ragged, hungry, welcomed, acclaimed, and loved, the Confederates swept yet another time down the Valley, routed the small force left to oppose them, re-entered Winchester on July 2nd, and on the fifth crossed the Potomac into Maryland.

They were only 11,000, with no hope of reinforcements, and enemy armies all around them. "It was so reckless," says Douglas, "that historians are still examining figures to see if it can be possible." In the lush fields of Maryland, on the untouched farms, they filled their empty stomachs, and rolled on; until they passed through Silver Spring and camped in front of the breastworks around Washington. On clear days they could see the white dome of the Capitol, gleaming like a mirage. They could also see the hastily summoned reinforcements filing into the breastworks. After two days, Early withdrew, and brought his army back unscathed to the Valley, just ahead of the returning Hunter.

The temper of the war grew steadily grimmer. Now the Confederates put into practice some of the new technique they had learned. General McCausland, who six weeks before had to retire from Lexington, crossed the Potomac to demand damages of $100,000 from Chambersburg in Pennsylvania. The money was not forthcoming, and he burned the town. General Hunter returned to the Valley in no conciliatory mood. With the sullen fury of a man worsted in many a dinner-table argument, he set fire to the houses of his relations and his acquaintances, beginning with the home of his first cousin, the Honorable Andrew Hunter, in Charles Town. The elderly Andrew, wearing a gold ring inscribed with

David's love, was taken into custody by David, and the family were permitted to save nothing from the flames.

Hunter also burned Fountain Rock, the home of Colonel Boteler of the Confederate Congress. His two daughters, one a widow with three children under six, could not save anything—not even the baby's cradle, not even the poor bundle of a little servant girl's clothing, hidden behind a hedge. Miss Helen begged in vain for her piano, seated herself at it and began to play and sing a hymn.

> My God, my Father, while I stray
> Far from my home in life's rough way,
> Oh teach me from my heart to say,
>   Thy will be done.

As the flames licked closer, a soldier took hold of her and tried to lead her out. She pulled away from him, sat down, and sang the second verse. Then she closed the piano, locked it, and stepped through the window to join her sister and the children under the trees.

General Hunter also burned Bedford, home of General Lee's cousin Edmund, where his own niece had been a refugee guest of the family throughout the war; and Mrs. Edmund Lee wrote him a letter in which the mildest term was "monster." "Were it possible for human lips to raise your name heavenward, angels would thrust the foul thing back and demons claim their own."

General Hunter did not answer this, but he burned the home of Mrs. Brown, she who had smuggled in the quinine in her daughter's doll. She asked for a sofa for her invalid father, and was refused. She started upstairs to get her baby, and a soldier stopped her.

"You let me go. My baby's up there."

The soldier took her by the wrists and swung her over the banisters.

"Let the damn little Rebel burn."

Mrs. Brown came back at him in a rage which gave her a sense of supernatural power, of force sufficient to kill without weapons. The soldier saw it, and gave way.

It was not too long a reign of terror. Washington had not been pleased when General Hunter allowed Early to come so close to the city. On August 8th, Hunter at his own request was relieved of his command, and another man took charge of crushing the resistance in the Valley.

His name was Philip Sheridan.

21. The Starving Crows

Up from the South, at break of day,
Bringing to Winchester fresh dismay,
The affrighted air with a shudder bore,
Like a herald in haste, to the chieftain's door,
The terrible grumble, and rumble, and roar,
Telling the battle was on once more,
    And Sheridan twenty miles away.

But there is a road from Winchester town,
A good, broad highway leading down:
And there, through the flush of the morning light,
A steed as black as the steeds of night
Was seen to pass, as with eagle flight;
As if he knew the terrible need,
He stretched away with his utmost speed;
Hills rose and fell, but his heart was gay,
    With Sheridan fifteen miles away.
      —THOMAS BUCHANAN READ, "Sheridan's Ride"

GENERAL SHERIDAN'S ARMY, assembling 50,000
strong at Harpers Ferry, was named the Army of the Shenandoah, a fact which gave small satisfaction to the inhabitants of the region. The hearty new commander, a West Pointer with a bluff and humorous face, born of Irish parents at Albany, roused the loyalty and admiration of his troops in a way that his predecessors had failed to do. He had fought Indians, he had done fine work with his cavalry in the west. Now he had an army of his own—the usual G. I.'s, tired of fighting, tired of four years of defeat, still coming back with the same wry jokes, the same hardened determination,

255

ready to die if necessary, and hoping that they would not have to. For them the Shenandoah was still the "Valley of Humiliation," and around their campfires originated the classic exchange, any Yank to any Rebel, meeting on any road in Virginia, during any year.

"Where are you going, Yank?"

"Going to Richmond."

"You'll never get there."

"Oh yes, we will. Swap generals with us and we'll be there in three weeks."

Now the disillusioned but determined fighters had found their generals—and they had a new song, charged with a fateful and ominous meaning for the South.

We are coming, Father Abraham, three hundred thousand more,
We are coming, we are coming, our Union to restore.
We are coming, Father Abraham, three hundred thousand more.

Grant had recognized clearly that attrition was his infallible weapon. When he lost sixty thousand men around Richmond, where Lee opposed him with only sixty-eight thousand, he did not falter. He saw in the Shenandoah Valley a green and fertile oasis from which year after year the Confederates drew provisions and comfort for their straightened army. Operations in the Valley constantly threatened his plans at Petersburg. When Early withdrew from Silver Spring, he was already writing:

If the enemy has left Maryland he should have upon his heels everything that can be got to follow to eat out Virginia clear and clean . . . so that crows flying over it . . . will have to carry their provender with them . . . Should make all the Valley south of the Baltimore and Ohio a desert . . . If the war is to last another year, we want the Shenandoah Valley to remain a barren waste.

Sheridan was the right man to carry out such orders, to pass them on to General Torbert, commander of his cavalry, in no uncertain terms.

In compliance with the instructions of the Lt. General commanding, you will make the necessary arrangements for the destruction of the wheat and hay south of a line from Millwood and Winchester . . . You will sieze all mules, horses, and cattle . . . Loyal citizens can bring in their claims against the Government for this necessary destruction. No houses will be burned, and officers in charge of this delicate but necessary duty must inform the people that the object is to make this Valley untenable for the raiding parties of the rebel army.

As the Union reinforcements poured into the Valley, the Confederates watched them from their signal station on top of Massanutten. During the first two weeks of September, the cavalry fought almost daily, "handsome dashes," Sheridan called them. He lived at Rion Hall near Charles Town, where the woodwork is still decorated with saber cuts, and a woman who came to sell pies found the family portraits cut from their frames and rolled for shipping. She smuggled them out instead and hid them until the Bedingers came back. On September 15th, Grant himself visited Charles Town, for the weary Mr. Lincoln had told him "there will be nothing done unless you watch it every day and hour and force it." But after one talk Grant felt satisfied that Sheridan would need no order save "Go in."

The armies feinted, advanced, withdrew, advanced again. Early's thin cavalrymen were never at rest two days in succession. The Valley people called the Pike the "soldiers' racetrack," called the Blue Army of the Shenandoah "Harpers Weekly," because it showed up at the Ferry every week. By mid-September, Sheridan had 56,764 men against Early's 12,509, and Early was writing with a poignant optimism: "No wheat has been burned in this county, and if we can stay here, we can live."

The first large battle of the last campaign was fought just east of Winchester on September 19th. It was not a clockwork battle. The Federal divisions came up slowly, and at least two of the subordinate Union generals considered that they had saved the day by attacks undertaken on their own initiative. Nevertheless, Sheridan had the proper presence, the spirit the men had been waiting for. When the shells burst near him he laughed, "Damn close, but we'll lick hell out of them yet," and the men cheered. Accounts of the battle are controversial, both Early and Sheridan have been criticized by uninhibited subordinates, but the Confederate defeat was unquestionable. The sun set on a retiring Rebel line, with smoke coming out of it in ragged patches as the men fired and fell back; and on a thin straight line of ordered fire along the Union front. Once the Rebels started running, they went fast. In Winchester the beautiful Mrs. Gordon, wife of a Confederate general, rose from a sickbed and rushed into the street vainly exhorting the fleeing men to stand. It was a rout. The Union soldiers roared approval of the general who had shown them how to win. They hugged each other with delight, and the bands played wildly.

"We sent them whirling through Winchester, and we are after them tomorrow," Sheridan reported exultantly. "This army behaved splendidly."

"Sheridan should have been cashiered for this battle," grumbled Early in retrospect, "for a skillful commander . . . would have destroyed my whole force." But that is not how John Casler saw it, John, now the last man left in Company A, tramping wearily southward up the Long Gray Trail, defeated on the very fields where he had won under Old Jack. He remarked that Sheridan outnumbered Early five to one, and blandly added that Early was entirely to blame for the defeat, since he should not have fought such a large army where the Valley was wide enough for them to get at him. "The corps never had much confidence in him afterward, and he never could do much with them."

The Confederates halted and dug in at Fisher's Hill, where Early felt reasonably secure in a strong position, but Sheridan had enterprise, and he knew something about flanking movements. He sent Wright's corps by night to hide in the timber on North Mountain and surprise Early's left. The battle was ordered for four A.M., but by six P.M. the night before all was ready, and Sheridan clapped his hands together and exclaimed, "By God! We'll jump them tonight!"

Again the Rebels ran, this time in disorder, up the Pike, through the Narrow Passage, back up the Valley, back to the old camp at Brown's Gap. Sheridan was made a brigadier general and confirmed in permanent command. "Keep on," Grant wrote him, "and your good work will cause the fall of Richmond."

Sheridan pressed on to Harrisonburg, on to Staunton, with his cavalry everywhere carrying out their work of destruction. Every barn, every mill, every haystack, they burnt; every cow, every steer, every horse, pig, sheep, or hen, they slaughtered or drove off. The military necessity did not console the inhabitants.

There were some darker episodes. Lieutenant Meigs, a member of Sheridan's staff, was shot near the village of Dayton, and Sheridan ordered the village and all houses within five miles burned to the ground. The Confederates insisted, and history supports them, that Meigs fell in a fair fight between cavalry scouts, but the general blamed bushwackers, and insisted on revenge.

A regiment of cavalry rode in with heavy hearts to carry out the order, and were met by the weeping women and children. The officer in charge hesitated. His men hastily got up a petition which they signed and presented to him protesting against the duty imposed on them. Still he hesitated. Two women succeeded in making their way to the headquarters of General Custer, who personally took the responsibility of rescinding the order, and the troopers cheered with relief. But the lonely houses on the surrounding farms had no one to plead for them, and they burned. At about this time, two of Mosby's men, one only seventeen, were captured in an attack on the Federal wagon train, and hanged without trial by Custer's orders. Mosby retaliated by hanging some Union prisoners, and leaving their bodies to swing by the roadside.

At the end of September, Sheridan decided that his supply lines were too extended, and withdrew back down the

Valley, burning as he went. He scorched the countryside "clear and clean," he "carried off their stock and Negroes to prevent planting," he "made it a barren waste." The crows would need their rations in flying over, but the people of the Valley could not fly, and they were offered free transportation north with the receding Army of the Shenandoah. Only the oldest or the most fainthearted availed themselves of the opportunity. The rest stayed on their land to face down starvation.

At Fisher's Hill, little John Fisher, one of twelve children, saw his old grandfather knocked down by a trooper, saw their mill set afire, saw the machinery broken and carried off. He helped to put out the flames after the soldiers left, and remembered crawling back into the old bolting chest to scrape up a bushel of flour dust which had accumulated there for years. His mother sifted the worms out of it and made bread for the little ones, but he preferred to clean the black grease off the crackers and eat them instead. Near Harrisonburg the three Baugh girls put their old parents into one of Sheridan's wagons, and stayed behind to work their wrecked and blasted farm. (John Casler married one of them later.) At Mount Jackson, Mrs. Wayland recorded the passing and repassing in her diary—the little boys gathering the nails from the burnt barns, the increasing devastation—and continued to wash her yarn, to weave and dye, to spool her linsey chain, pick apples, and bake bread.

Sheridan reported that he had burned 2,000 barns, 120 flour mills, destroyed or carried away 874 barrels of flour, 22,000 bushels of oats, 460,072 bushels of wheat, 51,380 tons of hay, 157,076 bushels of corn. He drove off 16,438 head of cattle, 16,141 hogs, 17,837 sheep, took 10,000 pounds of tobacco, 2,500 bushels of potatoes, tore up 947 miles of railroad. The damage was estimated at twenty-five million dollars, houses were not spared, whatever the original intention had been, and the destruction included the Luray and Fort Valleys as well as the main Valley. Well satisfied with his achievement, Sheridan left his army in a strong position north of Fisher's Hill, and made a hasty trip to Washington, where Congress passed a vote of thanks to him and his brave men.

As Sheridan withdrew, Rosser's Laurel Brigade (once Ashby's) came through Brown's Gap to reinforce Early. Looking down from the mountains they could see a cloud of smoke across the Valley from the Blue Ridge to North Mountain. The smoke rolled up from the rich fields, from the well-remembered situations where the barns had been. By night the sky glared redly and the earth was starred with bonfires. Most of this command were Valley men, who now saw their own homes burning.

The pursuit wasted no time, and legend says that if they caught a party of the burners they took no prisoners. They saw women and children whom they knew weeping by the roadside with no roof but the sky, they saw young girls who had entertained them cursing hysterically as they watched the flames. Where they could avenge, they gave no quarter.

"The assurance with which Rosser challenged Custer all the way down from Harrisonburg showed that he had no conception of Sheridan's mounted strength," said the Federal George Pond. "His fatal zeal was probably due in part to the excitement of his men at seeing their barns and houses in flames." Excited indeed, in the end Rosser's men found themselves twenty-five miles ahead of Early, with the Federals between them and their commander. At Tom's Brook 1,500 of them fought 4,000 under Custer, and were soundly beaten. "The Laurel is a running vine," said Early grimly when he heard of it.

On the morning of October 19th, Early attacked Sheridan's army where he had left it just above Cedar Creek, a right flank resting on the North Fork of the Shenandoah where it loops around the spurred foot of Signal Knob. Only a Valley man would realize that infantry could defile between the river and the mountain, and reach the loosely guarded fords above—but there were plenty of Valley men in Early's corps.

General Gordon, General Pegram, General Ramseur, led their men by night through that narrow passage, leaving even the canteens and dippers behind for fear a rattle would betray them. At two in the morning the pickets of the 5th New York Artillery heard a tramping across the river and informed General Crook, who ordered his front line into the trenches, but sent out no reconnaissance, left gaps unfilled, and did not even make sure that the sleepy men had loaded their muskets. By four o'clock the Confederates could see the Union tents gleam whitely in the moonlight, and a dawn fog coming up. General Ramseur, still in his twenties, was joyful at the last staff conference. "Douglas, I've got to survive this fight, for I must get back to my wife and baby"—a first child whom he had never seen.

The attack began at 4:30 and the light fog added to the confusion. The surprise was complete, the Rebels passed the pickets without returning fire, and took the breastworks in five minutes. The sleepy 19th, U.S.A., breakfasting in the darkness, heard the Rebel yell, and ran to take over the trenches. As the fog lifted, they saw the whole gray army in front of them. They held gallantly until bullets flew from their rear, and their general sent an aide in haste "to tell the First Division to stop firing." But the aide came back more quickly than he went, for the men at the rear were Rebels too, and he "did not tell them to quit firing, as he did not think they would give a damn."

Within an hour, the whole Federal army was pouring down the road in disorder, with the Rebels after them, but not so hotly as Early wished, for the grays again gave way to their fatal propensity for plundering. Good food, good clothing, sound equipment, offered an irresistible temptation, and thousands tarried to be fed and covered. The irate Federal prisoners declared that even the officers relieved them of their coats, their shoes, and the money in their pockets. One Yank was smart enough to slit the uppers of his boots, and so preserve the soles for his own use.

Meanwhile in Winchester, some fifteen miles from Cedar Creek rather than the twenty of poetic license, at six A.M. a courier brought news of the battle to General Sheridan, who had stopped there for the night on his way back from Washington. The evening before his scouts had reported to him that Early's old camp was empty, and that the Rebs were retiring up the Valley. Sheridan was at first inclined to think the morning action just a skirmish. He breakfasted comfortably, and mounted between eight and nine. But he had not covered more than three or four miles when he began to meet the flying stragglers, then the wagons, with the drivers lashing sweating teams, then the hurrying confusion of the army itself. He ordered guards to stop the fugitives, put spurs to his black charger, and flew up the Pike.

"Face about, boys, and follow me, and we will lick the whole damn Rebel army!"

The men cheered and turned back, and as the general galloped on and others saw him, the cheers rolled up the Pike from regiment to regiment and division to division, and the men took fresh heart. They remembered Winchester and Fisher's Hill, and they knew that there would be no more falling back.

After a spirited gallop of about five miles, Sheridan met his main body at Newtown, and ordered them back to the position they had just vacated, riding himself along the re-formed lines, encouraging them in his animated earnest way, smacking his right fist into the palm of his left hand.

"Boys, if I had been here, this never would have happened. I tell you it never should have happened. And now we are going back to our camps. We are going to get a twist on them. We are going to lick them out of their boots."

The slackening of Early's pursuit around midday gave time for reorganization and a fresh attack was beaten off.

"That's good! That's good! Thank God for that . . . Now go after them and follow them up and sock it to them. Give them hell. We'll get the tightest twist on them yet that you ever saw. We'll have all those camps and cannon back again."

Sheridan was right. He breathed his spirit into his men and they responded nobly, counterattacking and breaking the Rebel charge. After fighting all day in the hot sun without food or water, evening found the Yankees back in their old camp, where they flung themselves down and slept among the dead. The cavalry pursued the flying Confederates as far as Woodstock. In the old Hite home, Belle Grove, General Ramseur, who had wanted to live, lay dying. He had been wounded in the morning, and his staff were taking him from the field together with a captured Federal officer, when the reversal came. The staff promptly turned to their prisoner. "Sir, we surrender to you"—and the Federal made arrangements for the general's care. He died holding the hand of the Union Colonel Dupont, who had been his friend and classmate at West Point.

Sheridan reported the battle modestly. "Hundreds of men, who on reflection found they had not done themselves justice, came back with cheers." But his men were sure where their salvation had lain. "The only reinforcements which the Army of the Shenandoah received or needed to recover the lost field of battle . . . was one man, Philip H. Sheridan."

So the last thrust had been tried, and had failed. Sheridan took his army back to Winchester, where he was made a major general. Early camped for two months near Newmarket, then withdrew to winter quarters at Staunton.

That was the starving winter. In the homes up and down the Valley, beside the blackened embers of the barns, the women found that life could be sustained all day on a roll and a cup of chickory coffee, that milk and mush made a royal supper for the children after beans and sorghum molasses. Some edibles had been saved, buried in gardens, driven up the mountains, hidden under floors—and since one can live on so very little, the Valley people were not ready to give up.

The cavalry was still active. In October, Mosby's men made their "Greenback Raid," on a train near Harpers Ferry, and captured $75,000 in gold from two Federal paymasters. The train was full of German immigrants going west, who refused to leave the cars until the raiders scattered newspapers up and down the aisles and set them on fire. The enraged General Sheridan wrote to Halleck:

I will soon commence work on Mosby. Heretofore I have made no attempt to track him up, as I would have employed ten men to his one, and for the reason that I have made a scapegoat of him for the destruction of private rights. Now, there is going to be an intense hatred of him in that portion of the Valley which is nearly a desert. . . . The people are beginning to see that he . . . causes a loss to them of all they have spent their lives in accumulating. Those people who live in the vicinity of Harpers Ferry are the most villainous in this Valley and have not yet been hurt much. If the railroad is interfered with I will make some of them poor . . . I will let them know that there is a God in Israel.

General Sheridan was mistaken in one supposition. It was not Mosby whom the Valley people were going to hate.

When the frost had killed the grass and the cold rains started, it looked as though Rosser's cavalry might have to disband for lack of forage. The troopers could tighten their belts and live on a handful of flour, but they could not stand it when their horses began to die in camp of starvation. So that they might be fed, Early let a quarter of his command go home on leave as soon as the roads became impassable for armies. Others were detached for duty at Petersburg, and his task became daily more hopeless. In January he made one of his rare appearances in church at Staunton, and when the minister rhetorically inquired what his congregation would do if the dead should rise and confront them, the general audibly remarked:

"I'd conscript every damned one of them."

Rosser let three hundred men go on a raid into the South Branch valley across the Alleghenies. They fought in the hail, they fought in freezing rain and mud, they fought when their uniforms were stiff with ice, and the ice rattled under their horses' bellies as they moved. They lost only one man, Fontaine Hite, who had followed them on foot all the way, hoping to get a horse for himself, and was killed at the door of a tent in the camp they surrounded. They did find horses and food, enough to last for a while, for a little while. They took nearly six hundred prisoners, many of whom died on the cold march back, while others froze their hands and feet and had to have them amputated. General Crook in a rage ordered the Federal officers who had allowed themselves to be surprised dismissed for disgraceful neglect and incompetency—which was fine, except that a few weeks later another little band of the same cavalry, aided by McNeill's Rangers, rode the surprised Generals Crook and Kelley out of their hotel in Cumberland and brought them as prisoners into the Confederate lines.

But it was all unavailing, all the endurance, all the gallantry, all the unbelievable determination in the face of hardships. They could not win. While Rosser's two thousand were barely managing to keep alive, the Federal Government complained because they had sent Sheridan's cavalry 8,265 remounts between December 1st and February 20th. The Rebels could not win. It was not right that they should win. They were fighting against Time, against the future, against the greater dream. But let America take a due pride in their courage, for they were her sons.

In that same bleak winter another young man from the lower Valley, John Beall, got himself hanged as a spy in New York City. Invalided out of the army by wounds and tuberculosis, he had gone to Canada, and after capturing two lake steamers had attempted to free the prisoners of war on Johnson's Island in Lake Erie. The plot had failed. A month or so later, he was caught at Buffalo in civilian clothes, tried, and condemned. When he faced the gallows, like another John, he turned his face skyward, and saw that life was good.

"How beautiful the sun is!" said John Beall.

They made him stand on the scaffold, where he turned toward the south, while they read the charges against him, and the order of execution.

The Government of the United States, from a desire to mitigate the asperities of war, has given to the insurgents of the South the benefit of rules which govern sovereign states in the conduct of hostilities . . . and he who in a spirit of revenge or with lawless violence transcends the limits . . . should be visited with the severest penalty.

At this point John Beall, remembering the burning, remembering the Valley, was seen to laugh aloud.

"I die in defense of my country," said John Beall.

At the end of February, Sheridan moved again, attacked Early at Waynesboro, flanked him, destroyed the remainder of his command. The Federals took eleven hundred prisoners, and Early himself barely escaped through the underbrush. Rosser made a flying attack on the Federal column to allow the prisoners to escape, but they did not want to escape. They had had enough.

So ended the movements of large armies in the Valley. On March 6th, Sheridan crossed the Shenandoah and departed by way of the James River Canal, which he destroyed. Rosser followed his blazing trail down into lower Virginia, but could not stop his progress, flaming with glory, crowned with success. "But, General Sheridan," said one of Rosser's men, "your march was through the Confederate graveyard, and the bones of dead soldiers could do you no harm."

Now only Mosby's troopers hung on, without a camp or headquarters, raiding when they could and returning after each sally to the shelter of the Blue Ridge, "that beautiful blue mountain," which was their safety and their home. Desertions increased, for the men drifted back to their starving families. The generals felt sure they would return as the spring operations began.

But the spring brought Appomattox, where on April 9th General Lee surrendered the last eight thousand of what had been his army.

It was over. Americans no longer had to kill each other. Out of an army of two and a half millions the Union had lost nearly five hundred thousand. Out of a million the South had lost nearly two hundred thousand. At Gettysburg ten thousand more men died than at Waterloo. Frequently both sides lost from thirty to fifty per cent of the forces engaged in a battle. Eighty-two per cent of Hood's Texicans died at Antietam. Let these things be remembered by those who think Americans cannot endure slaughter.

It was over, and the beautiful Valley lay a barren waste. The weary soldiers limped home to blasted trees and blackened fields, stark chimneys rising out of crumbling walls, eyeless windows, silence, and devastation. All that men could do to ruin the Valley had been done.—But the Land remained, the limestone and the river, the courage and the hope in human hearts, as frail and as persistent as the grass.

"Let your men keep their horses, general," said Grant to Lee. "They will need them for the spring plowing."

PART III

Recovery

22. The Hero

Furl that Banner, for tis weary;
Round its staff it's drooping dreary.
Furl it, fold it,—it is best.
For there's not a man to wave it,
And there's not a sword to save it,
And there's not one left to lave it
In the blood which heroes gave it,
And its foes now scorn and brave it.
    Furl it, hide it,—let it rest.

Furl it! for the hands that grasped it
And the hearts that fondly clasped it
    Cold and dead are lying low.
And that Banner,—it is trailing
While around it sounds the wailing
    Of its people in their woe.
        —FATHER RYAN, "The Conquered Banner."

O NE AFTERNOON in the early autumn of 1865, a solitary traveler, wearing a gray military coat from which the buttons and insignia had been removed, rode into Lexington on an iron-gray horse. Although his arrival was as unostentatious as possible, a few passers-by recognized him, and turned to follow him quietly. When he stopped at the hotel two or three ex-soldiers ran forward eagerly to hold his horse, and a little boy, with the impiety of his kind, tweaked a long hair from the tail and told his mother afterward that he intended to have it set in a brooch for his hypothetical future bride. Then Professor White happened by, objected strenuously to the traveler's plan of staying at the hotel, and bore him off after a courteous argument. So with the utmost simplicity General Robert E. Lee began his tenure as president of Washington College.

ROBERT E. LEE

He had not come because of a tempting offer, for the fortunes of the little college had never been at so low an ebb. He had come to discharge a responsibility which his conscience laid upon him.

All through the Valley that summer, all through Virginia, all through the Confederacy, the boys were coming home—riding their broken-down horses, tramping their dusty lanes, returning not to efficient hospitalization, mustering-out pay, a bonus from a grateful government—but to silence, poverty, labor, bitterness, defeat.

When Robert Page of Clarke County had ridden away at seventeen, his colored mammy tried to believe that he had not gone. Every evening at dusk she walked down the lane as usual and called him as though he were still a dirty-faced little boy who might run home to be washed for supper. After Appomattox, Captain Robert Page came home on foot over the long miles. He found the fences around "Saratoga" gone. A weed-tangled common stretched where the fields had been. Silence lay blankly over the pastures and the blackened foundations of the barns. The house stood alone and staring. Then in the twilight, in the thin spring air, he heard his mammy call him, and answered, "Here I am."

Henry Douglas stacked arms with the last brigade to surrender, and went slowly back to camp, where he heard that his Negro Buck had run off with his horse, bridle, saddle, and trunk. He had been so sure of Buck's fidelity that he found this hard to believe, but it was true. He started to walk home. When he had tramped as far as Lexington, he found Buck waiting for him. If the Yankees arrested Marse Henry, Buck had thought, they should not get his horse and his things. Buck had swum the river, climbed the mountains, and brought all safely to the Valley. Now they could go on together.

"But I can't pay you, Buck."

"Doan want no pay."

"You don't understand, Buck. I must learn to do without a servant. I can't even feed you, Buck."

Buck began to cry.

"Tell you what you do, Buck. You take the horse. You've surely earned it."

They parted then, and Henry Douglas walked home alone.

These were the young men who had left their youth behind them on the bloodstained fields, who had learned nothing since their boyhood save to kill and to endure. Half their brothers slept beneath the wheat, but the homecomers could not sleep. They had to find what they could do in their ruined land, what aptitudes they had for which society would pay them with bread. They had to train their minds and school their muscles—but most of all they must learn to forget, to forget the terror and the glory, the lost vain hopes, and to forget the bitterness. They had followed Lee bravely, giving all the bright young morning of their lives. Now he would dedicate his evening to their service.

The general was a defeated warrior, a paroled prisoner of war, excluded from the general amnesty. Many voices in the North were calling for his blood, insisting that he ought to be hanged. The radical party in Congress might have succeeded in having him tried for treason had not General Grant threatened to resign his commission if the terms of surrender were violated. For reasons of personal safety, Lee might well have felt it necessary to go abroad as many others did. Of his personal fortune nothing remained. His house and lands were confiscated, his career as a professional soldier was closed to him. By any worldly terms he was completely ruined. He had retained nothing except the unanimous love and veneration of his people in the South.

He lived quietly that first summer with his invalid wife and two daughters in a four-room cottage on a friend's place near Richmond, and ignored the threats which constantly appeared against him in the northern press. He refused a country home in England, a somewhat illusory hacienda in Mexico. He also refused all commercial offers. His reputation was not for sale, and what remained of his life belonged to his own country, to that impoverished Virginia with which his fortunes were irrevocably involved. He declined the presidency of Suwannee in Tennessee, because it was a denominational college, and of the University of Virginia, since it was a state institution. When the offer came from Washington College, he hesitated also—not because it was struggling, depleted, and comparatively unknown, but because he was "an object of censure to a portion of the country, and my connection might be injurious to it."

The board of trustees soon overrode his objections. They had been conscious of an unparalleled temerity when they offered him the presidency. When he accepted they could hardly believe their good fortune. Individually and collectively, they were in a state of absolute poverty. The faculty was reduced to three, the students to not more than fifty. Most of the equipment had been destroyed by General Hunter. Judge Brockenbrough had to borrow a suit before he could go to Richmond and make the offer. They promised Lee a salary of $1,500 a year and a house, but they felt obligated to explain that the college was $4,000 in debt and that they counted on an increased enrollment under his presidency to pay their bills. It was a beginning from behind the beginning, and Lee so understood it.

A letter which he wrote to Mrs. Lee shortly after his arrival in Lexington shows the spirit in which he accepted his changed circumstances. "Life is indeed gliding away, and I have nothing of good to show for mine that is past. I pray

I may be spared to accomplish something for the benefit of mankind and the honor of God." He put the past behind him and marched forward with a calm serenity. "Misfortune nobly borne is good fortune," he quoted to the sculptor Edward V. Valentine. Only once did someone see his composure broken. He left chapel one morning with a look of extreme distress, and a lady with more concern than tact asked him what could be the matter. He answered her directly.

"I was thinking, madam, of my responsibility to God for all of these young men."

General Lee's broken-down college had a long history. The Scotch-Irish, as concerned about education as they were about religion, founded in 1749 a "classical academy" at Timber Ridge, where Latin, Greek, algebra, and geometry were taught in a one-room log cabin. In 1774 their Presbytery decided to further this good work, and sent a Princeton graduate, William Graham, to head it. Two years later upon examination of his students, they were sufficiently satisfied to give him one hundred and sixty pounds. With this he bought a telescope, a microscope, a globe, an air pump, an electrical machine, a quadrant, surveyor's instruments, and two hundred and ninety books. Alexander Stuart and Samuel Houston, father of "Texas Sam," presented eighty acres of land to the school, and its name was changed to "Liberty Hall" in accordance with the spirit of the time. For a tuition of four pounds a year, and a board of fifteen, a youth could be educated. When hard times closed the academy in 1780 and the Presbytery withdrew its support, Mr. Graham took some of the boys into his own house, and continued to teach.

After the Revolution the school resumed independently, and continued in the face of an outcry about the "wild young people," the "juvenile delinquents," the young men who had been to war "losing their primitive innocence," and learning instead to drink, to play cards, and to swear. An intractable boy threatened to kick one of his fellow students, to "fly at him like the devil and carry him away to Hell."

The shocked authorities advised the other students to avoid his company. By 1793 religion had revived a little. In 1796 General George Washington himself, with more faith in the younger generation than had some of his contemporaries, made Liberty Hall a present of his shares in the James River Canal and permitted the name to be changed to Washington College.

By this time they had four professors and four departments, Languages, Mathematics, Natural Sciences, and a sort of omnibus curriculum of Logic, Moral Philosophy, Belles Lettres. Mr. Graham was allowed to retire at the ripe old age of fifty. The young men paid seven pounds a year for a breakfast of bread and tea, a dinner of meat and vegetables, a supper of bread and milk, and they recited once a day in one subject only. But despite this frugality of bread and thought, it was deplored that there were too many "gentlemen's sons" among them to give the necessary tone of seriousness and hard work. Neither the gentlemen nor their sons kept the college out of debt. After a great fire which necessitated a move to town, bankruptcy would have been imminent had it not been for an unexpected benefactor, John Robinson.

Robinson began his life as an itinerent Irish weaver, a quondam horse trader, who grew rich after the Revolution by buying up the certificates of the penniless veterans and collecting their bounties and their lands. Although he had no children, he interested himself in education and gave Washington College the money for a new building. When they laid the cornerstone, in the early 1800's, Robinson set out on the campus a forty-gallon hogshead of rye for the benefit of the trustees and their guests. In that lusty age seven out of eight of the church elders had their own distilleries, and such justice was done the occasion that the college hill soon resembled a battleground strewn with bodies. Tradition allows that John Robinson was shocked, but he did not withdraw his support, and when he died left the then handsome endowment of $46,000. "Although without a child to provide for . . . in the trust that I have done something to protect the sons of others from ignorance and vice."

For about fifty years thereafter, the college proceeded quietly on its way, while students came and went to the accompaniment of complaints about the lack of respect they showed their elders. Then the Liberty Hall Volunteers marched off in the spring of 1861.

When General Lee took over the ruin that four years of war had made, he knew that the South's greatest need would be for education, and his ideas on the subject were clear-cut and consistent. While bigots in the North fulminated against his unfitness to lead young men, he deliberately turned away from military discipline, and placed the responsibility for good behavior on the boys themselves by establishing an "honor system" which is the basis of the university today. "We have but one rule here," he said, "and it is that every student must be a gentleman."

This was not to be interpreted as an invitation to laxity. General Lee tried to know all his students personally, even when he had eight hundred of them. He talked in warm and fatherly terms with any who offended by misconduct or idleness. But if reformation did not follow, the young man was dropped. "A young man is always doing something," he said, "if not good then harm, to himself and to others." He sharply checked a student with a bevy of thin excuses for an absence. "Stop, Mr——. Stop. One good reason is enough for an *honest* mind."

Between 1865 and 1870, the South discovered that the war had been more bearable than the peace. Then at least they had had the relief of action. Now all was impotence. Because they had fought in the Confederate Army, the fathers of the youths at Lexington were disfranchised, and so were many of the students themselves. Virginia was neither in the Union nor out of it. She had become Military District One. She had not been allowed to secede, but now she might not be represented in the national Congress. Even her state officials were held incompetent to serve because of their connection with the rebellion. Four thousand offices were vacated when this proviso was put into effect by act of Congress, and were filled with northern appointees. The Southerner, dispossessed of control, retained only one right, that of paying taxes.

The Negroes were enfranchised, and Congress provided for the election of a new state constitutional convention to meet at Richmond and set up a regime which would be acceptable to the radical northern leaders. The military supervised the election, appointed election officials, and the result of the "plebiscite" was as expected. The "Black and Tan" convention duly met at Richmond. Of its one hundred and four members, twenty-five were colored. The white leaders were Northerners who had come to the state as sutlers or clerks in the wake of the Union Army, or as workers in the Freedman's Bureau. The South, viewing all this helplessly but not in silence, had a bitter word for them: "carpetbaggers."

"The carpetbagger," said the Winchester *Times,* "is a two legged animal of the male species which travels without a trunk, wears paper collars, and carries a great portion of his baggage on his back . . . has a fine nose for offices, (but) invests no funds anywhere 1) because he has none, 2) because he would not settle anywhere." Negro suffrage they saw not as an issue, but as an accomplished fact forced upon a prostrate people. "The radicals have accumulated their outrages upon our constitution with such rapidity that they have *fatigued* the indignation of our people."

Free speech was by no means suppressed in this conquered territory. The *Spirit of Jefferson* in Charles Town reported freely and sourly on the attempted impeachment of President Johnson and the candidacy of General Grant. It quoted without comment the long speech of a colored member of the Black and Tan convention, on the superior construction of hogpens in Massachusetts, and the consequent necessity of a land tax. It reported the confusion of a white member who came out for a capitation tax and against a poll tax. It quoted from another Negro member: "De power of dese disloyal men whose larnin and houses has been gained by de labor of blacks, and de very stones under dere feet has been got from dere blood, must pass away."

Yet in spite of obvious ignorance, in spite of naïveté

exposed and long words misused in the speeches which were reported without sympathy, the convention at Richmond did struggle toward some liberal ideas which are now commonplaces: an eight-hour day for labor, legitimate status for children born in slavery, higher education for the Negro. The Southerner, however, saw no good in his despoilers. On its front page *The Spirit of Jefferson* published the two-column story of an elderly gentleman whose children had committed every crime in the calendar; yet he held his head up until the youngest crowned their infamy by the ultimate offense of sitting in the Congress of the United States. Nor was this the only sample of the editor's sense of humor, for on March 31, 1868, the following small advertisement appeared without comment near his editorial matter.

All those interested in the organization of a Society of the Klu Klux Klan are requested to meet at the U.M.S. tomorrow Wednesday a.m. when the object of the organization will be fully explained.
By order of the eminent Khi Kho Khan.

A week later the editor remarked blandly on the excitement aroused among the military by this paragraph—one which he had obviously intended merely as an April Fool since it was published on that date. He declared himself astonished at the success of his little joke.

Those were the lawless years. Throughout the Valley neither property nor life was safe after dark. Horse stealing reached such a pitch that the death penalty was demanded for it. Livestock of all kinds disappeared, public property was smashed by vandals. The drifting and embittered Negroes did some of this, but more was done by the ex-soldiers, the young men who had had four years of taking what they wanted. Civil authority commanded no respect, for its representatives were removed or appointed at the will of the military. The new county courts were referred to in the county papers as "emigrant trains" or "menageries." General Stoneman succeeded General Schofield, General Canby followed General Stoneman, as the controllers of Virginia. Henry Wells, a Northerner who had settled during the war in Alexandria, was appointed governor, and an Ohio Negro, J. D. Harris, as Lieutenant Governor. But within a few weeks this farce of statehood was played out, and General Stoneman resumed the powers of the executive.

Alexander H. H. Stuart of Staunton organized a "Committee of Nine" to attempt a compromise along the lines of "universal suffrage and universal amnesty." He engaged the interest of General Grant, but otherwise accomplished little. The Valley people were for the most part so sunk in apathy or stubborn bitterness that they ridiculed his efforts. When Grant was elected president in 1868 the people of Virginia were not allowed to participate in the election, but soon after his inauguration he accepted the proposals of the Committee of Nine and allowed an election of civil officers throughout the state. In January of 1870 Congress passed an act "to admit the State of Virginia to representation in the Congress of the United States." This restored a measure of calm, although under Grant the security was to prove illusory.

Through the snarled warp of this most tragic era in American history, ran the dark and tangled woof of the liberated Negro. Uneducated, unprovided for, confused, this unhappy people had lost their old world, confining but secure, and had as yet found no foothold in the new. In their first delight at knowing the war over and their freedom assured, they flocked to the Federal camps, sure that their liberators would take them to Canaan in the North. But the northern army did not want them. When the numbers grew so large that they could not be employed, the soldiers discouraged newcomers by tossing them in blankets. The boys were a little rough and some of the Negroes died.

Still the black men were free, and this was glorious, but in their freedom they could not be expected to stay on the farms where they had been slaves. They crowded into the towns "as if they could not be free in the country," wrote one observer in Augusta. In the towns they went hungry. Some died, and others fastened themselves to the better class of southern whites who still felt a responsibility for them. The efforts of the Freedmen's Bureau touched only the sur-

face of the problem and did not reach the roots. Now that the
Negroes were free, most of them did not know where to go
or what to do.

Sometimes amid the naïve bombast of the speeches in the
Black and Tan convention, a sentence would strike to the
heart of truth like jagged lightning in a blue-black sky. "You
will never get the colored man out of Virginia while the sun
shines. This is heaven enough for him." And again, "The
blacks has got to root or die."

So great a social upheaval could not be accomplished
without violence. In Darkesville a Negro shot a white man,
and in Lexington, and in Front Royal. In Clarke County a
Negro girl who had decided to stay with her white family
was abducted in daylight by a gang of eight or ten blacks.
In sleepy Charles Town they had a race riot one Saturday
afternoon, when thirty Negroes who had been drinking set
upon five whites. The Irish fought the Negroes in Winchester.
In Rockbridge County the murdered and violated body of a
Miss Hite was found beside a road, and a Negro admitted
the crime. For the first time in Valley history, a man was
lynched. But against other offenders no mob violence was
attempted.

Amid these dark currents of hatred, fury and revenge;
amid ruin, lawlessness and pillage; amid apathy and despair
—General Lee at Lexington stood like a beacon by which
men could steer. If he felt regret or sadness, he did not utter
it; if he noticed a difference in his circumstances, he did not
refer to it; if he felt critical of the new authorities, he did
not say so.

Quietly he discharged the duties of his new post, finding
no detail too small to be beneath his notice, whether it concerned a new woodpile or a new school of law or journalism.
He asked for no praise and no attention, but gently rebuked
both adulation and bitterness by word and by example.

He summered at White Sulphur Springs for the benefit
of Mrs. Lee's arthritis. He had hoped to be unnoticed there,
but when he first entered the hotel dining room the entire
company rose in silent respect. Once during the evening

promenade he noticed that a party of Northerners with the wartime governor of Pennsylvania were sitting alone. He asked if they had been made welcome. No, and why should they be? He asked some lady to introduce him. Silence. "Then I shall introduce myself and any lady who will accompany me." Miss Christiana Bond of Baltimore went with him, and halfway across the ballroom asked the question for the others. "But, General Lee, did you never feel resentment towards the North?" The general stopped under the crystal chandelier. "I believe I may say, speaking as in the presence of God, that I have never known one moment of bitterness or resentment." There were no more Yankees snubbed at the White while General Lee was there.

On another occasion after talking to a run-down man who seemed pleased by his attention, he remarked: "That was one of our old soldiers. He fought on the other side, but we must not think about that." When the student orators overdid it, he corrected them. "Young gentlemen, your remarks about the government of the United States had best be left unsaid, as tending to prolong bitterness. Your praise of me is distasteful to me, and your compliments to the ladies had better be paid in private."

To all the parents who sent their sons to his institution, he gave the same advice: "Remember that we form one country now. Abandon all local animosities, and make your sons Americans."

In her most bitter moments of humiliation, the South could look at General Lee and feel proud again—feel that he justified the civilization that had produced him. All classes had the same respect for him. A mountaineer stopped him once on the daily ride on Traveller which was his only relaxation.

"General, I fit for you. I feel like cheering for you now."

"But we are alone, and there is no occasion for cheering."

"I don't care. I'm a-going to cheer."

As the general galloped off in embarrassment he heard

the Rebel yell shiver the leaves behind him. "Yai-ai-ai! Three cheers for General Lee!"

For five years he guided, built, encouraged, led—and then death came for him, not stealthily or suddenly but as a last antagonist whom an old soldier might calmly face. One evening he came home from a vestry meeting and as he stood to say grace before tea, he found himself unable to speak, and sank back in his chair. Afterward he lay quietly in bed for two weeks, perfectly conscious and apparently in no pain, rarely speaking, never complaining, but "neither expecting nor desiring to get well." In his last hours his mind wandered slightly. "Strike the tent," he said. "Tell Hill he must come up."

They laid him in the crypt of the new chapel. Today above his ashes rests the recumbent statue which Valentine carved out of white marble. Not as a warrior has he been preserved for the young men of Washington and Lee, but in the dignity of a perfect self-control, in an illumined rest.

Dr. Pendleton, Sandy's father, selected the text for his funeral sermon. "Mark the perfect man, and behold the upright, for the end of that man is peace."

Even then the people of America knew that he belonged to all of them, not only to the South. Julia Ward Howe wrote a commemorative poem for him, Charles Francis Adams and Gamaliel Bradford had paid him tribute. In the summer of 1943, Washington and Lee was taken over by the Army of the United States, and young men in uniform from all over the Union acquired in Lexington a part of their education as soldiers. As their khaki-colored figures moved briskly about the campus under the old trees, a custom persisted as it has now done for three-quarters of a century. Whenever they passed the ivy-covered chapel, the hands from Maine or Michigan, Kansas or California, went up in a salute to the sleeping general.

It is a good thing for Americans, with their worship of success, to have one hero who was magnificent in failure.

23. The Faith

No more shall the war-cry sever,
Or the winding rivers be red;
They banish our anger forever
When they laurel the graves of our dead!
    Under the sod and the dew,
    Waiting the judgement day:—
    Under the laurel the Blue,
    Under the willow the Gray.
   —FRANCIS MILES FINCH, "The Blue and The Gray."

ANOTHER distinguished Confederate taught at Lexington during the postwar years, although he did not come there until after the general amnesty in 1868. Matthew Fontaine Maury, "Pathfinder of the Seas," held a chair at the Virginia Military Institute until his death in 1873.

He was descended from that Fontaine who so obligingly kept a diary of Governor Spotswood's trip, but his father had migrated from Virginia to Tennessee when he was five. Two fortunate accidents colored his career. At twelve he fell out of a tree and injured his back so that he was unfit for work on his father's farm, and consequently was allowed to amuse himself by study. Later, after he became a naval officer, an injury to his knee retired him from active duty to the Department of Charts and Instruments at the Observatory in Washington. There he originated the signal service, and made the first charts of winds and currents, by means of which voyages under sail might be shortened twenty per cent. Foreign governments recognized his work, decorated him, imitated his system, but he was lost to the

United States Navy when, like so many others, he felt that he could not fight against Virginia.

During the war he tried to build up a Confederate Navy, worked with torpedoes and mines, and was in Halifax on a mission when the conflict ended. He was one of those whom the Emperor Maximilian beguiled to Mexico, but that plan proved as illusory as the rest of the emperor's hopes, and after a brief stay in England, Maury came home—home to Virginia, home to the Valley, the refuge that war could not destroy. His connection with the Valley had begun early in life when Samuel Houston procured his appointment to Annapolis. In the Valley he lived out his closing years in peace and competence, and his dying request was that his body should be carried through Goshen Pass when the rhododendrons were in bloom. In Goshen Pass his monument still stands.

Not all the Confederates had Maury's well-developed talents to sustain them during Reconstruction. For most of them life was reduced to a basic struggle for a living. "We had to begin at the bottom—and it was out."

Major Edward Allen, he who had resigned a colonelcy to be a private, who had commanded without a commission, and who had ended as a major in Ashby's cavalry, came back to find his home gone, his family dead or "refugeeing," his only assets two war-worn horses. The resourceful major started a livery stable. When some of the colored people wanted to be driven to a social in the country, he and his brother were glad to oblige. The night grew cold, the festivities protracted, and after a brief hesitation the hackmen went in to warm themselves at the stove. Some of the Negroes soon came up to them.

"Would you gen'lmen min' steppin' outside? You smells so of de hosses."

A dollar was a dollar, and the major went.

In Lexington, Mrs. Angus McDonald also was discovering that pride had no market value. The Yankees had ruined her home in Winchester beyond repair, Colonel McDonald had died as the result of his stay in a Yankee prison, and after she lived through the first two years of the peace she could be glad he had been spared them. When relatives offered to take some of the children, she refused to divide her family, saying that God had sent them to her, and of her hands would he require them. She could imagine the question on the Day of Reckoning: "Where is thy flock? Thy beautiful flock?"

She had three hundred dollars in Confederate money, worth about fifteen in Federal silver, and it went quickly. She gave lessons in drawing and French, held classes to read poetry and history. Harry chopped wood for the Federal quartermaster. He used to take little Roy with him as company, and when it snowed he carried the child on his back for the toes were out of Roy's boots. When the woodcutting ended, Harry and Allen went to work on a farm, plowing with and paid like the Negroes, falling asleep in their chairs from exhaustion when they got home at night.

For breakfast they had bread and water; for dinner, bean soup and bread. Weak with constant hunger, watching the slow degradation of her family, and seeing no hope of better circumstances, at times Mrs. McDonald wished that God would sweep her and her children from the earth. "There seemed no place on it for us, no room for us to live." Then she would reproach herself for her want of faith, and struggle on. When the summer ended and the college opened, she found it bitterest of all to live surrounded by good schools and have no hope of securing an education for her sons.

One late October afternoon, as she went for her daily walk, she felt too forlorn to face people in the street. She retired to the cemetery and sat by Sandy Pendleton's grave, watching the purple shadows darken the mountains as twilight fell. When she went out at dusk, she met Mrs. Pendleton at the gate and, taken off guard, her face showed what she felt.

"What can be the matter, Mrs. McDonald? You look so dreadfully. Come home with me and tell me what it is."

The kind words broke down the last of her self-control,

and she began to sob while Mrs. Pendleton held her hands. It was impossible to hide the situation any longer.

"We are starving. I and my children."

And by a miracle, Mrs. Pendleton knew of one hundred dollars which she might have, from a source which could not be divulged. She learned long afterwards that it came from a fund sent to Canada for secret-service work, and now to be dispensed for Confederate widows and orphans. This proved the turning point. Soon another friend received a quarter of beef and sent her a roast. One of her older stepsons found a bond of his father's and cashed it for enough to pay the rent. Someone else lent her three hundred dollars.

With a light and happy heart I set about making provisions for the winter . . . Harry was old enough to go to college, and I had determined to send him . . . Here ends my account of my trials; and though they were not at an end entirely, I was able in various ways to take care of my family till they were fitted to be of use to themselves; and when they were able to bear the burden they took it up manfully and acquitted themselves well.

The Valley had been ruined, but the Valley was coming back. Descendants of the Scotch-Irish, accustomed to a new debacle in almost every generation; descendants of the thrifty Germans, who had made a garden out of a wilderness by their own hands; descendants of English gentlemen, who "adventured" rather than accept defeat or meager life—all the people of the Valley dug down to the limestone rock and planted their feet thereon. They had thrown everything into the battle for a cause in which they believed, and they had lost. This might be tragic, but it had happened before to their own ancestors, who had survived. They also would survive. "Well, the upper Valley still flourishes in spite of the drought and General Canby," wrote an Augusta County newspaper in 1868, "The hardy Scotch-Irish above us are used to persecutions, and the Dutch below are constitutionally phlegmatic, and the soil of the Valley is generous still. We have never been dependent on the institution of slavery."

In truth they had not been dependent on the slaves.

They had never depended on anything save their own characters, and they never would. This was their secret, and the source of their recovery. For they did recover.

In such a complete upheaval, such a reversal of accepted values, it could not be expected that all would have the necessary strength to make adjustments. There were some vaguely wandering minds in crumbling houses, there were some suicides in lonely homes. Most families had a cousin or two who drank themselves to death, often requiring seventy-five or eighty years to complete the agonizing process. But most of the Valley people during the eighty years since their disaster have done one of two things: they have stayed on their land and rebuilt their homes and their ample way of living or they have sent their children to succeed in far places, but never quite to lose contact with Home.

During four years of desperate fighting, followed by four years as a subject people, they ate the last black crust of bitterness, and discovered that it need not choke them. They had lost everything except the ground beneath their feet, and yet they found that something remained to them, for defeated but unbroken they still had their pride, their truly integrated self-respect.

This pride has at times been misunderstood. It is not based upon a memory of a glamorous past, which in point of fact they had never had. Like most Americans, they had maintained themselves through hard work and enterprise, and by good luck they had done so with gaiety rather than with Puritan grimness. But the lean spirit which sustained them for the next fifty years was not based on that. It was the fierce and hungry stare of a man who has defied fate once, withstood the ultimate misfortune, and is willing, by God, to do it again. Valley tradition held that a man might be called upon to die for his country. Valley tradition holds this true today. From Germany to Iwo Jima the Valley men are doing as their fathers and grandfathers did. It has been said that the proved readiness of Southerners to enter the armed forces is the result of economic pressure, but it can be demonstrated that the roots lie deeper. They lie in a code which considers no material advantage worth a loss of self-respect.

The people of the Valley kept their self-respect. Even under the military occupation, when the carpetbaggers and the Negroes seemed to have the clutch of death on Richmond, they adopted no lickspittle philosophy. Their newspapers and their leading men openly discussed measures of resistance and denounced oppression. This courage was assisted by the magnanimity of the conquerors, who took no direct steps against defiance, despite legislative decrees.

The Valley people had lost the easy power which they had taken for granted, the peaceful living, the control of circumstances which were pleasant if limited. They retreated to the impregnable citadel within themselves, which their traditions had taught them how to defend. It is old-fashioned to speak of "a Christian gentleman," but the phrase still has a meaning in the Valley, and all classes have been to some degree permeated by the ideal behind it: responsibility toward others, integrity within oneself. The Civil War had ruined the world as they knew it, but truth was still true, courage and loyalty still duties. They had never been irresponsible. It was now only the scope of their responsibilities that had changed.

One of the first steps in readjustment was to accept the situation realistically. It took a little time for the first shock to pass, and time for hope to die. Nothing pointed up the altered situation more forcefully than the position of two counties in the northern end of the Valley; their people were informed that they now belonged to the new Union-sympathizing state of West Virginia.

The fate of Jefferson and Berkeley counties was peculiar. To this day they like to consider themselves a sort of American Alsace-Lorraine. When Virginia seceded, her counties beyond the Alleghenies objected bitterly. Their rugged soil had not encouraged slaveholding, they were tired of being "poor relations," and their sympathies were with the North. In August of 1861 they held a convention at Wheeling on the Ohio, and formed themselves into the Union state of

West Virginia. When in November they set up their government and defined their boundaries, the Baltimore and Ohio
Railroad clamored for protection in the two Virginia counties which it crossed east of the Alleghenies. It was a vital
carrier for the new state, so West Virginia readily agreed to
include them and declare them Federal territory.

Such action seemed a joke to the residents of the two
counties, who, since they were Confederate sympathizers,
had no voice in the proceedings. By law the consent of Virginia had to be secured, but this was arranged through the
self-styled "government-in-exile" of Virginia, which had set
itself up at Wheeling. In May of 1863 it was considered advisable to hold a popular vote in the disputed territory. The
area was at that time occupied by Union troops, no one was
allowed to vote who did not first take the oath of allegiance,
and most of the men were away fighting on the Rebel side.
The result of the plebiscite was never in doubt. It took only
seventy votes to transfer Jefferson County into the new state,
and even so, according to the records of Colonel Boteler in
Shepherdstown, one hundred and seventy votes were added
after the polls had closed. At last all the red tape was tied,
and in June of that year President Lincoln proclaimed West
Virginia the thirty-fifth state in the Union.

The citizens of Jefferson and Berkeley counties observed
all this with amusement, while their real interest was centered
on the movements of their army. Then the war ended, and
they faced the horrid fact that these political shenanigans
could be made to stick.

In 1865 Virginia sued for the recovery of the two lost
counties, but without success. The citizens of Jefferson
County tried to vote for a Virginia legislator, and were
forcibly restrained by Federal troops. Two-thirds of their
electorate signed a petition asking that the act ceding them
to West Virginia be repealed, and the radical government of
West Virginia circulated a counterpetition saying that the
Baltimore and Ohio Railroad would leave them if this were
done. The matter went before the Congress of the United
States, which, over the objections of President Johnson, re-

ported overwhelmingly in favor of West Virginia. In 1867 Virginia took her suit to the Supreme Court, which divided on the question four to four. In 1871 it was argued again, and this time Virginia lost by a vote of six to three.

In 1871 the *Spirit of Jefferson*, the county's leading newspaper, changed its masthead from "Charlestown, Virginia" to "Charles Town, West Virginia." But it is easier to change an address than a heart. "West Virginia can offer no price," they said, "which would prompt us to submit willingly to the deep damnation of our taking off from our dearly loved mother." They ignored the change as much as possible, and many still ignore it, sending their children to Virginia schools, their ministers to Virginia synods, sweetly asking visitors from across the mountains: "When are you going back to West Virginia?" and describing their place of residence as "in the Shenandoah Valley, near Winchester."

But they cannot get back. Their separation is permanent. In one of those anticlimactic footnotes which history appends to the most heroic situations, Virginia sued West Virginia for expenditures made before the separation, and won her case. The two lost counties hoped that they might be returned to Virginia in payment of the debt, but the suggestion was never made, for it appeared that the mother state preferred to have the money. Perhaps in another hundred years it will have ceased to matter.

In the decade following the war, even the skies turned against the Valley people, even their river betrayed them. In September, 1870, the Shenandoah rose in its greatest flood, which took out every bridge and covered every bottom, and cut the railroad lines. At Lexington it washed away an undertaking establishment and all the coffins. General Lee lay dying while this was going on, and they would have had nothing to bury him in had not a farmer found one coffin washed up on the bank several miles down the river. In Rockingham County the damage was estimated at a million dollars. In Shenandoah it took away all the mills, the Shenandoah Iron

Works, the homes at Slabtown and Honeyville, the Kite family, the Dorrough family.

Near Front Royal, J. C. Blakemore sat in his house with his children and three guests and watched the river sweep away the mills which he had just rebuilt after Sheridan's burning. As he remembered the sweat and anguish that had gone into their reconstruction, it seemed to him that he could not bear it, and he cried out: "I am ruined!" But his distress was to endure only two hours.

He had often seen water run over the lowland behind his house, and before he realized that this was no ordinary flood, he was cut off. His two boats were moored at low-water mark, and when he thought of building another, he had no nails. The water reached the second floor, and the house floated away from its foundation and moved off with the current. The brick chimney held it for a moment, and one of the visitors floated on ahead, perched on the detached porch roof. Mr. Blakemore removed the sash from a second-story window, and stood by it in silence with his wife and three daughters, while his young son lay on the floor praying.

He told his family to go to the attic, but before they could reach the stairs the house suddenly sank in the water, and they were thrown against the ceiling. When the house rose again, the young boy found himself alone in the room. He climbed out the window and swam to shore, but he never saw any of the others again.

On the evening of the flood a Professor Kidd had spoken on Free Schools in Harpers Ferry, and had called attention to the faulty construction of the schoolhouse in that district. He declared that he wished for a convulsion of the elements to remove it so that a better one might be built. The river, with overzealous promptness, attended to his request before nine o'clock. It removed the schoolhouse, and all the buildings on two islands in the river, as well as the railroad bridge. Mr. Fitzgerald, supervisor of the track, went over on the last train and saw his wife screaming at her window. But he could not reach her. A Mr. Williams, who had been one of the hostages taken by John Brown, sat in his house until the front of it fell off, a rope was cast to him, and the family ridden out one by one in a basket. Mr. Williams was an imperturbable man, who had already lived through a great deal. All the lower streets were ruined in the little town, and forty-three were drowned.

More damage was done in one night by the water than had been done in a year of war. But the untouched areas sent help to the stricken, and they built the Valley up again. There is nothing man has ever built which cannot be rebuilt —so the Valley people said.

24. Fool's Gold and True Gold

URING the last thirty years of the nineteenth century, the people of the Valley were concerned with one absorbing problem—the necessity of making a living. The variety of solutions which they found proved their vitality and sturdiness.

The land was there, and hands and backs could work it; but parceled out among the members of a family it could not answer every need. Inquiring minds found an economic resource in education. Although Virginia had had some of the first free schools in the nation, she did not inaugurate a free school system until 1870. Now that children could no longer be sent away to expensive institutions of learning, the older generation who had had such advantages set up schools. The spacious old houses accommodated the scholars, and at Cool Spring, at Woodberry, in the house which General Milroy took from Mrs. Logan, in many other places, the schools began. Some were later discontinued, but many survived, and by 1940 eighteen boarding schools or colleges still flourished in the Valley, most of which were established or resuscitated during Reconstruction days.

At Harpers Ferry there is Storer College for colored students; in Winchester, the Shenandoah Valley Military Academy; at Front Royal, the Randolph-Macon Academy for boys; at Newmarket, the Newmarket Academy, the Lutheran Seminary, and a Seventh-Day Adventist school; at Woodstock, the Massanutten Military Academy (Reformed Church); at Bridgewater, Bridgewater College (Dunkard). Harrisonburg has Madison College, a normal school for women teachers, and Waynesboro the Fishburne Military

School, and Fairfax Hall for girls, named with unconscious humor for that stanch misogynist Lord Fairfax. Staunton is rich in the Mary Baldwin College, Stuart Hall, Staunton Military Academy, Augusta Military Academy, and the State School for the Deaf and Blind. At Lexington, Washington and Lee University continues its traditions, and the Virginia Military Institute still turns out top engineers and soldiers.

Besides the land and a tradition which valued education, the Valley had iron in its mountains and timber on their slopes. Jedediah Hotchkiss, the enterprising Yankee who had made Stonewall Jackson's maps, organized a company to develop these resources and, like Fernando Fairfax half a century earlier, put out a glittering prospectus. He planned to lease one hundred thousand acres in Page and Rockingham, on which he would mine iron, manganese, and limestone. At that time iron could be extracted for $44.44 a ton —less than in the Lehigh Valley, including transportation by barge down the Shenandoah to the railroad—and sold in Baltimore for $52.00 a ton. A miner would receive the handsome wage of seventy cents a day—quite sufficient since he could get board for thirty cents—while the manager would be handsomely recompensed by a salary of fifty dollars a month.

At Staunton, Major Hotchkiss published a magazine which he called *The Virginias: A Mining, Industrial, and Scientific Journal*. It procured articles written by northern geologists to describe the manganese, copper, iron, slate, clay, and ocher of the region. It pointed out that the cheapness of local labor more than compensated for the lack of transportation, since the Negroes preferred working in gangs and so were flocking to industry and away from agriculture. (It was added rather smugly that nearly every former slave now paid more in taxes than his master had been taxed for him). As for transportation, the Shenandoah Valley Railroad already had fifty-four miles of track and would soon have more. And at this point the *Journal* really let itself go: "furnishing easy access to one of the richest and most delightsome portions of the far famed Shenandoah Valley, its charming scenery, wonderful caverns, and famous battlefields, and to the immense far stretching beds of iron ore that rib with metallic wealth the sides and flanks of the mountain ranges that on either hand border that land of agricultural plenty."

Before long Major Hotchkiss scored a triumph by securing for Staunton the annual meeting of the American Institute of Mining Engineers. The ladies of the town, justly renowned for hospitality, rose to this opportunity of promoting national amity. The high spot of the convention was a brilliant evening entertainment at the new Asylum for the Deaf, Dumb and Blind, where the Stonewall band of the old brigade furnished the music, and the major made an address, telling "how his corps charged across the Trenton limestone, and climbed with many bruises a mountain of that confounded Medina sandstone; how victory perched on the Silurian, and defeat lurked in the Trias."

Union, accord, and progress were to be the keynotes for the coming century—and in this forward movement the river played its part. Although the hope of making it navigable had never been completely realized, it carried a considerable volume of freight on barges which were poled down and broken up for sale at Harpers Ferry. Much of that town is built from wood so acquired.

In May of 1880 they shipped by water from Riverton where the North Fork and the South Fork join, 1,000,000 pounds of lime, 48,000 pounds of mill feed, 40,000 pounds of corn, a carload of sheep, another of crossties, 268 barrels of flour, 1,191 sides of sole leather, 10½ tons of sumac, and also a quantity of wool, brandy, dried fruit, and tanbark. This was not so much as the 5,623 barrels of flour which "River Commodore" Jacob Sipe boated out of Port Republic in 1841, or the forty-one barges which sailed in one week of 1861—but it was creditable.

The river men had a life of their own, lusty, gusty, and cheerful. They called their barges "gundalows." A good barge, nine feet wide and seventy-six feet long, would bring

$25.00 at Harpers Ferry. Between fourteen and eighteen men were needed on it, and the trip took four days going down, and three days walking back. The voyage was not without dangers and adventures, for the barges went in chutes around the dams, and sometimes in the rapids they sank clear to the bottom. Then the boys had to wade around and fish for the iron as best they could. They blew tin horns eight feet long so that the people for five miles around could hear their tunes and know that they were coming. Zack Raines, Coronel Comes, Dug Dovel, Columbus Kite, Bogus Lucas, Bax Bugan, Sharp Good, Cap Dofflemoyer, Shinnol Croft—the river boys were plenty tough, and when they hit town on a Saturday night you knew somebody was there!

In these days of recovery all the leading newspapers reflected a spirit of optimism. The railroads were going to open up the Valley as they would have done a hundred years earlier had not friends of the James River Canal prevented it. "Happily the day of local prejudice has passed away, and the most sanguine can hardly conjecture what great things the future has in store for us. Slavery, the bugbear that frightened off Northern capital and enterprise, has now ceased to exist, and we already see a new era dawning upon the South."

While the people of the Valley thus unitedly contemplated a roseate future—no more averse to earning a dollar than the people of any other section—they found themselves almost without volition squarely in the middle of a land boom. It happened in 1890. When the same fever broke out in Florida thirty years later, the Valley people were able to view it with a calm tutored by experience. Perhaps these sporadic eruptions are a necessary concomitant of American enthusiasm.

This sudden mushroom ballooned forth almost simultaneously in the upper, lower, and middle Valley. Research does not reveal in what mind it originated, nor what was its cause. It had no basis in fact. No new discoveries of natural resources had been made, the climate remained in winter cold and in summer hot—yet overnight, by a kind of mass hysteria, Valley land seemed to have become immensely valuable. Every little town was to become a metropolis, and the surrounding fields were netted with signposts marking prospective avenues, boulevards, and even streets. Since the Valley people themselves had always believed that they were living in the American Eden, they found it easy to think that the rest of the country had awakened to this fact and would rush down to demand a foothold between the blue mountains.

Along the curving reaches of the river, beside the springs, and in even more unlikely places rose huge rambling hotels, crowned with wooden gables, cupolas, and fretwork. Hundreds of thousands were spent on their construction and publicity, hundreds of chairs rocked on their wide porches, they opened with ceremonies, music, and dancing; but their season was brief. Within a decade they were ramshackle and deserted. Some of them survived to be converted into schools or institutions, to fail again, to slide a little farther into decay, eventually to burn. With their seasoned timbers and thin wooden walls, they made brighter bonfires than the stubborn old stone houses on which General Sheridan had tried his hand.

The promoters came with brassy voices and bright promises, and culled their harvest from the gullible. "Mining, Manufacturing and Improvement" companies were formed all over the Valley. In Charles Town they built a three-story brick building to house the real estate offices. Jamie Ransom sold his 365-acre farm for $200 an acre, and bought back 200-foot lots for $300 each. The Powhatan Hotel was built and opened in the bare fields, and an auction of lots from its steps brought in $450,000 on paper. When one farmer's team ran away during the sale, he shouted: "Let 'em run! Selling lots pays better!" A real flurry was occasioned by the discovery of coal oil floating on the water in a ravine on R. D. Lamar's farm, until it was discovered that some boys had poured it there for a joke.

In Lexington a cheerful young newcomer announced that his mission was to buy a site and erect a tool plant. Local businessmen welcomed him and agreed to put in several thousands when the work of construction had advanced to a certain stage. He bought property and began to grade it. He solidified his position by attending the Presbyterian church and singing in the choir—the most infallible passport to favor and respectability. Before long, somewhat to the consternation of the native swains, he was taking the conventional first steps in courtship by walking the prettiest soprano home from choir rehearsal. The grading of the factory site was completed, the cement foundation laid. The businessmen fulfilled their contract and paid him their thousands. And then one day the young man did not appear to direct operations. Like Enoch, he was not. Missing also was the money painfully raised within the town. Washington and Lee now uses the graded site for its tennis courts.

Shenandoah Junction consisted of a railroad station and a house or two until in the sudden burgeoning of belief it threw out a checkerboard of streets, optimistically named. Options were secured on 5,000 acres in the neighborhood. They talked of bringing water from the Potomac, five miles away; they talked of a mammoth steel plant, and a second plant for "Russian steel," which was to turn out 150 tons daily; they talked of building a $35,000 hotel at once. The signposts shone among the corn while harvests ripened around them. Twenty-five years later some could still be found, lying on their backs in the alfalfa. Today Shenandoah Junction consists of a railroad station and a house or two.

Every Valley town grabbed for its slice of pie. They built Basic City, Buena Vista, Glasgow. At Grottoes, then called Shendur, they installed a track and a horse-drawn streetcar so as to be able to reach the hypothetical suburbs. Partridge hunters used to ride out and shoot from it. At Goshen, a crossroads near the Alleghenies, Jim Aldred invested in a lot, but was permanently frightened away by meeting a bear on the supposed main street of the imagined city.

Then it was over. As mysteriously as it had begun, the

vision faded. The Valley remained a countryside of quiet fields and limestone outcrops. Many were disappointed and some were poorer, but their poverty had kept them from plunging too deeply—and ruin had become for all time there a comparative term. The young, who had observed without participating, were ensured against future booms, and their elders buried the subject, even in conversation. The boom is forgotten, although many families still are paying taxes on lots bought at that time. The land smiled on, and in the rich soil there was wealth enough—but it was never to be attained without much labor.

But the Valley was to have a source of revenue more solid than the paper real estate—a tangible, fragrant, succulent basis of income. The earliest settlers had discovered that apples would thrive there. Lord Fairfax stipulated that some of his tenants should plant two hundred trees and fence them in. Braddock's ill-starred army brought back some trees from Pennsylvania. Jacob Funk, the musician of Singer's Glen, cultivated apple sprouts in 1843 for his daughter to take with her when she went out to Missouri. Apple Pie Ridge runs from Martinsburg to Winchester, crosshatched with trees for more than one hundred years. Queen Victoria gave an impetus to Virginia apples because she so relished a barrel given her by an American ambassador that she removed the tariff on their importation.

The early worthies, however, used their fruit for making brandy, and apples were not grown on a large scale until the same bustling nineties which struck the fool's gold of the land boom. Miss Lizzie and Miss Julia Terrill, cousins of John Yates Beall, were saving their money to go to the Philadelphia Centennial of 1876 when an apple tree salesman arrived at their door. They never got to the centennial, but they put in one of the first big orchards in the county. Now Virginia is the third state in apple growing, with a crop worth twelve millions yearly, most of which comes from the Shenandoah Valley, with two million apple trees, and a payroll of three million dollars for the industry.

Apple growing is a business for patient and laborious

men. The farmer must plant yearling twigs, then wait from seven to twelve years before they bear. How long does it take? "How long is a string?" say the apple growers. Then there are the spring frosts to destroy the blossoms, the summer droughts to dwarf the apples, the coddling moth, the scab, the scale—and in a good year perhaps a labor shortage to make picking impossible, or an overproduction which gluts the market and sends prices down below profit. In spring the trees are sprayed, and sprayed again. And now the experimental bureaus pessimistically suggest that the coddling moth is developing an immunity to arsenic since its members are increasing in spite of stronger sprays. At least three times each season, the spraying machine plods slowly between the long rows, and for weeks on end the farmer comes home smelling of fish oil and sulphur, and whitened by the flying poisonous mist. Then he must prune the trees and thin the crop if the fruit grows too heavy on the bough.

There follow the months of waiting, the anxious consultation of sky and cloud, the sun too fierce, the summer storms too violent, the hail, the beating wind and rain, the lack of rain. The long hot days pass in a nervous dependence upon the blind resistless weather—which is never right.

But there are compensations in this business. In spite of foreboding, anxiety, and moments of depression, the fruit does ripen. By autumn the trees are jeweled with red and yellow, the branches sagging in the mellow light, the countryside enveloped in rich fragrance. The farmer moves amid abundance under a bright blue sky, and feels his own roots nourished in the soil as are his trees. He takes an apple in his palm, a sun-warmed globe, curved to the hand, firm, smooth and spicy, admires and sniffs it before he bites into it, and knows himself enriched with the harvest of creation.

The hardest labor is still ahead, for now the fruit must be picked, packed, and marketed. Into the quiet Valley pours a flood of itinerant laborers, thousands of them, as migratory as locusts, settling over the landscape for a brief two months. Hundreds of Americans, men and women, earn a plentiful if precarious living by following the fruit and vegetable harvest from Maine to Florida and back. Usually unmarried, not too young, not too dependable, they seem satisfied to move with the warm sun from boardinghouse to labor camp without a foothold anywhere, earning good money at times, and retaining little during the seasons of idleness. After the Florida oranges and the Georgia peaches, they strike the Valley at apple-picking time. In the packing houses the flat rate is $4.20 a day, but in the orchards they are paid ten cents a crate, and a rapid picker can earn from eight to ten dollars. The farmers point out hopefully that wages have never been so high, and that when war conditions are past, and the mountain labor on which they formerly depended returns to the orchards, the scale should drop to something more normally reasonable. Meanwhile they manage as best they can. In the summers of 1943 and 1944, crews of Bahamian Negroes were imported. They lived in their own camps—near Martinsburg one is a reconverted cattle market—were furnished transportation to and from the orchards, and paid at the current rate. Their government withheld seventy-five cents a day for each of them to make sure that they do not return home penniless, and their food was handled by their own manager. The orchardists say that they were about like any other labor, some good, some bad, a few impossible.

The picking is a grueling season for the farmer, a time when he must rise before dawn to be first on the job, and work after dark with his last reserve of strength; for nature moves on relentlessly, fruit falls to rot as soon as it has ripened. For two months the farmer, surrounded by noisy crowds and busier than an ant, driving himself harder than he drives his men—forgets that breathing community with Earth which he once felt and shared.

At the packing plants the round and shining apples are poured onto conveyor belts, pass over a wide steel net through which the small ones drop, roll into an acid bath which washes off the spray and leaves them gleaming, are pushed on by wooden paddles and carried past the long tables where the sorters pick them over. The little culls which fell through the net tumble along a trough toward their destination in a cider mill, the choicest apples are wrapped in tissue paper and preciously handled for a fancy price, the average are stored in barrels, bushel baskets, or more recently in crates. Bright, gleaming, kaleidoscopic in color, the river of fruit flows swiftly through its complicated process. Grimes Golden, York Imperial, Delicious, Winesap, Pippin, every red apple that a city school girl bites has had the service of perhaps a hundred hands before it reaches her.

At last it is over. The freight cars roll away heavily laden, the apple sauce and cider factory has its quota, the greater portion of the crop has gone into the four cold storage plants at Winchester, which can hold over a million bushels to be released during the winter as the demand occurs. But all the hazards of the apple grower are not past. The prices vary with the months and years, and remote international situations may have a surprising effect. In 1932 at the Empire Conference in Quebec, England decided to give preference to Dominion apples, and the Virginia fruit lost its favorable position. The growers had to tighten their belts, alter their methods of growing and packing, and win themselves a place in the domestic market, which demanded a different type of product. In 1943 the OPA set a ceiling price, the crop was so small that in order to fill army demands for canned and dried apples, growers were forbidden to sell more than five bushels individually. Under such favorable conditions, profits were excellent, and many growers made in one season more than in four years previously. In 1944, on the other hand, the ceiling remained, but the demand was so poor that the growers could not get a price anywhere near it. Owing to the drought four-fifths of the crop were stunted low-grade apples, and no one wanted them. The outlook for the growers was gloomy, but they are used to that.

The dry leaves fall and winter quiet settles on the orchards. Under the cold moon the gnarled trees sleep with their crooked branches baldly exposed. There is no one now to walk between them and to tend them, only the little round-eared field mice gnawing at the roots like a bad thought. Dormant and windswept, the orchards await in patience the annual and accepted miracle.

Then, long expected and unhurried, spring arrives and dyes the guardian mountains with a deeper blue. The rolling earth stretches itself, and overnight the gray trees throw a veil of blossom across ridge and hollow. The whole world is aflower until even the bees are drunk with the perfume of it, and the farmer stands watching the lazy impalpable snow of the white petals, and looking at a spray he has broken off. He looks at the round white petals with their blush of pink, curving like love around the stamens, looks at his orchard, fairer than a garden, and in spite of the toil to come, feels that to be an apple grower is the highest good.

25. Past Into Present

AND AGAIN time passed into another century, and another great war was just a story for old men. They sat under the oaks, the aging soldiers, and saw their children grown, their land restored. They had known the hardship of war, and the long labor of the peace, and they had not perished, neither they nor their families. Now in the early 1900's their hands were relaxing slowly. Some of them slept already in the thickly settled churchyards, under the shadow of those old blue mountains which had once been their refuge and their home. The remainder had not long before they too would join in the quiet wait for the last muster. They had known the ultimate in danger, comradeship, love, toil, despair and happiness, and this was the end of it—a dream beneath the oaks.

They had not much to say about their past experience, for the heart of it could not be communicated to those who had not shared it.

"We came across those fields," a veteran might tell a grandchild, pointing with his stick, "and the Yankees were waiting in those woods—but you go now and play, you are tired of listening to me."

Sometimes visitors asked for the old stories. "Captain, I hear you captured six Yankees singlehanded. How did you do it?"

And the captain might answer, after spitting accurately into the round-bellied iron stove, "Well, dammit, I surrounded 'em."

The time had passed for caring. Too many new things engaged the attention, telephones, automobiles, even an air-

plane which flew across the Valley. Mosby was only an old
man with a patch over one eye and a dashing hat, who talked
gallantly to the ladies at the horse show. The round-eyed
little girls stared at him, and observed that when he greeted
a former comrade something electric flashed between them,
a secret not to be apprehended by the rest. Out of the battles
and the marches, the charges, and countercharges, the last-
ditch tenacity, nothing remained save the young look in a
grandfather's eyes while he played "Dixie" for the children
on a paper-covered comb.

The women talked more about the past, for since they
had seen fewer Yankees they could hate them better. They
had hoped until hope turned to bitterness; they had worked
until work gnarled their hands and bowed their shoulders;
they had gone without and made a virtue of their necessities. They reared their children and preserved their gracious
manners. It was vulgar to be rich, they said. Nice people
never had any money. Money could not make a home, or
family love, or pride and self-respect—and these were all that
mattered. Serenely conscious of "who they were," they
scrubbed their kitchen floors without complaining and wore
their battered hats like flags.

"Never let me hear you call it the Civil War, my child.
It was a most *un*civil war."

The tempo of life moved slowly in the Valley, the old
houses slipped a little farther into decay, the old brick side-
walks became a little more uneven. In every hall or parlor
hung an engraved portrait of Lee or Jackson, a painting of
Confederate flags around verses from "The Conquered Banner" or "The Blue and the Gray," framed with a spray of
dried laurel from a general's tomb. The homes might lack
conveniences, but they had atmosphere. The owners reveled
in the mellow brick or stone, the creaking floor boards, sagging doors, worn doorsills, the cool and musty smell where
sunlight never penetrated, all the revered evidences of age
and of survival. Cool the houses were in those days, with a
scrubbed smell, and dark, always with some rooms little aired,
where old mahogany furniture and family portraits crooked

on the walls, hair wreaths and peacock-feather fans, glass bells over dried flowers, seemed to have embalmed the past. Large widows dressed in unaired black dwelt in such rooms, drowned in a pool of motionless air, and rude children referred to them irreverently as "the gorge of gloom."

In this reminiscent quiet, this tranquillity undisturbed by progress, characters allowed no fear of eccentricity to hamper their development. Where everyone knows you and knew your grandparents, you feel no compulsion to be other than exactly what you please to be. You have no identity to establish, no front to maintain.

There was Miss Rosella Hartridge,[1] whose weight did not deter her from wearing trousers and working her place like a man, and Miss Lacey Granville, who had painted in Florence and added a cosmopolitan assurance to the impregnable satisfaction of Valley birth. Miss Lacey once decided to visit a nephew in New York, exhumed her mother's ermine tippet and a blue chiffon veil from the attic, mounted her ancient Ford, and sallied forth. The miles did not discourage her, nor did she quail at the Hudson Tunnel, but sailed through with her hands firm on the steering wheel, and emerged boldly into the hurly-burly of Seventh Avenue. As she proceeded she became aware of shouts and much hooting of horns and sirens behind her, but she ignored them as a lady should until a motorcycle policeman, on fire with rage, drew alongside and forced her to a halt. Miss Lacey bent down and greeted him graciously.

"Did you want me, officer? Is something wrong?"

"What's de big idea running through all dem red lights?"

"Red lights?"

"Yeah. Red lights."

"I saw some red and green lights overhead, officer, but I assumed that they were Christmas decorations, since it is so near that season."

The policeman pushed back his cap, and taking time

---

[1] Only the names are fictitious.

to look at her, now perceived that he had collected a rare human specimen.

"Lady," he asked, almost in awe, "where in hell are you from?"

"I'm from the Shenandoah Valley."

The cop put his foot on the running board and leaned toward her confidentially. "Lady," he breathed, "will you please for God's sake go back?"

The colloquy ended in the utmost amiability on both sides. The cop collected a patrol car, and with himself as motorcycle escort, conveyed Miss Lacey back through the tunnel to a New Jersey garage where the car was safely housed. Then the police deposited her with her baggage at her nephew's door.

Miss Bettie Allenby had a little income of her own, but made a career of visiting relatives. Invited for Thanksgiving dinner, she would arrive and stay until Easter, contributing to the family in that time perhaps one bag of flour. The major called her "Blizzard Bet," because she always came to call just as the weather was turning so bad that she could not reasonably be expected to leave. When she died her body was carried to the church in a snowstorm, and they were not able to get her out and bury her for three days. Blizzard Bet to the last.

Cousin Julia lived alone in the family house, wearing on weekdays black and white calico with sunbonnets to match, and on Sundays an immemorial black taffeta as spreading and slippery as a haircloth sofa. When the younger branches of the family called on her—as why should they not, she having no direct heirs—she would leave her garden of untrimmed boxwood and sprawling roses, open the shutters, and receive her callers in the parlor with the hand-carved wainscoting brought from England, and a framed reproduction of the "Last Supper" worked in needlepoint upon the wall. In time she fell mortally ill, and a neighboring relative went to look after her. Always a just woman, Cousin Julia aroused herself enough to say: "It is good to see you,

Mary, but I must tell you, I have left you nothing in my will."

Mary nursed her to the end, as Mary would, but when she died the relatives far and wide were filled with consternation to discover that the old lady had devised the family place to be sold at auction "for the benefit of educating indigent young men for the ministry." "Encouraging mediocrity," said one of the more acrid tongues. None of the family had the means to buy it in, and it was purchased by a hardworking Pennsylvania Dutchman, whose sons had labored when other people's sons were wasting time at college, who had eaten frugal meals when other families were having parties, who had risen early and toiled late, while others danced or went to picnics. The relatives removed the heirlooms, the willow china, the crested silver, and that was all. Now in the wainscoted parlor beans are spread for drying, and the new owners live in the kitchen wing.

The ladies had no monopoly on individualism. Mr. Hal Weatherby, an aging bachelor, did not allow either years or three hundred pounds of flesh to discourage his attentions to the fair sex. If a young woman was known to be visiting in the county, Mr. Weatherby would arrive as inevitably as the sunset, bearing a nosegay of sweet peas (picked in a cousin's garden). He would play the piano and sing, between compliments, until the night was far advanced, and in accordance with the country custom he would be invited to remain. He would accept with charming dignity, and in the morning he would arise betimes and depart before the household stirred, not neglecting to remove the sweet peas from the parlor table so that he might carry them off to the next object of his attentions.

Old Judge Barden collected trees until his grounds resembled an arboreum, kept thirty cats and fed them by pouring milk on the dining-room floor until their rough little tongues scraped hollows in the boards. The old judge died, and the trees pressed more and more closely upon the house, shutting out light, shutting out air. The porches began to rot and fall away, and in the musty attic the ghost of an unexplained baby wept in the night. One of John Brown's pikes hung above a plaster cast of a clutching hand, and Sheridan's saber cuts still marred the banisters, but no young children fingered the scars, for the last of the family was a spinster, although all the beds in the house were large enough for three. After she also died, the house stood empty, with the trees pressing ever more closely and the shutters hanging on a broken hinge, until a huge magnolia at the back forced out a glass by steady pressure, thrust in an arm, and pushed a great leafy bough through the upper hall, as one who might say, "This is mine!"

It would be possible to pry into the walnut wardrobes and drag out some family skeletons and scandals, to tell the story of the man who beat a slave to death, and of the curse which the Negroes say still follows his descendants, or to relate other whispered incidents. But such things give no more understanding of the Valley than the shore-tossed and battered hulk of a wrecked vessel gives of the sea. The truth of the Valley is found in the soil, the limestone, and the river, and the thousands of brave and industrious people who have kept themselves erect and moving forward through good times and bad.

On Valley farms the owners worked in muddy boots and sweat-stained shirts. After the Civil War, Negro farm hands were scarce, and nonexistent the idyllic picture of "singing blacks returning from their labors." The Negroes preferred mines or factories, and the farmers preferred white workers who would take more initiative, work more steadily, and need less watching. At harvest time the "Page County men" came down from the mountains to the lower Valley, riding the freights, locally called "Page County Specials," and dropping off to walk across the fields to farms where they were needed. Rough men, mountainmen, "they never took off anything but their hats when they went to bed, and not even that much on Saturday nights." They had their own ideas as to what work was suitable. It was all right to reap, to swing after the machine and pile the nutty golden bundles into shocks, all right to thrash, and see the chaff and straw flying like golden rain while a molten river of grain poured out of the thresher into sacks—but there were other tasks not so acceptable. On one farm a fourteen-year-old boy was left to lead the men out to work one morning.

"What's on today, bud?"

"Cutting corn."

Cutting corn is slow, arduous, hand done, the left hand seizing stalk after stalk, the right swinging the crooked knife through with one blow, the left throwing the stalk aside, seizing another. Hard, unremitting, unglamorous work, closed in by the tall corn, cut off by the broad leaves from the breezes, from the other men, from conversation, from everything but the direct burning sun. The Page County men trudged down the lane in silence, then one of them stopped and cupped his hand to his ear. In the middle of an empty field, he went through all the motions of attentive listening.

"Bud, I hear somebody a-callin' me. I'll be right back."

He swung off with his mountaineer's lope, and although that was nearly forty years ago, he has not yet returned.

Somehow each year, by some laborious hands, the wheat was garnered, the corn husked or chopped for silage, the sheep sheared, hogs butchered, the hay mowed. The endless cycle of the seasons, of the turning earth, wheeled across the Valley and the Valley men and women. Much they had lost and much they had retained. In the old houses the dinner tables were elastic, the fried chicken and ice cream always could serve one or two more. Gaiety had not vanished, only the cost of gaiety was lower. To give a dance meant only to move the furniture aside, to bake a cake and make some lemonade, to turn on the victrola. There would be candles in the windows and Japanese lanterns swinging under the tall trees. There would be well-chaperoned camps on the river with canoes and singing. In the balmy nights, bought with long sultry days, in the honeysuckle-laden air, in the silver effulgence of the moon, the girls and boys played out the old story, danced the old dance of meeting and avowal. This did not change among the other changes. This remained constant like the river and the rocks.

The surface of Valley life, however, altered slowly. The mud-stained buggies and tired horses which once lined both sides of the main streets gave way to equally mud-stained automobiles. The roads had not yet improved in proportion to the new rapid transportation, which was to end isolation in the country. Still in spring the deep mud folded back like batter from the wheel's rim, still the deep ruts twisted the axles; still in summer the thick dust flew like a smoke barrage and smothered those behind. They soon macadamized the lower Pike, but in some upper sections the old plank road of rotting logs remained until the second decade of the twentieth century, and in these areas communication with the outside world was so difficult that the region lingered as if frozen in its past. Not until 1918 were the tolls abolished which had made it cost $4.75 to drive from Winchester to Staunton.

A Charles Town man in 1896 took a great step toward ending rural isolation, when Postmaster General William L. Wilson established the first rural free delivery route in the United States. The service followed a plan made by John Wanamaker during his preceding term. Congress appropriated $40,000 and the first route was started in Jefferson County, followed by fifteen others all over the country. The carriers were each to cover twenty miles a day on horseback, and it was not until one of them complained of having to open and shut sixty-three gates on his route that the farmers were asked to put mailboxes along the public road.

By now peace meant prosperity and progress in the Valley. Peace dwelt in the blue air cupped between the mountain ranges, in the shaded towns surrounded by the fields. Prosperity also, if the measure of prosperity be that a man and his family live pleasantly, in surroundings agreeable to them, maintained by work which they find not too difficult. But then and now, if a man wished to grow really rich he had to travel, to make a fortune merchandising in New York, like Charles ("Broadway") Rouss, or in California, like

Thomas Marye, or in Chicago, like Joseph Swearingen. The Valley may be a seedbed for ambitious men, but it is not a ladder on which they can climb to their destiny. Yet these men who prospered by leaving it never quite broke the tie with their green cradle, often preserved the family homesteads in which they no longer found it convenient to live, often sent contributions for fire companies, libraries, schools or hospitals—and usually returned to the Valley for their long and final rest.

If no one grew rich in the Valley, no one starved, white or black. The Negroes, never more and usually less than one in ten of the population, had their own system for getting through lean times by attaching themselves to white families whom they served at will and victimized at pleasure. Tradition is a strong tie, not to be broken in a single generation. Tradition said that a Negro who worked for a white family became that family's responsibility. And so the Negroes lived in a strange blend of dependence and independence. They worked for wages and had their own cabins, never in the country, always on the fringe of town where they could gratify their sociability. They worked when they felt like it, sometimes well, sometimes badly, and stopped when they pleased, which was usually at the most inconvenient moment for their white employers. Their wages were low, for the money to pay them came from lean pockets, but if illness or idleness brought them below the level of subsistence, a small "darky" would arrive at the "big house" with the news, and the white man would ride over to check the necessities of the situation, to deliver a ham and a basket of food, to tide the black family through. If the provender thus obtained should be used in one night for a barbecue, a scolding might be administered, but never the harsh discipline of cutting off further supplies. That would have been considered cruel, unusual, and reprehensible on the white man's part.

It was not a perfect system, but as a transition it had some merit, for evolution has never been accomplished solely by legislation. The Negroes protested loyalty and devotion, and did not hesitate to pilfer. The white man protested affection, took responsibility, but "kept them in their place." And the two races lived in friendship, for they found each other useful, and a mutual usefulness builds up a mutual respect. Above all, they saw each other as individuals, not as faceless masses of black or white, which might be impersonally hated.

Although free schools for Negroes were established in the Valley after the Civil War before free schools for whites, the black man who wanted broader horizons had to migrate like his white brother. "Aunt" Christian's son wrote her from Wyoming that he had married a white woman, and she came to her white folks in some agitation.

"What kine o' white woman goin' to marry herself wid a black man? I tole him not to bring her home. I don't want no white trash in my house."

In 1912 a man born in the Shenandoah Valley was elected President of the United States. Woodrow Wilson arrived in this world on December 28, 1856, at the Presbyterian manse in Staunton, where his father was the minister. The historic event occasioned no excitement at the time, and the family moved on before Woodrow was three. But Staunton claims him, and has turned his birthplace into a shrine.

Because he grew up in the shadow of one great war, he set a great value on peace. By the time he reached the Presidency all the old quarrels were healed, most of the veterans dead, the old wounds forgotten. The leaves and the grass had covered the trenches and the bones. Peace lay on the Valley as deep as the mile of limestone beneath it, and the earth would not vibrate again to the tramp of marching men. Civilization seemed to have moved beyond such primitive methods of settling disputes. If the Blue and the Gray could compose their difficulties, other hereditary enemies could do the same.

But across the world the winds were piling up another tidal wave, and again the peaceful Valley was swept into the storm. This time her sons were taken far away. They went willingly. In one county, out of the 565 called for examination, only five claimed any exemption; in other counties more than half the registered saw actual service. Many volunteered before the draft-boards reached them. A Shenandoah County boy filled out his questionnaire in France.

Q. Are you an expert in any occupation?
A. Fighting Huns with a bayonet.
Q. What language do you speak?
A. Pigeon French.
Q. How many persons are employed in the plant where you work?
A. Ten million.
Q. How many persons live on the land?
A. NONE, VERY LONG.

In 1917 the Valley fought again—the Valley which had been for a generation a home for old soldiers. The streets were brave with flags. For the first time in fifty years the Stars and Stripes floated above the doorways. But at doorway after doorway it was crossed with the Stars and Bars.

This was natural and it was right, for in the Valley they know that the past and the present are coexistent in time, and that no man walks into the future without both of them.

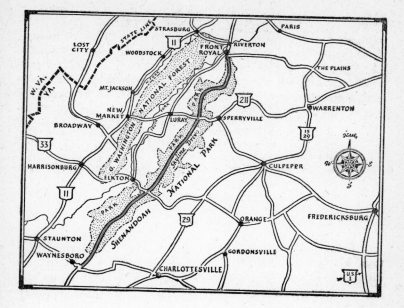

26. Valley Tour I

THE PRESENT and the past have flowed together. There is a new road now along the crest of the old blue mountains. From Rockfish Gap near Waynesboro almost to Manassas Gap near Front Royal, the Skyline Drive climbs for one hundred and seven miles along the summit of the ridge —over the lava, the basalt, the granite, the inestimably ancient volcanic rocks which antedate these on the Valley floor. The slopes which Lederer and Spotswood painfully climbed are now accessible to fat women in cushioned seats. The modern traveler can see the panorama of the Valley from the points where the explorers saw it, and like them can behold that it is fair.

317

THE SKYLINE DRIVE

From Hazeltop and Stony Man, from Old Rag Mountain, Hawksbill Head, Big Meadows, Thornton Hollow, and Hogback—a man may look down as the birds look down, ancient volcanic rocks which antedate those on the Valley spreading to the far waves of the Alleghenies. It is all there, the checkered rolling fields, the toy house towns, the occasional smokestack with a gray plume, the frowning bulk of Massanutten making the Luray valley dear and close, and the Shenandoah twisting grandly through the fertile land. It is there, and it is beautiful. Adjectives are exhausted after the first thirty miles, voice after sixty, eyes before the end. A traveler grows blind to scenery before the car rolls down into Front Royal.

The wooded mountains around the Skyline Drive have been made into the Shenandoah National Park, to belong forever to all the people of the United States. In 1924 Hubert Work, secretary of the interior, appointed a commission to find a park site in the East. Although skeptical, they were persuaded to come to Skyland, a camping resort near Stony Man Mountain, which provides cabins, trails, horses, fishing, and all the other advantages of roughing it smoothly. After they left, they voted unanimously for the Blue Ridge.

The government of the United States did not buy the land, but merely promised to improve it after it had been donated. In a truly American spirit of voluntary co-operation, the citizens of Virginia raised a million dollars by subscription to buy the mountains from the mountaineers. The legislature of the state voted a million more, 183,311 wild acres were set aside, and the drive built. President Roosevelt conducted the ceremony of dedication at Big Meadows in 1936.

The legal boundaries of the park read like a mountain song. From the Crinora manganese mine to the mouth of Dry Run, past Deep Run, Swift Run, Elk Run, Huckleberry and Piney Mountains, Furnace Postoffice, and Naked Creek. From Grindstone church and graveyard to Pumpkin Hill, Pass Run, and Neighbor Mountain. Past Over All and Matthew's Arm, through Brown Town to Hominy Hollow. To Sandy and Hogback, Hazeltop and Ragged Mountain, past Old Tom Mountain, to the Dunkard church. Through the dry legal document, the dusty title deeds, runs the descriptive chant of the back-country names, salted with unconscious poetry, tangy as mountain air.

Willingly or unwillingly, the mountaineers sold their homes—the crooked cabins, the clearings, the steep patches, where (as they say) a man has to hang on to a root with one hand while he hoes with the other and has to plant his corn by shooting it into the hill. Like their compatriots in Kentucky or Tennessee, these were real mountain stock, whose forebears, early settlers from the British Isles, had reached the mountains and holed in as bears do, either from a lack of initiative or from a love of solitude and independence. Isolationists par excellence, they had preserved until the era of the automobile their quaint speech, their old ballads, their dulcimers, their weaving, their tribal jealousies, their fierce and peculiar code. Now the hard-surfaced roads brought civilization to them whether they liked it or not, and most of them welcomed the change.

Some moved when they had sold their homes, others stayed on by a lifetime agreement with the government, but the old mountain ways were broken and in a decade or two the people will be standardized to the movie pattern. The old handicrafts will vanish, the picturesque speech, the old songs and dances, along with the poverty, malnutrition, and ignorance in which they thrived. As the highways go through, the mountain people outside the park are selling solid log houses and good land to move into plywood shacks near the big road. There they have no room even for gardens, but they can watch the cars go by, and can walk or hitchhike down to town on Saturday night.

The men have found work in the towns. When at the Viscose rayon plant in Front Royal they have family night once a month, the tribes roll in ten or twenty strong in battered jalopies and handmade trucks. The babies sleep in corners while the others dance square sets, drink, and eat. The only serious strike the plant has had came from a mountain feud. The Lucases and the Cubbages do not get along, and if the Lucases were willing to accept certain terms, the Cubbages would not have them. Labor and management, the lion and the lamb, may lie down together, but while the sun climbs over the mountains if something suits a Cubbage a Lucas cannot agree to it.

There are several missions in the mountains, one at Pine Grove in Page County and another just above the Shenandoah on the road to Leesburg. The latter was founded by the Episcopal Church in 1886, and after several changes is now in the hands of the Reverend Temple Wheeler, who has converted it into a children's home. He is a small stocky man, whose working clothes contrast oddly with his cultivated voice. He gives his life to the mountain people, but sees them without illusions. They are so ingrown, so full of jealousy and gossip, so suspicious of each other and so allergic to co-operation that they cannot be coaxed into clubs or organizations—except the 4-H clubs, which offer tangible benefits. Tangibility is appreciated, and when the mission ceased giving handouts to its parishioners, the falling off among the faithful was disastrous. But Mr. Wheeler let them go, and held his course. Parents are even jealous of their children, if the children improve beyond their environment.

And yet they can improve. The children of one family which had to be separated did not recognize one another after the girls had had a year of mission life and wore habitually clean faces. The work is small, but it is growing. All mission work by its nature touches only a fragment of conditions caused by circumstances which it cannot control. The hard roads will succeed in changing mountain life profoundly, as the missions have failed to do for fifty years. The hard roads will bring the people out of the hollows, will secure for them more education, more ways of earning money, better living conditions, perhaps even plumbing—that current *sine qua non*. They will be introduced to the benefits of civilization, and also to its vices. Whether the mountaineers will choose the good way or the bad will depend as always on the individual. Perhaps the missions can help them in their decisions. The hard roads will not heal their souls.

Meanwhile on the mountainside above the Shenandoah there is a solid old stone building in a clearing, with the hardwood trees cut back far enough to make room for swings and seesaws and a basketball court. The children wander about informally. The air smells new-washed, and there is the freshness of pine in it. Blue jays, finches, thrushes, flicker and sing in the oaks, and under them Mr. Wheeler smokes his pipe—a man at peace.

The mountain world calls to peace. It is a high clear untroubled world where the complications of life seem to drop away—and the children of civilization avail themselves of it with as much eagerness as the mountaineers display in leaving it. In the first year after the opening of the Shenandoah National Park it had 776,880 visitors, seeking exactly the conditions which had bored the mountaineers. It is the city people now who love the narrow trails which twist secretly through the flower-jeweled woods, who like to lie in the sun on the high rocks and see the buzzards hanging in the air below them, and the valley spread out like a rich carpet.

Few of them recognize the hardened lava under their feet or find a shell print left by the long vanished sea when these mountains were the ocean floor. Some peer into the hollows hoping to find the far more modern relic of a mountain still—but they will not come upon that either. They will not find any bears or wildcats, only the luckiest will glimpse a deer, for the popularity of the park has spoiled it as a wildlife sanctuary. The little people flourish, the squirrels, chipmunks, weasels, minks, raccoons, oppossums, woodchucks, rabbits—but the big important ones, who cannot hide in hollow logs or under fallen leaves when clumsy boots tramp past, now stay away. There are fourteen deer in the park, as familiar as friends to the wardens. They survive, but they do not increase.

For the botanist or the ornithologist, however, the park is a paradise. Every sort of plant flourishes in the moderate yet varied climate, and the migratory birds all stop there on their annual journeys. During a single May one hundred different species were counted. Eighty varieties of trees grow on the slopes, tulip and chestnut (for the chestnut is coming back after the blight), maple, oak, holly, hickory, hemlock, persimmon, locust, dogwood, cherry, sassafras, mountain ash, black gum, shad, nine different evergreens. The wild-flower families number more than a thousand. Spring brings the Judas tree and the dogwood like puffs of pink and white smoke along the hills, and summer the faint rose and glossy green of rhododendron and of laurel. In the damp ferny hollows are hidden all the small shy flowers, hepatica and bloodroot, orchids, anemonies, wintergreen, ladies' tresses, and some rare plants not found elsewhere outside the Arctic Circle. It is thought that the seeds may have been dropped there by the migratory birds.

Most of this the tourists miss. The secret of the mountains, human and animal, is driven into hiding by their laughter and their chatter, by the roaring of their engines and the rushing of their wheels. As this book is being written the mountaintops are quiet again, for gasoline shortages have forced the resorts such as Skyland and Big Meadows to close; but when the war restrictions have been lifted, the visitors will flood in once more. Again they will spin along or stop

SHENANDOAH NATIONAL PARK

to climb in keen enjoyment, for here on the heights above the Shenandoah they grasp for a while the illusion of something which has never existed save as a hope still glimmering in the mind of man—the illusion of perfect freedom.

Roll down into the Valley from the Blue Ridge, and see it—not hurrying through on the good hard roads which would have pleased that hastening general Stonewall Jackson—but slowly and quietly, taking time to discover its secrets. It is possible now in a four-motored transport plane to cross the Valley at its widest in ten minutes, seeing it only as an interruption between the dark waves of the mountains, saying, "Could that be the Valley? Yes, it must have been, because now we are over the hills again." It is possible to whirl by car along the full length of the river in one day of driving, to see only a hasty panorama of smiling fields, punctuated by billboards about caverns, by gasoline stations, and by such gruesome aspects of commercialism as "John Brown Candy," advertised at Harpers Ferry.

But the face of the Valley is still best revealed along the narrow curving back roads which wind between honeysuckle-covered banks and wander along the reaches of the Shenandoah under the willows and the sycamores. Lost quiet little roads, which cross the river casually on low-water bridges, only a foot or two above the swirling eddies. If the river rises, the road is cut in two and traffic along it must wait until the water falls again. It always does fall, sooner or later. Why should man be more troubled than the bright red, blue and yellow birds which flit above the swift green stream? At night the land exhales, drenched by the moon, and by its scent the countryside is still perceptible field after field: the nuttiness of wheat, the sweetness of apples (with a slightly chemical overtone), the fragrance of new hay, the damp freshness of a little brook, curling around its water cress. This is the Valley of the Shenandoah, a deep sweet land, where the evenings are full of loveliness, the mornings fresh from heaven, and it is best to stay indoors behind closed shutters during the long hot dusty afternoons.

Front Royal, where the Skyline Drive ends, is a progressive town. Its past is Mosby, the local hero or demigod, and the marker by the roadside where General Custer hanged seven of Mosby's men. (There is no marker at the place where Mosby hanged seven prisoners in reprisal, but he wrote a letter to the *Spirit of Jefferson* after the war saying that certainly he had done it, and why not?) The past is Belle Boyd, with the flying curls, and Jackson, and behind them the early British soldiers ordered to "Front the royal oak," or the river boys making it Helltown on Saturday night—or farther still, mild John Lederer, peering through Manassas Gap. All these things are over and done with long ago, and the present of Front Royal is the Viscose plant, a branch of the American Viscose Corporation.

Flat, red, sprawling over many acres, the plant lies rawly on what were fertile fields. A child of the depression, opened in 1940, it planned first for a limited capacity of thirty-four million pounds a year of rayon yarn—now mushroomed up to two hundred and forty million pounds, and perhaps to end with thirty per cent of the spun rayon in the country. Rayon has gone to war. This plant spins Tenasco, a high-tenacity yarn woven into suits for paratroopers, and Rayflex, which makes tire cordage for the motorized army. With these wartime activities comes secrecy, and admission only by permit.

The plant employs about two thousand people, and two thousand more have come to the town with a construction company which is building neat raw workers' homes. They have an open shop, with a voluntary union, and little labor trouble, unless it be that old dispute between the Lucases and the Cubbages, or a mild racial disturbance when one of the colored workers drank from a fountain reserved for the whites. If the corporation had realized how the plant was to grow, says the manager, they might not have placed it at Front Royal, where the local labor supply is relatively limited. Now they must import workers from New Jersey and other industrial centers, and acclimate them to the Valley.

Inside the plant all is modern efficiency, from the brisk northern manager down. The endless miles of shining rayon yarn spin on, wound on their giant reels. The wood-pulp and cotton linters are soaked, crumbled, churned, and spun into an intricate gossamer which threads the air like moonbeams. In an air-conditioned atmosphere, under the ghastly blue of vacuum lights, the workers tend the incessant machines as they revolve and plunge and whirl blind arms with unerring accuracy. The ingenuity of man has shut the hot sun away from these people, has flattened the rugged earth beneath their feet into the smooth rigidity of concrete. The machines spare them exertion and the necessity for thinking. If their hands will move six inches or a foot this way or that the machines will do the rest. The roar of the motors makes conversation impossible.

This is the new world, the future, superimposed on the past without reference to what has gone before. Here everything is orderly, finite, known and understood, measured and precise to the last gram or millimeter. Each person knowns exactly what to do and does it. Here reason and intelligence have won their battle with inert matter, and have excluded the unruly elements of sentiment and instinct. Breathing a purified air only slightly tinged with sulphuric, protected from changes of light and temperature and from the unpredictable variations of growth, of life, the workers happily fulfill the measured hours in each shift. Every hour clicks off $1.85, and this is good sure money, not dependent on the whims of nature. No hail will spoil the crop, no drought will blast it, no personal fatigue will halt the endless spinning. In the even temperature of the cafeteria, 4,500 meals are served each day and eaten without the fatigue of doing more than lift a plate, while the latest swing blares from the loud-speakers. The plant has drained off labor, both men and women, from the fields and kitchens in the vicinity into this clean new world, where time goes on, the machines go on, where everything moves as if foreordained, and the gleaming dreamlike substance rolls out endlessly.

The chemical waste from the plant spews into the Shenandoah, and the Valley people say that it is killing the fish, the black bass and the catfish. They add that it makes bathing impossible, sickens the bathers, and erodes their skin. The gentle fair-haired girl who is the plant's public relations representative says that she cannot understand these rumors, for the plant has installed a reconversion process which should take all the acid from the waste. The Virginia counties have not raised objections, she says (she is a Virginian). Only the West Virginia counties, far down the river, have complained.

Everything has to be paid for, even progress.

27. Valley Tour II

Not far from Front Royal, where the hills begin to rise into the mountains, is a remount station of the United States Army, which breeds and trains horses for the cavalry. Fine stallions, treated like gentlemen, some Arabians, some Morgans, some thoroughbreds like Gallant Prince, a son of Gallant Fox, serve selected brood mares to produce the three-quarter breeds considered best for army service. Neighboring farmers may bring their mares for a nominal fee of ten dollars and put them to the best of stallions. Some of the stock serves for experimental purposes such as making serum. Stout hickory fences divide the bluegrass-covered hills into paddocks where long-legged foals can race beside their mothers and grow into battle chargers.

> The glory of his snorting is terrible
> He paweth the valley and rejoiceth in his strength—
> He swalloweth the ground with fierceness and rage—
> As oft as the trumpet soundeth he saith, Aha!
> And he smelleth the battle afar off,
> The thunder of the captains, and the shouting.

This is still altogether true, but the modern army is mechanized, and tanks are more terrible than the horses of war. Consequently many of the mounts at Front Royal have been "surplused," sold off at auction or otherwise disposed of. The station would be inactive if it had not developed two new services—the training of mules for pack animals in rough country and the training of dogs for the K-9 corps.

In the paddocks built for the aristocrats of horseflesh, the mules move with the dignity of their wisdom. Some train easily, others guess how their trainer wishes them to go— and go in the opposite direction. A good mule-dozer has to be more artful than his charges, and that takes guile indeed. The mules learn to obey signals, to follow a leader, they submit themselves to heavy packs, but they do not surrender their personalities. They do not enjoy showing off as a horse does, nor have they a horse's engaging foolishness. Their mild eyes regard man steadily with a reserved cynicism. They will learn no more than they have to, and walking or halting they will remain themselves.

Far different is the dog, who is but half of himself without a master. The dogs at the remount station have been donated to the army, and are sent there for basic training. Several hillsides are covered with the individual hutches to which they are chained, and the air is shattered with their barking. Most of the medium-sized breeds are represented, Dobermans, Alsatians, collies, coach dogs, and each is branded and assigned to the branch best fitted to his character. Bird dogs and similar breeds are no longer accepted, as they have been found too sensitive and nervous.

They take their basic training like good recruits, learn to come, go, heel, to lie down, to be quiet. In a few months they are ready for advanced courses. They learn to be scouts who warn patrols of snipers, to be messengers trained with two men always to find one when released by the other, and to be medical aides who find wounded that might otherwise be passed over. A canine medic has a simple form of diagnosis: to him a casualty is any man who is lying down. In the early days of the corps the dogs were trained to attack enemies, but this has been abandoned, for a dog's political beliefs are too liable to confusion.

Because they are dogs, their hearts must respond as well as their intelligence, so the soldier who trains one usually stays with his charge. Man and dog go together to the Philippines or Germany—a long way from the green hills of Virginia.

Fourteen miles down the Page valley from Front Royal lies Luray, another town which has stepped cheerfully into the present, for there are "The Beautiful Caverns, Miles of Subterranean Splendor, Brilliantly Lighted by Electricity, a Playground of Giants, a Garden of Fairies! You can never forget them, nor would you if you could!" The Luray Caverns are a series of limestone caves, channeled out by vanished rivers, decorated by the patience of eternity with stalactites and stalagmites. They have been a gold mine for their owners.

In 1878 Andrew Campbell and Benton Stebbins of Luray decided that Cave Hill, where a small cave was already known, might conceal a larger one. They searched the surface until they found a sinkhole out of which cold air was flowing. Here they dug until they made a fissure through which they could lower Mr. Campbell on a rope "into the dark and mysterious chambers of silence." When he touched bottom he lit a candle and dimly saw a great hall filled with statuary built by water; the fluidity of water congealed into stone.

Many such caverns have been discovered under the Valley of the Shenandoah, some by accident and some by diligent search. In 1818 a man digging a ground-hog trap found the Grand Caverns near Port Republic. Endless Caverns in the middle Valley were discovered when Reuben Zirkle's dog chased a rabbit behind a boulder. The Indians knew some caves, and Mary Greenlee used one as a hiding place for the White Dove. At present, up and down the Valley, a conscientious tourist may (for from 75 cents to $1.50) gaze upon one underground marvel after another: Grand Caverns, Blue Grottoes, Crystal Caverns, Shenandoah Caverns, Melrose Caverns, Massanutten Caverns, Endless Caverns.

None is larger than Luray, and in none has the imagination whipped itself into greater flights in describing the marvels. The visitor is instructed to feel "curious sensations of wonder and admiration," which may give way to "awe and reverence." From the Elfin Rambles to Titania's Veil, from Diana's Bath to the Saracen's Tent, to Dream Lake! The Sacred River! The Silver Sea!—the cement walks wind dry and safe, with an iron handrail at the difficult portions, and well marked flights of steps. The magic touch of the General Electric Company has worked out a really fine system of indirect lighting, and the guide will entertain the visitors with ancient jokes and up-to-date information on plans to convert the cavern into an air-raid shelter. The temperature is 54° winter and summer, the tour fills an hour, and one hundred thousand people take it every year.

Luray is ready for them with a fine hotel where all the more strenuous forms of relaxation can be practiced. Adam Miller's house is on exhibit, and there is a museum of Indian relics to provide safe shudders at far-off massacres. There is a Singing Tower. In 1937 a Mr. Northcott, then ninety-three years old, built a stone tower in memory of his first wife, fitted it with a carillon of forty-seven bells, and endowed it perpetually. The present carilloneur is Charles Chapman, a native of Luray, who gives a recital every day throughout the year.

A side road out of Luray leads to a narrow ravine called the Ida valley, between the Blue Ridge and an escarpment, where the New Deal has erected a resettlement project for the mountaineers dispossessed by the park. About twenty small houses have been built on farms of from eight to twelve acres, water has been brought by gravity from the mountainside, and electricity provided by the benevolent government. But the mountaineers are not community people. They like to choose their own way, and not all the homes are occupied. The residents of Page valley comment restrainedly: "The cost of building the homes was rather high compared to the cost of building like homes in this section."

There is another side road out of Luray, a twisted, gravelly, unimproved, radiator-boiling track, which climbs across the ragged bulk of Massanutten, with the trees pressing in on either side and the air growing perceptibly thinner and purer as it ascends. On the crest of the mountain is a narrow footpath which smells of the damp green forest, leading to a skeleton lookout tower erected by the enterprising Daughters of some War. From the tower the main Valley and Page valley are magnificently revealed, with the Shenandoah opulently curving in the Seven Bends, and that hidden vale within the mountain, Powell's Fort.

It is a little golden valley, not more than ten miles square, where clean toy houses, clean toy fields, a white-spired church, are enclosed forever from the world, enfolded in perpetual security. There an Englishman named Powell once stamped out his counterfeit money, which is said to have assayed higher in silver than the legitimate coin of the era; and there, according to the legend, General Washington planned to make his last stand in the event of failure. So green, so sweet, so safe it appears from the mountaintop that it is easy to understand how it might linger always in the mind of a driven man as the ultimate refuge. It would be best perhaps never to descend into Fort valley, but to let the imagination possess it always as the epitome of safety and of peace.

The highway south from Luray hugs the mountains, skips over the winding green river on short bridges, sails through a little town where once there was a popular resort, Bear Lithia Springs, and another where once there was an ironworks; passes near a house where once lived Gabriel Jones, king's attorney, "the man with the celestial name and the very uncelestial temper," crosses the Spotswood trail from which a royal governor once viewed the Valley, and comes at last to Port Republic, where once was fought a battle.

Twenty miles below the frowning southern front of Massanutten, the town of Waynesboro is converting itself into an industrial center. Steam shovels have torn a great naked wound in the green mountainside above it, a bald scar visible from one side of the Valley to the other. A du Pont rayon plant has been installed, and a ship-fitting company which flies the navy E. Within a few years Waynesboro has grown

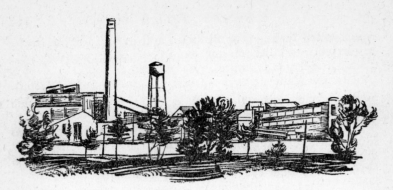

DU PONT RAYON PLANT AT WAYNESBORO

from a sleepy village to a population of ten thousand. When
the ship-fitting plant recently laid off five hundred of _its
suddenly acquired twenty-five hundred, the du Pont took
them on. There are nineteen other manufacturing establish-
ments in the city.

Waynesboro is still faintly astonished at this sudden
growth, and with some reason. It can look back to many
eras of enthusiasm, since it was named in 1798 for Mad
Anthony Wayne. In the early part of the nineteenth century
it was visited by Claude Crozet, Rochambeau, and Betsey
Patterson Bonaparte. It learned some caution in the fervid
nineties, when Basic City rose from "a hayrick, a cowshed,
and a cider stand," to a purported worth of $700,000. The
huge hotel built in that optimistic era has been converted
into Fairfax Hall, the girls' school named for the woman
hater. In 1923 the remains of Basic City were incorporated
with Waynesboro.

On the mountaintop above, near Rockfish Gap, is the
site of Leakes Tavern, where on a summer day in 1818 some
twenty-eight gentlemen of Virginia, among them Jefferson,
Madison, Marshall, and Monroe, met to select the site for the
new State University. Today the mountainside is orna-
mented by a white marble edifice in the style of the Italian
Renaissance, built by a Major Dooley of Richmond, later

transformed into a country club, and in 1939 about to be converted into "a center for the promotion of world peace." Today it still stands empty.

In the Valley they have seen the dreamers and the enterprises come and go. One thing they have learned. In the marrow of their bones, where it is inaccessible alike to reason and to despair, they know—what people could know better? —that the dream matters more than the achievement. Man does not always realize his aspirations, but the important thing is to build a new hope on the ruins of the old one, to go forward, to fight on.

The road winds on across the rolling fields of Stuart's Draft where that stout sea captain James Patton settled himself after he had done with bringing colonists from England in his rolling ship. Thirty miles from Waynesboro lies Lexington, home of the sleeping generals. There Lee rests in his ivy-covered chapel, and Jackson under his monument in the green cemetery.

Valentine modeled Lee recumbent in white marble, and has let Jackson stand in bronze above his grave, thoughtful rather than triumphant. It was long after the battles before the South could gather money for this monument. When they at last erected it, the surviving Confederate soldiers came to a reunion, and the elderly remnants of the Stonewall Brigade chose to sleep in the open among the graves, holding a last bivouac with their commander. They were not ashamed of wet cheeks when they left next morning.

"Good-bye old fellow," one called. "We've done all that we can for you."

Lexington does not lack memorials. Moses Ezekiel, once a cadet who charged at Newmarket, made the bronze statue of Virginia mourning for her children which stands before his institute. Benjamin West Clinedinst, a Valley boy named for an artist from Nantucket, painted a mural of the famous battle. George Washington's effigy has been brought back from Wheeling, where the Yankees took it, to crown again the cupola of his university. Cyrus McCormick stands upon the campus by virtue of an endowment. But Lexington does not depend on dead heroes and on memories. Lexington is youth, and youth is the future.

The hotel, inevitably named the Robert E. Lee, is cleanly standardized. The boys entertaining their dates in the cement-floored coffeeroom are not talking about history. In peacetime the students and cadets engage in an endless war between the university and the institute. In war the courses at both have been shortened, the graduates are getting younger—it has happened there before. V.M.I. looks backward with a reasonable pride, but does not depend upon its past, for it can still train officers. General George C. Marshall, chief of staff, is a V.M.I. graduate, General George S. Patton had a year there before going to West Point, and there are many others.

One road from Lexington leads to Goshen Pass, through which Maury asked to have his body carried when the rhododendrons bloomed. A granite stone with an anchor and an anchor chain commemorate him there today.

> The stars had secrets for him; seas
> Revealed the depths the waves were screening,
> The winds gave up their mysteries,
> The tidal flows confessed their meaning.

The way lies past the ghost of Rockbridge Springs, a resort whose glory has departed, and crosses the Alleghenies to "The Warm" and "The Hot." In 1853 Rockbridge Springs sold for the then staggering sum of $150,000. Four hundred visitors a day rolled up in carriages during the season, men of distinction tarried with their families on the fashionable "tour of the Springs"—so necessary to satisfy their wives and marry off their daughters. Now the population is not more than a hundred and only a few shabby houses cluster around the ruins of the hotel.

Most of the gay resorts in the mountains around the Valley are now memories, but a few still operate in a reduced style. The Shenandoah Alum has one hundred acres in the

George Washington Forest area, Orkney Springs preserves something of Victorian decorum in its "Ladies Parlor," at Massanetta the Presbyterians hold an annual conference, and Capon Springs is still alive. Berkeley Springs, which as Bath was the first of them all, is enjoying a revival.

In another direction from Lexington is Natural Bridge, an unhewn stone arch over Cedar Creek. Thomas Jefferson was so impressed with it that he bought it from King George for twenty shillings, built a log cabin and installed a guest book there. The young George Washington climbed it and cut his initials in the rock and, according to the legend, threw a silver dollar over it, as over the Potomac. (Posterity is asked to believe that this was his usual response to a natural phenomenon.) Harriet Martineau, Washington Irving, and many other articulate travelers have visited Natural Bridge and succumbed vociferously to the appropriate sensations.

It is not to be expected that the enterprising mind of modern man would be insensible to the value of this marvel. Never has the "Bridge of God," which saved the Monacans from the Powhatans, been so appreciated as at the present day. Never have its approaches been so closely guarded as they are now, in the effort to keep off the desecrating feet of those who have not paid their dollars to behold it. There is a large hotel with a battery of rocking chairs on the veranda, there is a pavilion full of souvenirs (many made in Japan). A thoughtful management has even provided a rack full of black rubber raincoats for guests in inclement weather. Once every hour a party descends the long flight of rustic steps past the 1,500-year-old arbor vitae. They sit in rows of wooden chairs on the broad asphalt by brawling rocky Cedar Creek and hear a mechanical voice recite the first chapter of Genesis, interspersed with incidental music.

People who live in the neighborhood find it eerie to sit on their porches of a summer evening and hear a voice boom in their ears about the darkness which moved on the face of the waters. But at the Bridge, with a special lighting which ebbs and flows like the dawn of creation, the program is surprisingly impressive. And sometimes in the midst of these ceremonies the true moon rises and floats like a round golden lantern beneath the solid and immutable old gray stone arch.

On the way back to Lexington stand two "boom" towns of the nineties, Buena Vista, still active and industrial, and Glasgow, where a company, headed by General Fitzhugh Lee himself, built a hotel and a powerhouse, neither of which has ever operated. Glasgow is more worthy of notice for the homes, Green Forest and Glasgow Manor, built in the late eighteenth century by the Scotch immigrant who was the great-grandfather of the novelist Ellen Glasgow.

The Shenandoah Valley can (and does) feel a proud connection with modern American literature, for it has Ellen Glasgow anchored at one end by her ancestral roots and Willa Cather born at the other. The old brick Cather house, uncompromisingly rectangular, sits in a hollow below the road between Romney and Winchester. But neither of these talents has exploited the cradle of its origin, for the Glasgows have long been settled in Richmond and the Cathers moved to the Middle West when Willa was small enough to take on the color of her new environment.

Leave Old House Mountain and North River to the students, who will put them to the best of uses, and travel north down the main valley of the Shenandoah. The first important stop is Staunton, a town of steep hilly streets, and old houses which hide their gardens behind them. This time the modern hotel is named for Stonewall Jackson, and in its lobby presides the somewhat wooden portrait of Woodrow Wilson, illumined by perpetual light. His birthplace, the old manse, has been appropriately furnished and maintained, and Mrs. Cordell Hull, a native of Staunton, is one of the sponsors.

Staunton looks back to the grave of John Lewis, two miles out of town, and to the time when the Lewis sons were young and lusty, and the frontier ended at her door. "Nowhere is there such a superfluity of military personages as in the town of Staunton," wrote an Irish traveler in 1796. The Duc de la Rochefoucauld reported that they were "fond of gambling and betting like the generality of Virginians." But Staunton has a present also.

The Stonewall Brigade Band still gives concerts in Gipsy Park—though not with the original cast of players. They celebrated the death of prejudice when they played at the dedication of Grant's Tomb on Riverside Drive in 1897. There are plenty of young people in Staunton every winter, for there are four thriving schools, two masculine and military, two feminine and fashionable.—And Staunton invented the city manager form of government in 1908.—And the Gold Star Mothers of America meet every year in Staunton.

From Staunton to Harrisonburg the Valley is now broad and smiling—where once the trees closed in, where once the Indians terrorized Augusta by swooping down from North Mountain. The Old Stone Church which Dominie John Craig led and drove his congregation into building with their rifles handy, still stands square and solid by the highway. It is the oldest church except one in Virginia. The Presbyterians still worship there, although they have modified the length of their sermons. They also worship still at Timber Ridge, at Tinkling Spring, at Windy Cove, and at the other churches in Rockbridge and Augusta which the first Samuel Houston helped to found. This is still Scotch-Irish and Presbyterian country around Lexington and Staunton, but as the road runs into Harrisonburg the German element begins to dominate.

Harrisonburg, although not new, has a new look, a square-set neatness not always found in Valley towns. Here are no jagged corners of old stone, no flaking weather-beaten paint, no sagging walls. The gray limestone buildings of Madison College and of the courthouse are massive and orderly, the streets are freshly scrubbed. Industrious thrift and energy are patent everywhere. Rockingham County has discovered a new industry to make it prosperous again—the raising of succulent bronze-winged turkeys, and it has become the poultry center of the country. The fields of Rockingham are lush and wide, and by the side of one of them stands a marker: "Ashby fell here."

Rockingham clings to its old customs. It was here that German remained the language of the community for one hundred years after the new settlement. Near here in the summer of 1944 they held a riding tournament, although in the rest of the Valley such meets have disappeared. The Natural Chimneys, rock pillars carved by water like the caverns and Natural Bridge, stand just over the border of Augusta County. They are still as dear to picnickers as they were when John Lewis took the White Dove there with Oroonah, and last summer the annual Natural Chimneys Tournament took place as it has done for one hundred and twenty-three years.

Forty-one knights rode at the ring, suspended on a cord above the arena. In the morning the Knight of Moscow won and crowned his lady Queen of Love and Beauty. The Knight of the Golden Horseshoe, the Knight of the Silver Cloud, the Knights of the Dusty Trail, of the North River, of Cranberry Hill, also brought honors to their ladies. In the days when Walter Scott was the favorite author, when every village had its tournament, and chivalry was the ideal, Turner Ashby was the constant victor. He called himself Hiawatha, or the Black Prince, because of his swarthy skin. He carried off so many rings that they forced him to ride without saddle or bridle—and still he won. Then fate called him to a darker tournament, and a peerless fame.

In the summer of 1944 the Valley people were conscious of their tradition and of their responsibility. Many of the contestants who enjoyed this one hundred and twenty-third meeting were men who had been released from the service in order to get in the crops, and who would allow themselves no other free day that summer.

In the Shenandoah Valley the present cannot be separated from the past, for each contains the other, and the future is their child. It is not for nothing that the Valley Pike—the Long Gray Trail—runs north from Harrisonburg —for if the ghosts of long-dead soldiers ever walk, some will be marching here.

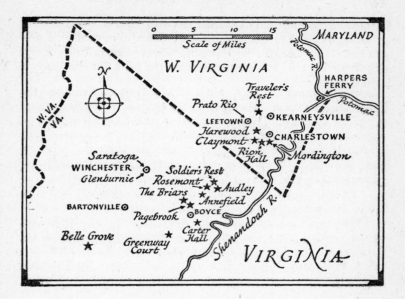

28. Valley Tour III

Go north then on the Valley Pike, where at least one man has died for every yard over which the automobile runs equably. You may try to see the present only, but the tread of the dead soldiers, blue and gray, still has power to shake the Valley hearts, and on this ground they cannot be forgotten.

Here is Newmarket, where the army bands played "Rockabye Baby" when the cadets came in. This is Mount Jackson, where Stonewall rested with his lemons and his Bible, where Sheridan once said to a dying captured soldier, "Aren't you McNeill of the Rangers?" and the answer was,

"I am." Five hundred Confederates still rest in this burying ground, more than one hundred of them unnamed and unknown. And here is Woodstock, where Peter Muhlenberg threw off his parson's gown to show the blue and buff of an earlier war.

But there were men of peace as well as warriors in this most peaceful Valley—and men of healing. In Edom, near the homestead whence the Lincoln family sprang, lived Dr. Joseph Bennett, who in 1794 performed a successful Caesarean operation on his wife, and saved both mother and child. This was fifteen years before Dr. McDowell's oöphorectomy. Dr. Walter Reed, the hero of yellow fever research, spent part of his youth in Harrisonburg. Dr. Wilmer, the eye surgeon, long had a country home near Berryville.

The law has its representatives also. In the high-ceilinged, fly-haunted courthouse at Woodstock, the record books are full of the copper-plate writing of Thomas Marshall, county clerk, and father of Chief Justice John Marshall. Edmund Randolph, the first attorney general, sleeps in the churchyard of the Old Chapel at Millwood.

But this tour is rolling through the Valley of today, the middle Valley, where the Shenandoah bends seven times through black alluvial soil. Shenandoah County comes next after Rockingham. In 1930 it had a population of thirty thousand, of which 97 $\frac{7}{10}$ per cent were native born white, 2 $\frac{1}{10}$ per cent were Negroes, and the foreign born were less than sixty souls. Their work was the production of food, with a few mills and canneries to complete the process. Seventy per cent of the farms have less than one hundred acres, but only ten per cent are worked by tenants. The average farm income is $1,642, and the homes in the villages rent for $8 to $30 a month. Dry figures which paint a picture of a settled and substantial population, industrious and independent—and that Shenandoah County is and has always been.

Once it had a group of famous potteries. Strasburg and Maurertown, just north of Woodstock, were nicknamed Pot Town and Jug Town. A family of Palatinate refugees, Angli-

cized as "Bell," potters by trade, followed the usual route
through Pennsylvania and Maryland to the Valley. Samuel
Bell set up his wheels at Strasburg in 1833. He was a patient
man, and skilled. His workmen earned $9 a month and really
learned their business. He was followed by sons and sons-
in-law, all with an honest love of their craft, who attracted
others until there were six potteries in operation.

The last wheel turned in 1908, and the industry has been
abandoned. Now if a collector should find an old blue jar,
a brown stone crock, a decorated mug or pitcher, it would
have to be at a dim old house or remote farm. The junk-
filled antique shops along the road have discovered the rarity
of these items, and have set a prohibitive price upon "the
Shenandoah Pottery." If Strasburg is to have a well-known
product again, it will be through its printing presses, for the
Shenandoah Publishing House has established itself there.

The road leads on through Middletown and Kernstown,
where Jackson fought his first Sunday battle, and suffered his
first defeat. Along this stretch Miss Charlotte Hillman
dropped her tollgate in front of Sheridan and his whole army.
The general humored her courage by paying for himself and
his staff, but told her that she would have to hold the United
States government responsible for the rest. And that is what
she did. She counted the soldiers as they passed, presented her
bill after the war, and collected.

Here on the gentle swells of land just south of Winchester begins the lower Valley, home of the English settlers, a
countryside of noble trees, old houses, long memories, and
gentle manners. In Frederick and Clark, Jefferson and Berkeley, the old houses tell the story, and it is not possible
to escape their meaning.

On Cedar Creek, a name full of sorrow and triumph,
stands Harmony Hall, built as a fort against the Indians by
Joist Hite's son-in-law, George Bowman. The rough stones
were roughly put together in 1753, and although the stockade around them vanished long ago, they have defied the
weather and marauders ever since. The little Miller girl ran
to this house on the day in 1764 when her family were

massacred. Here Bowman sired and reared four distinguished sons, one to be a colonel in the Revolution, two to go west with the Lewis and Clarke expedition, one to command militia in Kentucky.

A few miles northeast, Isaac Hite, grandson of the pioneer, built Belle Grove in 1787. Tradition says that Thomas Jefferson drew the plans, and certainly the house shows his influence. It is low, a story and a half, and handsomely proportioned. James and Dolly Madison stopped there on their wedding trip, for Mrs. Hite was Madison's sister, and the poor bride was taken with fever and ague. She recovered in a few days, however, and spent the rest of the fortnight "with great pleasure on our side, and I hope with no less on the other," as her husband wrote. Not all of Belle Grove's memories are happy. In the stone-walled cellar a Negress beat her mistress to death with a shovel. While Sheridan was using it as headquarters, young General Stephen Ramseur died there, his baby unseen, holding the hand of his enemy and schoolmate, Colonel Dupont. A noble young face, all life and fire, looks from his portrait. The baby whom he never saw is probably dead too by now, but Belle Grove goes on. In 1928 it was sold to a Honeywell of Boston and of Harvard University.

Pages and Washingtons, Carters and Burwells, Randolphs, Peytons, Harrisons, Meades, Nelsons, Byrds, Pendletons, seeded this ground. Pages or their descendants built Pagebrook, and Annefield, where the box, lilacs, and syringa planted more than one hundred years ago by "sweet Anne Page" still grow and bloom. Pages came to own Dan Morgan's Saratoga. Pages built the Briars where John Esten Cooke lived, wrote, and died after he married one of them. Cooke's histories and novels, in the Walter Scott tradition and overromantic for the present taste, were best sellers in their day. He served during the Civil War on General Jackson's staff, and *Surry of Eagle's Nest* and other books blended a vivid record of his experiences with a lush imagination.

A cousin of George Washington built old stone Fairfield, where he often visited. Brothers built Mordington and Harewood near Charles Town, nephews built Audley and Claymont. Of them all only Harewood is still in the hands of Washingtons today, and it is empty. Widow Dolly Payne Todd, Dolly Madison, was married there. (Her sister Lucy had married, at fifteen, the owner, George Steptoe Washington, the general's nephew.) The bride drove gaily down from Philadelphia in Thomas Jefferson's coach, with the groom and his friends on horseback beside her. The Madisons and Washingtons turned out in force, and at the last minute Light-Horse Harry Lee dashed up, "on the very finest horse in Virginia." They danced and frolicked so vigorously that the groom lost his ruffle of Mechlin lace, which the girls cut up for keepsakes. Then the bridal pair drove off up the Valley to "my sister Hite." When the Quakers "disowned" both Lucy and Dolly for their "misconduct" in marrying out of meeting, the gay young sisters were unimpressed. They had done well for themselves and they knew it.

When Charles Washington laid out his town, he built Mordington, and named it Happy Retreat. It has belonged for more than twenty years to the Conklins, two brothers and two sisters, all unmarried. One of them made beautiful hand-turned walnut furniture in the east wing until his recent death.

Claymont has passed through at least one fire and many hands since Bushrod Washington built it about 1820. Kercheval called it "one of the largest and most elegant edifices in our country," and the description is still true. A drive a mile long leads through the oak woods to a yellow brick house, vine covered, with exquisite portico and low-lying wings, in the Regency style which has never been bettered in grace and elegance for domestic architecture. Frank Stockton, author of *The Lady or the Tiger,* owned it once, and wrote and died there. Then it was bought by the Murphy family who had three public-spirited daughters, Elise, Yvonne and Lorraine. It has recently been bought by Mr. Raymond J. Funkhouser, who was born not far away in the hill country of Maryland, and began his business career at Shenandoah Junction.

He has made notable changes in the old place. The long drive is now hard-surfaced, nine miles of whitewashed fences have been installed, the thirty-four rooms have been redecorated. He has bought Blakely, a minor Washington house across the fields, for his son, and is negotiating for West Blakely. He has built $3,500 cottages for the Negro hands. Since he has numerous children and grandchildren, he hopes to entertain them at home, and so has installed a lake, a swimming pool, a tennis court, and even a juke box. Only the gardens, sprawled on their terraces, fragrant with box, have thus far resisted improvement.

Mr. Funkhouser has recently given to the town of Charles Town the site for a new hospital, the land on which the boom hotel, the Powhatan, once stood.

Audley, where Nellie Custis spent her last years with her son Lorenzo Lewis, and where she died in 1852, is a low white cottage with a long veranda. Outwardly it is unchanged, but the present owner, Mr. Mumford Jones, has redecorated the interior in the Italianate style, red velvet, heavy carving, ornate stone mantels. When Nellie Custis lived there surrounded by her descendants, as granddaughter of Martha and adopted daughter of George, she was the custodian of the Washington relics, and men of distinction, including two presidents of the United States, felt honored when she received them. They kept an unusual guest book at Audley by standing the visitors up against the front door and making them write their names at the height of their heads. Washington Irving stayed there, and so did Mrs. Robert E. Lee, a kinswoman, at the outset of the Civil War. When she had to flee from Arlington, there was plenty of room for her at Audley, because six young men of the Lewis family had just left for the Confederate Army.

The old doors have gone, and there is nothing left of Nellie Custis at Audley except a rumor about her ghost, and a holly tree which she once planted. The grass has obliterated the garden. The Joneses once bred race horses, but do so no longer, and their extensive stables are deserted. The estate has been put to raising hogs. A painted iron sign in the shape of a hog, lettered "Audley Farm," hangs at the end of the drive, and gives a great deal of pain to some of the Lewis blood who still live in the neighborhood.

Carter Hall, named for "King" Carter, still attests the magnificence of his grandson, Carter Burwell, who built it near Millwood in 1790. Mr. Gerard B. Lambert of Princeton bought it in 1929, and has remodeled the singing spiral of the staircase. James Wood's Glen Burnie stands, and Daniel Morgan's Soldier's Rest, but Angus McDonald's Glengarry has burned. Of Greenway Court there remains only the White Post which Lord Fairfax set up at a quiet crossroad a mile away, and the little stone office. Tenants live in Traveler's Rest, built by General Gates, and the silver waters of Prato Rio, retreat of that antisocial general, Charles Lee, have been turned into a governmental fish hatchery where trout and bass are spawned.

No list could cover all the old houses, there are too many of them hidden away down curving lanes, concealed by groves, retired behind long drives. They have survived prosperity, neglect, and desertion. Now they are drawing a new element to the Valley—the "rich Yankees". They are being bought up for good prices, by people from more prosperous sections, who want, or think they want, what the old houses have to give, and who bring with them their own accelerated tempo.

They have brought also another sort of aristocrat to the Valley, once familiar there, but for some decades absent— the thoroughbred horse. During the years of poverty the bluegrass grew from the limestone soil as sweetly as ever, but it takes a dew of silver coins as well to raise a thoroughbred. Now the horses are coming back. At Court Manor in Rockingham, Willis Sharpe Kilmer owned Sunbeau, the great money winner, and the famous Exterminator. The ancient sport of fox hunting had been revived at Millwood, at Front Royal, and elsewhere, until World War II sent it into temporary eclipse again.

But the new people are not only in search of sport and fun. They are trying experimental farming and introducing good strains of blooded stock. A New York woman who owns 175 acres of rich bottom land along the Shenandoah is raising beans and peas which are shelled by machine, quick-frozen in Winchester, and sold to the Viscose corporation in Front Royal for its cafeteria. This strikes a modern note. But she is also managing a 1,500-acre farm while her husband is in the navy, and that is in the Valley tradition—that has been done before.

The old and the new people are still inclined to assume toward each other a faintly patronizing tone. The Yankees find the Southerners quaint because they wear the same hats year after year and cling to antiquated customs. On the other hand, there persists in some southern minds an atavistic belief that it does no harm to take anything you can get away from a Yankee. After one newcomer of partly southern blood had coped with the simplehearted natives in a few horse trades, she wrote her family in haste for more pictures of ancestors in Confederate uniform. She has them on her mantel now, and in their reflected glory she can hold her own.

Sometimes the Yankees get in each other's way. One young couple looking for a house with just the right atmosphere found what they wanted at the end of miles of unimproved road, and telephoned in haste to an agent about their discovery.

"You can't have it," he said, unimpressed.

"Why not?"

"Because it already belongs to a vice-president of General Motors."

The new arrivals come in quickly, settle fast, protest appreciation of the Valley, but the inhabitants of long standing still regard them with reserve. They may have fallen in love with the Blue Ridge, and the old green Shenandoah, but will their infatuation last? To belong there they must love the Valley not only in its bridal veil of spring, in the embrace of honeysuckle-scented night, in the blue haze of autumn —but also in its less romantic aspects. When the cold winds and the rain bring in the winter and the mud, these strangers may fly off on the wings of dollar bills to some region where life is more "amusing." Will they love the land well enough to work it year after year under the blazing sun, to bear its treachery as well as its fruitfulness? In short, would they love the Valley enough to die for it? The Valley people will need the answer to that question before they feel entirely at one with the newcomers.

It is not hard to understand why the Valley still captures some prisoners every year with its snare of variegated fields and silver river, holds them behind a guardian wall of mountains. In the summer of 1944 the small golden hutches of reaped wheat stood long in the fields, for the threshers had gone to war. By the pellucid streams the weeping willows gently agitated their long green veils. The road banks were a flower bed of pink and blue, cornflowers and bouncing Bet —and the little roads wandered with apparent aimlessness, dipping, rising, curving around grove and meadow, tying the present and the past together.

By one such road in the lower valley stands a grove of dark cedars. This is "The Priest's Field," the land presented to the cleric who exorcised the phantom of Wizard's Clip. They have never plowed that field. It is given over to the cedars. Deep in the grove the Catholic Church has built a shrine where it holds a service once a year. The haunted village of Middleway lies ahead, the exact center of the county— once a thriving market, now a few substantial houses slumbering in abandoned gardens. The owner of one lives in Baltimore but keeps her old house richly furnished, arrives and airs it once a month for one day, closes the shutters and departs.

Well out in the surrounding countryside stands the red-brick church of Wycliffe Parish, once graced by a distinguished congregation, now with the tall grass deep around the portico and a frightened fledgling bird the only worshiper. Then unexpectedly the road arrives in Inwood, a town pervaded by the bitter-sweet tang of crushed apples, where the fruit rolls in by truck and out by freight car, and many thousand shining cans of applesauce march incessantly on the conveyor belt.

Another country road goes to the Bower, "ten miles from anywhere," headquarters for J. E. B. Stuart and his cavalrymen, who used a private ford over the Opequon. The Dandridge family still maintain the Bower as a home which any or all of them may visit in the summer. Between such occupancy, the house is empty except for a caretaker. The sheep graze up to the veranda, and a cool wind blows incessantly across the hill and rattles lightly through the prodigious oaks where Stuart's men tethered their weary mounts. Empty too is Woodberry, where Judge Tucker had his law school, empty and white and high, grass-grown the circular drive, moss-green the statues and the gravestones, fallen the trees.

A woman in search of the past had a flat tire on a rocky lane which meandered from nowhere to nowhere, and wanted a man to fix it. There was no one in sight. The vacant undulating fields, the distant mountains promised nothing. Then came the distant splutter of a tractor. She caught the driver as he turned in the hollow of an apple orchard, and he climbed down obligingly, leaving the motor running because it was too much trouble to start it up again. He proved to be a talkative and cheerful man who announced that he "was born right in Clarke County and lived there ever since," as though that piece of good fortune were enough to make anyone sunny-natured. As he knelt beside the wheel his sweat splashed softly in the dust.

"Seems like I need a water-spout over my eyebrows," he said.

When he had finished he waved aside an offer of remuneration, and went back to his panting tractor with a remark which seemed to epitomize the attitude of his neighborhood.

"Glad to help you out, ma'am. A little touch of manners don't hurt nobody."

Winchester is the largest of the towns in the Valley, and it is not dreaming about its past. It is busy with the apple-storage warehouses, the quick-freezing plants, the rubber-heel factory, the woolen mills and flour mills, the glove factory, and the brick plant. In the old portion of the town the streets are tree-shaded and the houses present a solid front and hide their gardens, but the new and growing districts are neat, comfortable, and raw.

Winchester has a good hospital. It has a modern hotel—this one is the George Washington. It has a fine high school and a handsomely domed library, the gift of a stranger who fell in love with the Valley. John Handley came to the United States from Ireland when he was nineteen, and settled in Scranton, Pennsylvania, where he prospered and became a judge. Soon after the Civil War he visited the Valley and succumbed to an infatuation for it which was strengthened by the fact that Scranton did not appreciate him sufficiently to pave the cobbled street before his house. He was not impractical enough to try to live in Winchester, but when he died without children in 1889 he left his money to the city with instructions which built the bequest up to almost a million dollars. Twelve Irish cousins protested promptly but vainly. The courts maintained the will, and the town has made good use of the money.

In 1926 they buried Lord Fairfax in Winchester—not for the first time. His bones had been lost for many years, and a lawyer of the town was interested enough to hire a Negro to dig in search of them. After several days of failure he was ready to give up the search, but the Negro came one morning and said that the whereabouts of the bones had been revealed to him in a dream. "If I finds 'em, you pays me. If I doesn't, you doesn't." It seemed a sporting proposition, and under the combined stimulus of dreams and dollars the bones were found and suitably reinterred in Winchester.

Winchester holds an annual apple blossom festival—which has been temporarily discontinued during the present war. Queen Shenandoah is crowned on the steps of the Handley School, and one thousand children put on a pageant for her. They parade with floats and bands, and visitors from all over the country attend the two balls. A flaming red-plaster apple five feet high was installed during one festival on the grass in front of Mrs. Logan's house, and there remains. (When General Milroy once returned to Winchester after the Civil War and attempted to make a speech he was shouted down with cries of "Where are Mrs. Logan's spoons?")

Each year some distinguished son of the Valley presents the crown to the apple-blossom queen. In 1932 it was Admiral Richard Byrd. Both Winchester and Berryville feel that they have a claim on the Byrds, Tom, Dick and Harry. All three grew up in Winchester, children of a brilliant father who was state's attorney and of a mother from whose strong and salty character they still draw refreshment. At the age of nine Richard went abroad alone to visit friends. It did not astonish his neighbors when he later turned up at both the North and the South Pole. Tom has avoided the limelight, but in partnership with Harry has built himself up into the largest applegrower in the world. Harry has been governor of Virginia, and is now one of her United States senators.

From the southern point of view, Harry Flood Byrd had two great political assets. He was both a poor-boy-who-made-good and an aristocrat. The Byrds have been involved with lost causes ever since Charles Stuart gave a grant on the James to William Byrd. A later Byrd left the Tidewater and came to the Valley because of an overzealous support of Lord Dunmore. During the Civil War the family of course lost everything. Harry stopped school at fifteen and took over the Winchester *Star*, which his father owned but could not be said to manage. Within ten years he had put it on its feet and bought out his competitor. From then on his progress has been steady and not at all mysterious. Here was a man who did not leave the Valley and make his money by incomprehensible methods, but who built himself up in ways his neighbors could understand. They honor him for it, and the respect which he commands among them is not tinged with jealousy.

Senator Byrd succeeded through the old virtues of in-

dustry, integrity and thrift, and his devotion to this un-
fashionable trio has made him some political enemies. He has
been called by Arthur Krock, the columnist (who also has a
place near Berryville), "the most effective opponent of the
New Deal." But criticism has never made the senator waver
in a course he considered right, nor has he ever shunned a
fight for a policy in which he believes. He knows where he
stands, and so do both his enemies and his friends.

Meanwhile, when he can get away from Washington, he
sits of a summer evening on the white-columned porch at
Rosemont and watches the moon rise over the Blue Ridge, a
floating golden apple in a black and silver sky. His dogs trot
over the terrace, his grandchildren visit him, his orchards grow
almost to his door. If the nation does not use him further, it
can be safely assumed that Virginia will. Senator Byrd is a
man integrated with his environment.

The Valley Pike leads on through Berryville past a gray
stucco church which the white people built in memory of
their colored mammies, who indubitably had earned it. There
was a startling rattle of gunfire just outside the town one
afternoon in June, 1944, and for a moment it seemed that
the past might be reawakening. But it was not. The day was
Confederate Memorial Day, and a salute was fired across the
graves of the dead soldiers.

Twelve miles beyond Berryville lies Charles Town, with
Martinsburg and Shepherdstown somewhat to the north and
west. On certain days Charles Town is crowded now, the
hotel (this one is named for Thomas Jefferson) jammed.
But the visitors are not looking for the courthouse where
John Brown was tried. They are on their way to the races at
the new track on the edge of the town. Even when pleasure
driving was banned, the crowds continued to come and the
cars might be found parked several miles away in the country
because they did not dare to appear at the track. The old
conservatives deplore this new enterprise, the businessmen
rejoice, and the horses gallop on.

Beyond Charles Town the gray steel ribbon of the Valley

Pike dips and rises more steeply, for the mountains grow nearer, change from blue to green, from hazy smoothness to the shaggy reality of rocks and trees. And here is Harpers Ferry, and the end of the Shenandoah River. The street along the river has been condemned because of repeated rising water, the armory has never been rebuilt, the site of John Brown's raid is marked only by a bronze plate.

But he has not been forgotten in this town where he played out his fierce drama. On a steep hill hanging over the river stands Storer College, one of the first institutions established to give higher education to colored people. And under the great trees on the campus the engine house where Brown made his last stand has been reconstructed brick by brick. The leaves drop lightly on the silent roof, and in the gorge below the river roars and rushes, just as it rushed past the bloodstained rocks in 1859. "I am worth more to die than to live," John Brown said—but he has not died. An inscription on his old engine house speaks of it as "the birthplace of racial liberty."

The college was founded soon after the Civil War by John Storer of Maine, who felt a responsibility toward the freedmen and offered to give ten thousand dollars if his gift were matched. He did not live to see the work begun, but he is commemorated for the initial impetus. For the last forty-five years the president of Storer has been a white man, Dr. Henry T. McDonald, a cultured Northerner who retired in 1944. When he arrived some of the old slaves were still living. He knew and talked with them and found in the old Negro a dignity and a comprehension which the new Negro lacks, and which he attributes to a closer association with the better type of white. The present has brought a greater equality of white and colored on the lower levels, but the better classes are more remote. In his first years at Storer Dr. McDonald found a wonderful devotion between teacher and pupil, but World War I brought great changes, and the present war has accelerated them.

After years of study, he is convinced that the Negro who has attended a white college, or had some white influence of a high type early in life, obtains a better understanding of his problems than one who has not. With this in view he kept his faculty half Negro and half white. He believes that there are only two solutions for the racial question, *patience* and *religion*. These ideals are not in harmony with some new theories.

It is clear that the educated Negro is still in a difficult position, for his opportunities have not kept up with his capacities. The Storer graduates who took up teaching have usually stayed in the South, where there are segregated schools, for they are not accepted for positions in the mixed schools of the North. The professional men have usually gone north, although some of them have succeeded in the South among their own people. Progress for the race has been exasperatingly slow, although there has been progress. Once Storer was laughed at as a "nigger college," now it is respected. "In this atmosphere," writes one of the students, "there is a tendency toward developing patience."

But now new winds of change are blowing across the world, and Dr. McDonald has been replaced by a Negro. The racial leaders have a new term of contempt, "a white man's Negro," and they use it inclusively. All the white teachers at Storer are to be replaced by colored people. The race again surges upward, and again they have no time to wait for the slow and peaceful processes of evolution. And the river rushing past the college has washed away the memory of the blood upon its stones.

29. Epilogue

THIS THEN, is the Valley of the Shenandoah, a fair land, long in memories and rich in peace. Stonewall Jackson's trenches on the hills above the Valley Pike are lost in woods and filled with rotting leaves. Yet the land can still breed fighters as it always has, for—make no mistake about it—up and down the old river, rich and poor, white and black, the Valley is fighting another war.

The men have gone and they went promptly. In every county ten to fourteen per cent of the population are in the services, forty to fifty per cent of the men of fighting age. The wheat lies long in the fields, for the reapers are few. High school children and imported labor pick the apples. Senator Byrd's three sons are on active duty, one a naval lieutenant, one a paratrooper, one a sergeant of infantry. "Aunt Ruth," a colored cook, has letters now from London, and there is a new and burning pride in her, a new level meeting of the eyes.

"Is yo' boy in England?" she asks. "Mine is too. I reckon he is in France by this time."

The old streets in the dreaming towns are full of children, children holding a grandmother's hand, children sitting on the curbstones with vague little colored girls (who according to their own new rules work for half a day only), children playing in groups, free and unhindered, or laughing in their mothers' arms. But the fathers are not in evidence. They felt themselves called upon to fight, left the distant places where they were earning their living, and have sent their families home to wait for them. Back to the Valley where children are not a nuisance or a liability but an asset,

354

the hope of the family, the guarantee of continuance. Back to
the security of the Valley, where life is established and not
too difficult.

The war has boomed the Valley industries. In Jefferson
and Berkeley, subsidiaries of Jones and Laughlin and of the
United States Steel Corporation are tearing out the limestone
and dolomite ribs of the earth to make a product used in
fluxing steel, to make rock wool, cement, agricultural lime.
The war has also brought in new activities. The Federal
government has built the Woodrow Wilson General Hospital at Staunton on a high pleateau overlooking both mountain ranges. It can care for sixteen hundred wounded soldiers.
The Newton Baker Hospital at Martinsburg, named for
another native son, has a capacity of seventeen hundred
and is being enlarged. The one-story brick buildings of "semipermanent" construction (what semipermanent can mean is
not defined) are all heated from one plant in a corner, and
cover eighty acres, connected by covered galleries. Seventeen
hundred attendants, doctors, nurses, laborers, are required
to look after the wounded. Everything has been thought of,
even to a house for the sheep which are to keep the grass cut
short. Also near Martinsburg a new airport has been constructed. All the hot summer the bulldozers plied back and
forth in clouds of choking dust, smoothing off four hundred
acres, laying runways a mile long. Casualties are expected to
arrive there by air, direct from the battlefields. After the war
the airfields will serve civilian purposes.

The Valley takes a pride in the large scale of these con-
structions. It takes pride also in the fact that it was one of
the first sections in the country to organize for civilian defense in 1940. The Valley people can be persuaded to talk
about these things and about their material progress, but
conversation has a tendency to slip into other channels, for
they will also talk—indeed, you cannot prevent it—about
their soldiers and their battles.

"Residents of the Valley have sent their sons to all of
our nation's wars from the French and Indian on down,"
they say. If they at times embark upon the narration of in-

cidents which seem remote, it is because the present conflict is not an isolated catastrophe in their minds, but merely a link in a chain as long as the human race. Their pride in the present is part of the old pride, the sense of having always "done their part, held their own, and earned their salt."

They still can claim this fairly. The Valley educated Marshall and Patton. General Eisenhower's mother was born in Augusta County. General A. M. Patch spent twelve years as professor of science and military tactics at the Staunton Military Academy, and there in October 1944 his wife received the notice that their only son had died in battle. Brigadier General James E. Wharton lived in Staunton until he was killed in France in World War II. In a little gray frame church of no pretensions in the open country near Leetown, two generals now fighting were baptised or confirmed—and also two men of peace, the present bishops of Virginia and West Virginia.

Not all the warriors are famous, nor will they all return.

In France a small gray town called Saint-Lo found itself suddenly a military objective of the first importance. The Americans wanted it and they took it. Nothing new in that. There was a Major Thomas D. Howie in command of some of them. When taking cover under a burst of mortar fire he delayed and looked back to make sure his men were safe. A piece of shell killed him. Such deaths are a commonplace of war, and where so many are dying daily need occasion no comment.

But his men would not have it so, because they loved him. They took Saint-Lo, and they carried him with them. When they marched in, weary, battle-grimed, without flags or bugles, his flag-draped casket headed the procession. They laid him among the fallen stones of a shattered church, and there the press photographers found him.

The soldiers who were interviewed had little to say about it. They had wanted him along, and so they took him, that was all. "We looked up to him," one said. "You always felt comfortable around him," said Sergeant Garelik of the Bronx.

In Staunton, where he had lived, married, and taught at the Military Academy, they had loved him too. Another young man of Staunton wrote home to his parents: "I suppose Mrs. Howie will want to know where Tom is buried . . . His grave is beside a private's which I believe would please Tom . . . He was a soldier's soldier."

They held a memorial service for him in ivy-covered Old Trinity Church, to which he had belonged. The same church once housed the Virginia Assembly when Tarleton drove it across the mountains in 1781. The rector spoke on courage, and what he said may serve to close the story of the people of the Valley, and to predict what still may come:

"The Christian must have fortitude and bravery, and they have been characteristics of this congregation since the beginnings of this church."

Postscript

In the spring of 1945 the Shenandoah Valley was threatened by a danger which would have made this book the story of a nonexistent river, and of a valley that had partly vanished. After the Civil War it seemed that men could do no more to ruin the Valley, but that was because no one reckoned with the powers of the Federal government.

In 1936 Congress authorized engineers from the War Department to make plans for flood control along the Potomac and the Shenandoah. After two years of study they drew up a project for fourteen immense dams, two of them on the Shenandoah, which were to cost an estimated $235,000,000 and to inundate 172,000 acres of fertile and historic land.

At Millville, a few miles above Harpers Ferry, the dam would have a maximum elevation of 483 feet, and 36,000 acres in the lower Valley would be flooded. The rolling Shenandoah would be converted into a blank lake fifty-two miles long and four miles wide. One-eighth of Jefferson County and almost one-quarter of Clarke County would disappear forever under deep water. The Baltimore and Ohio would be under ninety feet of water, hundreds of old houses would be lost, others would perch on isolated islands. The plan referred to all this territory as "the lake bottom." Since the dam was to have a fluctuating level of fifty feet it would inevitably be surrounded at low water with miles of mud flats.

On the North Fork of the Shenandoah, a huge reservoir was to be built at Brock's Gap behind a dam 216 feet high, which would cover 6,100 acres of Rockingham County farm land. The replacement of highways alone in that area would cost a million and a quarter.

The report of the engineers admitted that the dams would eliminate only twenty per cent of the estimated annual flood damage in the Potomac basin, and that ninety-two percent of the benefit would be the generation of power. But it also admitted that at the present time there is no lack of power in the area affected.

These facts were cautiously submitted at Winchester to a few selected citizens under pledge of secrecy, early in February. Within two weeks they were made more generally public. Then the people of the Valley rose again to defend their land.

With Senator Byrd as their leader, they held mass meetings in every town and planned their protest. They wrote to every official and organization which might have influence. Before long Governor Meadows of West Virginia instructed his attorney general to register an objection. The senators and congressmen from both Virginia and West Virginia came out against the plan. The West Virginia State Planning Board, Farm Bureau, and Public Service Commission opposed it. The National Capital Park and Planning Commission deplored the destruction of scenic beauty.

But the people of the Shenandoah were not satisfied that they had done enough. Not until their Valley was threatened did they know how much they loved it—the contour of the fields, the flowing reaches of living water, the history written on the land. This was the countryside their ancestors had farmed for over two hundred years in family rotation. The local newspapers were full of letters and editorials decrying man's destruction of God's handiwork.

"They propose to take our fields, the houses our fathers built."

"We are a part of the Shenandoah earth, when you kill that you kill us too."

"It is obligatory to fight the dam, for we have grandchildren."

On April 3rd a hearing was held in Washington at which

any interested citizens had a right to appear before the Board of Engineers for Rivers and Harbors of the War Department. This is a routine procedure in such matters, after which the board makes its report to the chief of engineers, and the chief of engineers reports to Congress. The plan then goes to the committee on commerce in both houses, and if passed by both branches of Congress and signed by the President is returned to the committee on appropriations to be passed again. All along the way interested citizens have opportunities to be heard.

But the Valley people are not the sort to give an enemy time to entrench himself. They had not been so moved since the Yankees marched across the Potomac in '61. "A defensive campaign can only be made successful by taking the offensive at the proper time," Stonewall once said. The Valley people have never been afraid to fight. On the day of the hearing in Washington a crowd of approximately two thousand attended it, with their arguments well prepared.

By noon of the next day, the Board of Engineers announced that it would make an adverse report in the matter of the dams. And so another cloud has rolled away from the Valley and the matter ends.

"I am gratified," wrote Senator Byrd, "that my confidence in the Board has been confirmed . . . by the fact that [they] carried out the democratic processes of government by giving full and proper consideration to the citizens."

ACKNOWLEDGEMENT

A WORK of this kind must have so much assistance, so many contribute help and interest, that it seems invidious to single out a few. Especial thanks, however, are due to Dr. John W. Wayland, who placed his compendious and accurate information at the disposal of the author, to Mr. Arthur Bevan, state geologist of Virginia, who corrected the geological chapter; to Mr. Vernon Eddy of the Handley Library, to Miss Rose McDonald, Mrs. R. T. Browse, Mrs. Raymond Guest, and Captain Marshall McDonald.

BIBLIOGRAPHY

ALERS, F. VERNON, *History of Martinsburg and Berkeley Co.* Hagerstown, Md., 1888

ALLAN, WILLIAM, *History of the Campaign of Gen. T. J. Jackson.* Philadelphia: J. B. Lippincott & Co., 1880.

ALLAN, ELIZABETH RANDOLPH PRESTON, *A March Past.* Richmond, Va.: Dietz Press, 1938.

ANDREWS, MATTHEW PAGE, *Women of the South in War Times.* Baltimore: Norman Remington Co., 1924.

ARNOLD, T. J., *Early Life and Letters of Gen. Thomas J. Jackson.* New York: Fleming H. Revell Co., 1916.

ASHBY, THOMAS A., M.D., *The Valley Campaigns.* New York: Neale Publishing House, 1914.

ASHE, SAMUEL A. COURT, Capt. *James Iredell Waddell.* North Carolina Booklet, 23 Sm V 13 No. 2.

BARRY, JOSEPH, *The Strange Story of Harpers Ferry.* Martinsburg, Va.: F. Thompson Bros., 1903.

BAYLOR, GEORGE, *Bull Run to Bull Run.* Richmond: B. F. Johnson Publishing Co., 1900.

BEVAN, ARTHUR, *Origin of Our Scenery.* Bulletin 46-A.

———— *Contributions to Virginia Geology.* Bulletin 46.

———— *Virginia Geological Survey,* Charlottesville, Va., 1936.

BOYD, BELLE, *Belle Boyd in Camp and Prison.* New York: Blelock & Co., 1865.

BOYD, S. G., *Indian Local Names.* York, Pa., (privately printed) 1885.

BRONSON, HOWARD, Shenandoah (A Drama). 1897.

BRUCE, PHILIP A., *Robert E. Lee.* Philadelphia: George W. Jacobs & Co., 1907.

BRUCE, THOMAS, *Southwest Virginia and the Shenandoah Valley.* Richmond: J. L. Hill, 1891.

BUSHONG, MILLARD K., *A History of Jefferson Co., W. Va.* Charles Town: Jefferson Publishing Co., 1941.

BUTTS, CHARLES, *Geology of the Appalachian Valley in Virginia.*

Virginia Geological Survey, Bulletin 52. University of Virginia, Charlottesville, 1936.

CADY, R. C., *Ground Water Resources of the Shenandoah Valley.* Virginia Geological Survey, Bulletin 45. 1936.

CASLER, JOHN O., *Four Years in the Stonewall Brigade.* Girard, Kan. Appeal Publishing Co., 1906.

CARTMELL, T. K., *Shenandoah Valley Pioneers and their Descendants.* Winchester, Va., 1909.

CHITTENDEN, L. E., *An Unknown Heroine.* New York: G. H. Richmond Co., 1894.

CLARKE COUNTY HISTORICAL ASSOCIATION, Vol. III, 1943 (Reprint of the trial of Dr. Berkeley's slaves).

COOK, ROY BIRD, *The Family and Early Life of Stonewall Jackson.* Richmond: Old Dominion Press, 1925.

COOKE, JOHN ESTEN, *Surry of Eagle's Nest.* New York: Bunce & Huntington, 1866.

——— *Virginia, a History of the People.* Cambridge, Mass.: Riverside Press, 1888.

CORBIN, DIANA F. MAURY, *Life of Matthew Fontaine Maury.* London: Sampson, Low, Marston, Searle, & Rivington, 1888.

CRESSWELL, NICHOLAS, *Journal 1774-1777.* Edited by Lincoln MacVeagh. New York: Dial Press, 1924.

DANDRIDGE, NATHANIEL PENDLETON, *The Discovery of the Valley of Virginia by Governor Spotswood.* Cincinnati: Robert Clarke Co., 1903.

DE HASS, WILLIS, *History of the Early Settlement and Indian Wars of Western Virginia.* Wheeling, 1851.

DOUGLAS, HENRY KYD, *I Rode with Stonewall.* Chapel Hill: University of North Carolina Press, 1940.

DU PONT, H. A., *The Campaign of 1864 in the Valley of Virginia.* New York: National American Society, 1925.

FAIRFAX, FERNANDO, *Description of Iron Estate.* Washington: J. Crossfield (printer), 1815.

FISHER, SYDNEY GEORGE, *The Struggle for American Independence.* Philadelphia: Lippincott & Co., 1908.

FITHIAN, PHILIP VICKERS, *Journal 1775-1776.* Edited by R. G. Albion & L. Dodson. Princeton, 1924.

FLINN, FRANK M., *Campaigning with Banks and Sheridan.* Lynn, Mass.: Nichols, 1887.

FREEMAN, DOUGLAS SOUTHALL, *Lee's Lieutenants, a Study in Command.* New York: Scribner's, 1942.

FREEMAN, DOUGLAS SOUTHALL, *R. E. Lee.* New York: Scribner's, 1934.

GORDON, ARMISTEAD C., *In the Picturesque Shenandoah Valley.* Richmond, Va.: Garrett & Massie, 1930.

GRAY, R. L., *The Wonderful Shenandoah Valley.* (privately printed).

GREENE, KATHERINE GLASS, *Winchester, Virginia, and its Beginnings.* Strasburg, Va.: Shenandoah Publishing House, 1926.

HART, FREEMAN H., *The Valley of Virginia in the American Revolution.* Chapel Hill, N. C.: University of North Carolina Press, 1942.

HENDERSON, G. F. R., C. B., *Stonewall Jackson and the American Civil War.* London, New York: Longmans, Green, 1902.

HOTCHKISS, JEDEDIAH, *Shenandoah Iron, Lumber, Mining, & Manufacturing Co. of Virginia.* Page County, 1878.

———— *The Virginias, A Mining Industrial & Scientific Journal.* Staunton, 1880.

HUNT, CORNELIUS E., *The Shenandoah, The Lost Confederate Cruiser.* New York: G. W. Carleton, 1867.

INDUSTRIAL SURVEY, *Edinburg & Madison District.* Blacksburg, Va.: Engineering Extension Division, V.P.I., 1930.

JACKSON, ANNA (Mrs. T. J. Jackson), *Life and Letters of Stonewall Jackson by his Wife.* New York: Harper & Bros., 1891.

JOHNSON, GEN. ADAM R., *The Partisan Rangers of the Confederate States Army.* Louisville, Ky.: G. G. Fetter Co., 1904.

JONAS, HUGH, *The Present State of Virginia.* London, 1724.

KEARSEY, A., *Shenandoah Valley Campaign.* Aldershot, England: Gale and Polden, 1913.

KELLOGG, SANFORD C., U.S.A., *The Shenandoah Valley and Virginia, 1861-1865.* New York: Neale Publishing Co., 1903.

KERCHEVAL, SAMUEL, *A History of the Valley of Virginia.* Woodstock, Va.: John Gatewood, 1850.

LAMBERT, DARWIN S., *Beautiful Shenandoah.* Luray, Va.: National Park Service, 1937.

Laws of Virginia relating to State Commission and Development on Conservation. Richmond, 1935.

LEDERER, JOHN, *The discoveries of John Lederer in Three Several Marches from Virginia to the West of Carolina, 1669-1670.* Translated out of Latin from his *Discourses and Writings.* Sir William Talbot, Bart. London, 1672.

LEE, CAPT. ROBERT, *Recollection & Letters of Gen. Robert E. Lee.* New York: Garden City Publishing Co., 1936.

Lewis, Margaret, *Commonplace Book of Me, Margaret Lewis, Nee Lynn of Loch Lynn, Scotland.* Reprint in Bulletin 3, Vol. B., Historical Society of Northwestern Ohio. Toledo, July, 1936. (Some historians question this, others accept it as authentic.)

Lewis, Thomas, *The Fairfax Line. A Journal of 1746.* Edited by John W. Wayland. New Market, Va.: Henkel Press, 1925.

Macdonald, Rose M. E., *Clarke County, a Daughter of Frederick.* Berryville Va.: Blue Ridge Press, 1943.

Maquire, Thomas M., *Jackson's Campaigns in Virginia.* London: Wm. Clowes & Son, 1913.

Mason, James M., *The Public Life & Private Correspondence of James M. Mason.* Roanoke, Va.: Stone Printing & Manufacturing Co., 1903.

McCarthy, Carlton, *Detailed Minutiae of Soldier Life in the Army of Northern Virginia 1861-1865.* Richmond: C. McCarthy & Co., 1882.

McCreath, Andrew S., *Mineral Wealth of Virginia.* Harrisburg, Pa.: Lane S. Hart, 1884.

McDonald, Cornelia, *A Diary with Reminiscences of the War and Refugee Life in the Shenandoah Valley.* Edited by Hunter McDonald. Nashville: Cullen & Ghertner, 1934.

McDonald, William Naylor, *A History of the Laurel Brigade.* Privately printed, 1907.

Memoir of John Yates Beall, Printed by John Lovell, Montreal, 1865.

Memoir of a Family in England and Virginia, The Yates Family. Privately printed.

Miller, Francis Trevelyan, *Photographic History of the Civil War.* New York: Review of Reviews Company, 1911.

Moore, Edward A., *The Story of a Cannoneer under Stonewall Jackson.* New York: Neale Publishing Co., 1907.

Morton, Oren F., *History of Rockbridge Co.* Staunton, Va.: McClure Co., 1920.

Norris, J. E., *History of the Lower Shenandoah Valley.* Chicago: A. Warner & Co., 1890.

O'Reilley, Pvt. Miles, *Baked Meats of the Funeral.* New York: Carleton, 1866.

Original Narratives of Early American History, American Historical Association. New York: Scribner's, 1907.

Papers Relating to Trial of John Brown. On file at Charles Town courthouse.

PAXTON, ALEXANDER S., *Memory Days.* New York: Neale Publishing Co., 1908.

PIDGEON, WILLIAM, *Traditions of De-Coo-Dah and Antiquarian Researches.* New York: Horace Thayer, 1853.

POLLARD, EDW. W., *The Virginia Tourist.* Philadelphia: Lippincott & Co., 1870.

POND, GEORGE E., *The Shenandoah Valley in 1864.* New York: Scribner's, 1883.

PUTNAM, GEORGE HAVEN, *Some Memories of the Civil War.* New York: G. P. Putnam's Sons, 1924.

REILY, EMMA CASSANDRA, *Reminiscences of the Civil War.* Mason, 1911.

RENIERS, PERCIVAL, *The Springs of Virginia.* Chapel Hill: University of North Carolina Press, 1941.

RHODE ISLAND SOLDIERS AND SAILORS HISTORICAL SOCIETY, *Personal Narratives.* Fifth Series, 1-10.

RICE, A. H., AND STOUDT, JOHN BAER, *The Shenandoah Pottery.* Strasburg, Va.: Shenandoah Publishing House, 1929.

RILEY, FRANKLIN L., *Gen. Robert E. Lee After Appomattox.* New York: The Macmillan Co., 1922.

SHENANDOAH NATIONAL PARK. National Survey Institute, 1929.

SNOWDEN, WM. H., *The Story of the Expedition of the Young Surveyors.* Alexandria, Va.: G. H. Ramsay and Sons, 1902.

Southwest Virginia and The Valley. Roanoke, Va.: A. D. Smith & Co., 1892.

STEVENS, WILLIAM OLIVER, *The Shenandoah and its Byways.* New York: Dodd, Mead, 1941.

STILES, MAJOR ROBERT, *Four Years Under Marse Robert.* New York: Neale Publishing Co., 1903.

STRACK, DR. CHRISTIAN, *John Lederer, der Endecker des Virginia Valley.* Washington: Deutsche Historische Gesellschaft, 1906.

STRICKLER, HARRY M., *Massanutten.* Strasburg, Va.: Shenandoah Publishing House. 1924.

SUMMERS, FESTUS P., *The Baltimore and Ohio in the Civil War.* New York: G. P. Putnam's Sons, 1939.

TEACHER, THE VIRGINIA, *The Geology of the Shenandoah Valley.* Vols. XVI-2, XVII-8, XV-1, Harrisonburg, Va.

THWAITES & KELLOGG, *Documentary History of Dunmore's War.* Madison, Wisc.: Wisconsin Historical Society, 1905.

Tourist Guide Book of Virginia. Strasburg, Va.: Shenandoah Publishing House, 1930.

TRACY, J. P., *Shenandoah.* New York: Street & Smith, 1895.

Travels in Virginia in Revolutionary Times. Edited by A. J. Morrison. Lynchburg, Va.: J. B. Bell Co., 1922. (Reprints).

TYRRELL, HENRY, *Shenandoah.* 1912. (A Novel). G. P. Putnam's Sons, 1912.

U. S. BUREAU OF AMERICAN ETHNOLOGY, *Information Regarding Indian Popular Names.* Washington, D.C., 1927.

VAN DEVANTER, J. N., *History of the Augusta Church 1737-1900.* Staunton, Va.: Ross Printing Co., 1900.

VIRGINIA: *A Guide to the Old Dominion.* New York: Oxford University Press, 1940.

VIRGINIA, *Department of Agriculture and Immigration of State of Virginia.* Richmond, 1931.

WADDELL, JOS. A., *Annals of Augusta County, Virginia.* Richmond, Va.: Ellis Jones, 1886.

Washington and Lee Historical Papers. Baltimore: John Murphy & Co., 1890.

WASHINGTON, GEORGE, *The Writings of George Washington from the Original Manuscript Sources, 1745-1799.* Edited by John C. Fitzpatrick. Washington: U. S. Government Printing Office, 1932.

WAYLAND, JOHN W., *A Birdseye View of the Shenandoah Valley.* Harrisonburg, Va., 1942.

———— *Art Folio of the Shenandoah Valley.* Staunton, Va.: McClure Co., 1924.

———— *The German Element in the Shenandoah Valley of Virginia.* Charlottesville, Va.: Michie Company, 1907.

———— *Historic Homes of Northern Virginia and the Eastern Panhandle of West Virginia.* Staunton, Va.: McClure Co., 1937.

———— *Historic Landmarks of the Shenandoah Valley.* Staunton, Va.: McClure Co., 1924.

———— *A History of Rockingham County, Virginia.* Dayton, Va.: Ruebush Elkins Co., 1912.

———— *History of Shenandoah County, Virginia.* Strasburg, Va.: Shenandoah Publishing House, 1927.

———— *The Master Sculptor: A Treatise on Erosion.* New York: Nomad Publishing Co., 1930.

WAYLAND, JOHN W., *Scenic and Historical Guide to the Shenandoah Valley*. Dayton, Va.: Jos. K. Ruebush Co., 1923.

WHITTLE, CAPTAIN WILLIAM C., *Cruises of the Confederate States Steamers Shenandoah and Nashville*. Privately printed, 1910.

WILLIAMS, FLORA MCDONALD, *The Glengarry McDonalds of Virginia*. Louisville: George G. Fetter Co., 1911.

WILLIS, CARRIE HUNTER, AND WALKER, ETTA BELLE, *Legends of the Skyline Drive and the Great Valley of Virginia*. Richmond: Dietz Press, 1937.

WINCHESTER *Times*, WINCHESTER *Evening Star*. Newspaper Files at Handley Library, Winchester, Va.

Spirit of Jefferson.

Newspaper Files at Charles Town Library. Charles Town, W. Va.

Index

Adams, Charles Francis, 283
Adams, James Truslow, 12
Akenatzy tribe, 24
Algonquin tribe, 17
Allegheny mountains, 9, 14, 55, 81
Allen, Edward, 171-172, 285
Antietam, 228, 268
Appalachians, 14, 15, 22-24, 192, 244
Appomattox, 24, 192, 244, 268
Ashby, Turner, 128, 161, 172-173, 179, 184, 187, 197-200, 202, 206, 211-212, 217-221, 224, 232, 237, 251, 337, 338
Augusta County, 11, 49, 55, 101, 104, 107, 129, 153, 337

Baltimore and Ohio Railroad, 128, 136, 160, 176, 290
Banks, General, 173, 176, 179, 185, 187, 195, 196, 199, 200, 202-204, 209-210, 213-215, 227
Bartow, Colonel Francis, 162, 167
Bath, 114-116, 335
Bayard, Ferdinand Marie, 114-116
Beall, John, 266-267
Beckham, Fontaine, 143, 144, 148
Bee, General, 167, 168
Bell, Samuel, 341
Bennett, Dr. Joseph, 118, 340
Berkeley, Dr., 131-132
Berkeley, Sir William, 22
Berkeley County, 11, 289-291, 355
Berry, Captain, 248-249
Berryville, 95, 98
Beverly, Sir William, 51, 53
"Black and Tan" convention, 278, 279, 281
Blakemore, J. C., 292-293
Blue Ridge mountains, 4, 5, 9, 10, 14, 16, 18, 24, 30, 77, 136, 138, 267
Blue, Willie, 165-167
Boone, Daniel, 117

Bowman, George, 33, 341-342
Boyd, Belle, 163-164, 175-176, 206-209, 236-237, 324
Braddock, General Edward, 66, 88, 97, 103-105, 301
Bradford, Gamaliel, 283
Brewbacker, Mrs., 73
Brown, John, 136-151, 244, 293, 311, 351-352
Brown, Mrs., 245, 254
Buck, 272-273
Bull Run, 164-167
Burden, Benjamin, 41, 44
Burgoyne, General, 98, 103, 104
Bush, Philip, 113-114
Byrd, Senator Harry F., 350-351, 354, 359-360
Byrd, Admiral R. E., 350
Byrd, Colonel Richard, 132
Byrd, Thomas, 350
Byrd family, 350-351

Candee, Colonel, 186, 191
Carpetbaggers, 278, 289
Casler, John, 165, 167, 193, 223-224, 227, 229, 239, 250, 258, 260
Castiglioni, Count, 10, 114
Catawba tribe, 17-19
Cedar Creek, 261-264, 335, 341
Chambersburg, 252
Chancellorsville, 237
Charles Town, 94, 136, 146, 278, 281, 291, 299, 344, 351
Chaulkley, Thomas, 46
Cherokee tribe, 18, 108, 118
Civil War (*see* War between the States)
Clarke County, 11, 281
Columbian Maid, 124
Conrad, Mr., 167
Constitution, 106, 111-112
Cook, John Edwin, 136, 137, 139, 144, 148

Cooke, John Esten, 342
Cornwallis, Lord, 100, 103, 108, 109
Cowpens, 99, 100, 108
Craig, John, 51-52, 70, 252, 337
Crook, General, 248, 262, 266
Custer, General George, 242, 259, 261, 324
Custis, Martha, 88, 92
Custis, Nellie, 119, 344

Dagworthy, Captain, 79, 86
Davis, Jefferson, 160, 179
Delaware tribe, 17-20
Dinwiddie, Governor, 68, 77, 81, 83-87
Doddridge family, 48-49
Dogs, training of, 328
Douglas, Henry, 137, 197, 199, 208, 231, 238, 252, 262, 272-273
Doyle, Mahala, 150
Dunkards, 33, 36, 107, 139, 171, 319
Dunmore, Lord, 95-96, 101

Early, Jubal, 239, 250-252, 254, 257, 258, 261-267
English settlers, 11, 12, 44, 64-65, 341
Evans, Mr. and Mrs. John, 71
Ewell, General, 198-199, 202, 218, 222-223

Fairfax, Lord Thomas, 33, 41, 45, 53-59, 64, 109, 111, 296, 301, 345, 349
Fauquier, Governor, 90
Fisher, Jacob, 75
Fithian, Philip Vickers, 96-97
Fontaine, John, 27-29, 284
Forbes, General, 88, 89, 91, 97
Forts:
    Cumberland, 81, 83, 84, 85, 86, 88
    Duquesne, 67, 90, 91
    Loudoun, 65, 85, 93, 103
    Sumter, 154
Franklin, Benjamin, 67, 112, 124
Frederick County, 11, 49, 55, 94
Frederick Town (see Winchester)
Fredericksburg, 204, 232, 237
Frémont, J. C., 179, 201, 204, 214, 217, 218, 221-223
French settlers, 64-65, 109, 120
French and Indian War, 64-69
Frietchie, Barbara, 227

Front Royal, 9, 95, 204-209, 217, 226, 295, 320, 324-327
Fulton, Robert, 124
Funkhouser, Raymond J., 343-344

Gates, General, 98, 99, 102, 103, 106, 110, 123, 131, 345
Garnett, General, 188, 195, 196
George I, 29, 30
Germans, 11, 31-34, 62, 94, 95, 225-226, 337, 338
Gettysburg, 238, 240, 268
Glasgow, Ellen, 336
Gooch, Governor, 33, 37, 38, 41
Graham, Dr., 174, 180, 213
Graham, William, 275, 276
Grant, Ulysses S., 242, 246, 256, 257, 259, 268, 273, 280, 337
Greenleaf, Charles, 209-210
Greenlee, Mary, 39-40, 329

Harpers Ferry, 9, 10, 16, 26, 121, 128, 136-139, 143, 146, 148, 155, 160-162, 243, 245, 293, 295, 297-298, 352
Harris, Major, 23, 25
Harrisonburg, 197-200, 202-204, 226, 259, 261, 295, 337-338, 340
Hayward, Shepherd, 143, 144, 148
Henry, Patrick, 100, 111
Hessians, 98-100, 114
Heydt, Hans Jost (see Hite, Joist)
Hill, Daniel, 157, 158, 231, 283
Hillman, Charlotte, 341
Hite, Joist, 32-33, 54-56, 111, 264, 341
Horses, training of, 327-328, 345
Hotchkiss, Jedediah, 182, 296-297
Houston, Samuel, 118, 275, 285
Howie, Major Thomas D., 356-357
Hunter, General David, 246-248, 250-254, 274

Ida valley, 330-331
Indians, 17-25, 29-30, 32, 37-40, 45-46, 61-78, 81-85, 88-90, 95, 101, 120
Ireland, Irish, 35-37, 95, 124, 281
Iroquois tribe, 17, 21, 37
Irving, Washington, 10, 119, 335, 344

Jackson, Andrew, 117
Jackson, Thomas J. (Stonewall), 135, 136, 151, 155-161, 165-240, 251,

296, 307, 324, 333, 336, 339, 341, 354, 360

Valley campaign, 11, 180-241

Jackson, Mrs. T. J., 158, 159, 174, 177, 179, 196, 213, 219, 238

Jefferson, Thomas, 4, 10, 14, 20, 154, 332, 335, 342, 343, 351

Jefferson County, 11, 94, 129, 136, 153, 289-291, 313, 355

Johnston, General Joseph E., 160, 178

Jonas, Hugh, 30, 33

Kelly, Patrick, 70-71

Kercheval, Samuel, 343

Kernstown, 187-189, 194-195, 341

Klu Klux Klan, 279

Knights of the Golden Horseshoe, 30

Lederer, John, 22-26, 317, 324

Lee, Charles, 102-105, 108, 345

Lee, Robert E., 145, 203, 227, 228, 232, 237, 238, 240, 242, 248, 251, 256, 268, 271-283, 291, 307, 333

Letcher, Governor, 178, 248, 249

Lethea, 216

Lewis, Alice, 38-40, 329, 338

Lewis, Andrew, 90-91, 95, 96, 101, 102

Lewis, John, 37-41, 55, 90, 100, 338

Lewis, Margaret, 37-41, 55, 90, 100

Lexington, 11, 108, 118, 155, 291, 296, 299, 333-335, 337

Liberty Hall, 111, 275-277

Lincoln, Abraham, 117, 154, 155, 179, 195, 203, 204, 217, 228, 246, 257

Livingston, Adam, 116

Logan, Mrs., 234, 295, 350

Loudon, Lord, 80-81, 84, 85

Luray Caverns, 329-330

Luray Valley, 9, 32, 53, 198, 221, 260, 318

McCausland, General, 252

McClellan, George B., 157, 179, 187, 195, 199, 214, 228

McCormick, Cyrus, 125, 333

McDonald, Colonel Angus, 95, 96, 102, 345

McDonald, Colonel Angus, grandson, 161, 173, 249-250, 285

McDonald, Mrs. Angus, 153, 174, 186, 189-193, 215-216, 235, 239-240, 249-250, 285-287

McDonald, Dr. Henry T., 352-353

McDowell, Dr. Ephraim, 118-119, 340

McDowell, General, 204, 213

McDowell, battle, 201

McGuire, Dr., 180-181, 188

McNeill's Rangers, 266, 339-340

Macon, Emma Reilly, 162, 174, 205-206

Madison, James and Dolly, 94, 131, 332, 342, 343

Manassas, battle, First, 166, 168, 170-172, 193, 229

Second, 227, 237

Marshall, General George C., 334, 356

Martineau, Harriet, 10, 335

Martinsburg, 18, 71, 128, 160-162, 228, 355

Maryland, 9, 25, 84, 136, 227-228, 252

Mason, James, 153, 186, 235

Massanutten Mountain, 9, 11, 12, 15, 21, 26, 28, 32, 55, 73, 183, 198-199, 203, 218, 221, 252, 257, 318

Maury, Matthew Fontaine, 284-285, 334

Mechlenburg, 31-32

Mennonites, 36, 46, 75, 107

Michelle, Louis, 26

Militia, 78-89, 99, 129, 145

Miller, Adam, 32, 330

Milroy, General, 201, 234, 235, 239, 240, 295, 350

Monmouth Court House, 105

Monocan tribe, 18, 335

Morgan, Daniel, 97-100, 102, 108, 118, 119, 342, 345

Mosby, Colonel John C., 247-248, 259, 264-265, 307, 324

Mount Vernon, 86, 87

Muhlenberg, Peter, 101-102, 340

Natural Bridge, 11, 16, 18, 335, 338

Negroes, 94, 129-151, 175, 243-245, 272-273, 278-281, 289, 311, 314-315, 340, 352-353

Newmarket, 117, 198, 204, 218, 245-246, 264, 295, 333, 339

Newtown, 247

Northcott, Mr., 330

Office of Price Administration, 304

Ohio River, 64-66, 72, 87-89, 91, 95, 125

Omayah, 38-40
Opequon River, 12, 32, 36, 46, 65, 75
Orange County, 49
Oroonah, 38, 40, 338

Page County, 12, 296, 311-312
Painter family, 74-75
Patch, General A. M., 356
Patterson, General, 160-161, 164
Patton, Colonel James, 44, 73, 333
Patton, General George S., 334, 356
Petersburg, 223, 244
Pond, George, 261
Pope, General John, 227
Port Republic, battle, 221-223, 331
"Porte Crayon," (see Strother, David)
Potomac River, 9, 12, 31, 55, 110-111, 123, 225, 231, 358
Powell's Fort, 11, 26, 122, 331
Powhatan tribe, 18, 335
Pratt, Captain, 191-192
Preston, Colonel, 136, 151
Preston, Elizabeth, 174-175
Preston, Willie, 156, 166

Quakers, 32, 33, 36, 46, 50, 83, 107-108, 171, 343

Ramseur, General, 261-262, 264, 342
Rayon, 320, 324-326, 331-332, 346
Reed, Dr. Walter, 340
Reilly, Emma (see Macon, Emma Reilly)
Revolutionary War, 93-112
Richmond, 159, 171, 173, 179, 195, 200, 202-203, 214, 223-224, 226, 237, 244, 245, 251, 256, 258, 278
Rickohockan tribe, 24
Robinson, John, 82, 86-87, 92, 276
Rochefoucauld, Duc de la, 10, 336
Rockbridge County, 11, 124, 281, 337
Rockingham County, 11, 33, 153, 291, 296, 337-338, 341, 358
Rodes, John, 75
Rommel, General Erwin, 180
Romney, 176, 178, 179
Roosevelt, Franklin D., 319
Rosser, General, 261, 265-267
Rumsey, James, 122-124

Salling, John Peter, 37, 40
Schoepf, Dr. Johann David, 114

Scotch-Irish, 11, 31, 34-44, 52, 94, 275, 287, 337
Senedo tribe, 18, 21
Seven Days, 224
Sevier, John, 117-118
Shawnee tribe, 18, 72, 93, 108
Shenandoah County, 11, 102, 340
Shenandoah National Park, 318, 321-323
Shenandoah River, 3-21, 41, 111, 318
  flood, 291-294
  Forks of, 9, 16-17, 74-75, 261, 297, 358
Seven Bends, 9, 16, 331
Shenandoah Valley, 3-5, 9-10, 12, 17, 22-59, 127-129, 298-357
  apple growing, 301-305, 349-350
  campaign, 11, 180-241
  dam project, 358-360
  slavery in, 129-151, 287
Sheridan, Philip, 242, 254-267, 292, 299, 311, 339, 341, 342
Shields, General, 187, 195, 204, 206, 214, 217, 218, 221, 222
Siegel, General, 242, 243, 245, 246
Skyline Drive, 18, 317, 318, 324
Slaves, slavery, 4, 94, 100, 101, 125, 129-151, 298, 311
Spirit of Jefferson, 278, 279, 291, 324
Spotswood, Governor Alexander, 12, 22, 26-30, 284, 317
Stanwix, Colonel, 86, 88
Staunton, 11, 37, 38, 44, 49, 50, 52, 53, 83, 100, 200, 245, 251, 259, 264, 296-297, 336-337, 355-357
Stephen, General Adam, 102, 105-106
Stockton, George, 72
Stockton, Isabella, 72-73
Stonewall Brigade, 169-177, 188, 212, 216-218, 229, 250-251, 297, 333, 337
Storer College, 295, 352
Stover, Jacob, 53
Strasburg, 218, 240-241
Strickler, Abraham, 53
Strother, David, 155, 246
Stuart, J. E. B., 145, 162, 251, 348

Talbot, Sir William, 22, 25
Tarleton, 99-101, 357
Taylor, General, 203, 208, 211-212, 218
Terrill, Lizzie and Julia, 301

Tidewater, 18, 30, 78, 100, 108, 153
Townes, Mr., 190
Tuscarora tribe, 18, 24

Valentine, Edward V., 275, 333
Valley Forge, 103, 105
Valley Pike, 10, 18, 124, 161, 189, 257, 263, 313, 338, 339, 351
Van Meter, John, 32
Virginia, 9, 25-30, 84, 136, 139, 154, 155, 277-291
Virginia Assembly, 56, 66, 79, 80, 82, 85-87, 89, 90, 92, 100, 101, 103, 357
Virginia Conventions, 101, 106, 111-112, 153-154
Virginia Military Institute (V.M.I.), 128, 136, 151, 155-157, 174, 200, 202, 238, 245-246, 248, 284, 296, 334
Virginia Riflemen, 97-100, 108, 118
Virginia, University of, 128, 274
Virginias, The, 295-296

War between the States, 127, 132, 152-268, 289, 307
Warren County, 12
Washington, D. C., 9, 195, 203, 214, 217
Washington, George, 10, 55, 60-69, 92, 94, 111, 112, 123, 137, 139, 145, 276, 331, 333
  French and Indian War, 64-69, 77-92
  Revolutionary War, 93-109

Washington, Lawrence, 55, 64
Washington, Lewis, 136, 139, 145
Washington and Lee University, 283, 296, 300
Washington College, 111, 118, 128, 248, 271, 274-277, 283
Washington family, 68, 94, 342-344
Wayne, Mad Anthony, 106, 332
Waynesboro, 295, 331-332
Welsh settlers, 44, 97
West Virginia, 9, 136, 160, 243, 289-291, 326, 359
Wheeler, Reverend Temple, 320-321
Whisky Rebellion, 119
Williams, Mr., 293-294
Wilson, Woodrow, 315, 336
Winchester, 12, 17, 32, 44, 49, 57, 61, 66-69, 77-88, 90-91, 94, 95, 107, 112, 161-162, 170, 174, 177, 184, 189-190, 195, 212-215, 226, 234, 244, 252, 257-258, 262, 295, 304, 348-350
Winder, General, 196, 212, 218, 237
Wintermeyer, William, 176, 177
Wood, Colonel James, 44, 49, 57, 345
Woodstock, 9, 34, 101, 226, 264, 295, 340
World War I, 316, 352
World War II, 345, 355-357
Wyndham, Sir Percy, 219, 220

Yorktown, 109